W9-CLR-580

PROLOGUE TO NEW ENGLAND
The Forgotten Century of the Explorers

PROLOGUE TO
NEW
ENGLAND

by Henry F. Howe

KENNIKAT PRESS, INC./PORT WASHINGTON, N. Y.

FERNALD LIBRARY
COLBY-SAWYER COLLEGE
NEW LONDON, N.H. 03257

F
7
H 85

TO

OLIVER H. HOWE, MY FATHER

*whose modest persistence in the lifelong pursuit
of local historianship has set the pattern
for this book.*

84502

PROLOGUE TO NEW ENGLAND

Copyright 1943 by Henry F. Howe
Reissued 1969 by Kennikat Press
By arrangement with Holt, Rinehart and Winston, Inc.

Library of Congress Catalog Card No: 68-26231
Manufactured in the United States of America

ESSAY AND GENERAL LITERATURE INDEX REPRINT SERIES

Acknowledgment

THIS IS NO book for the professional historian. Rather, it has been the result of a layman's probings into mysteries previously delved into by many a historian, but left strangely fallow for the general reader. Because of this, my only acknowledgments to historians appear in the bibliography.

But I do wish to render homage here to certain exceedingly human beings who have been kind enough to struggle with a reading and frank criticism of my manuscript. To Douglas S. Byers and Frederick Johnson of Andover I owe many hours of patient reading, annotation and comment, particularly in matters having to do with the New England Indians. To Frederick A. Fenger and to Dr. Donald Macomber I am grateful for many geographical and nautical suggestions, not to mention delightful opportunities for becoming acquainted with the coast of Maine. Stanley deJ. Osborne has been most helpful in checking matters regarding the fisheries, and both he and Ranald Hobbs have brought out certain structural weaknesses in the book which I fear have not been wholly corrected. To all these, to my patient wife, and to numerous others who have manfully listened to my tirades, many thanks.

Lastly, may I offer my most humble acknowledgment to that John Turner of the *Mayflower* who died in the first awful winter at Plymouth, and to his daughter, Marjorie, who later arrived at Salem, for these were my ancestors, together with Abraham Howe of infant Roxbury. This book perhaps also owes something to the chance that I was born in Cohasset, on the boundary between Plymouth and Massachusetts Bay, though discovered, and named, on Captain John Smith's map in 1614. One of my childhood memories was my father's dedication of Cohasset's Smith Memorial in 1914.

HENRY F. HOWE

Cohasset, Massachusetts
August, 1942

CONTENTS

PART ONE

New England in the Sixteenth Century

PART TWO

Precursors of the Pilgrims

Illustrations

Part One

NEW ENGLAND IN THE SIXTEENTH CENTURY

"It was the men of Devon, the Drakes and the Hawkins, Gilberts and Raleighs, Grevilles and Oxenhams, and a host more of forgotten worthies, whom we shall learn one day to honor as they deserve, to whom [England] owes her commerce, her colonies, and her very existence."

CHARLES KINGSLEY, *Westward Ho!*

CALENDAR OF VOYAGES

1498 John and Sebastian Cabot, Nova Scotia to the
      Carolinas
1502 Miguel Cortereal, Newfoundland to Rhode
      Island
1524 Giovanni da Verrazano, Narragansett Bay and
      Maine
1525 Estevan Gomez, Maine, Cape Cod and Long
      Island
1527 John Rut and the *Mary Guildford*, Newfound-
      land to the West Indies
1541 Diego Maldonado, Florida to Newfoundland
1542 Jehan Alphonsce, Cape Breton to Massachu-
      setts Bay
1556 André Thevet, Penobscot Bay
1565 John Hawkins, Florida to Newfoundland
1568 David Ingram, Mexico to New Brunswick
1579 Simon Ferdinando, Maine Coast
1580 John Wallace, Penobscot Bay
1583 Stephen Bellinger, Cape Breton and coast to
      the south
1593 Richard Fisher, Southwest of Cape Breton to
      latitude 44°

Chapter One

THE FORGOTTEN CENTURY
OF THE NEW ENGLAND DISCOVERIES

PLYMOUTH ROCK is often looked upon as the foundation stone upon which America's splendid democratic legend is solidly based. American reverence for the magnificent heroism of the Pilgrims is justly founded and unalterable. Anyone would be a fool who questioned it. But in the process of this reverence for the forefathers a grotesque thing has happened. Americans as a whole have practically ignored the first century of New England history.

Because of the coincidence of the Puritan emigration with the beginnings of successful settlement, it has been commonly assumed that this emigration was the whole and sufficient explanation of the colonial movement. Such was not the fact. In common justice we should recognize that a whole galaxy of New England heroes were searching out the possibilities of New England settlement for nearly a century before the Puritan emigration. It was in great measure upon the work of these "forgotten worthies" that the Pilgrim success depended. Many historians have recognized this, but the general public is not yet aware of it. Plymouth Harbor had been entered half a dozen times before 1620, the coast mapped, and Plymouth given its name. More than forty recorded voyages had preceded the Pilgrims to various parts of New England, and there is abundant evidence that many more remained unrecorded. At least fifty European explorers had died in the New England area be-

tween 1500 and 1620. A colony of a hundred settlers had wintered in New England a dozen years before the *Mayflower*
sailed. Yet the dominant Pilgrim tradition in historically-minded
New England has unwittingly contrived to thrust this whole
preliminary century into the shadows. Because of its colonial
failures Americans generally have ignored the century of the
explorers, forgetful that any brilliant success is ordinarily supported on many rough-hewn timbers of experimental failure.
We need to alter our conception of Plymouth Rock as a foundation stone. It was, rather, the pinnacle of a structure into the
building of which went heart-rending disappointment and economic ruin for hundreds of Englishmen who had never heard
of the Pilgrims. The Pilgrims, curiously enough, were quite as
little aware of their predecessors. Yet they were indebted to
these earlier men as surely as we are to the Plymouth founders.
Let us examine the New England of the explorers, whose failures
reared up Plymouth Rock to be a monument.

Chapter Two

CABOT AND THE
SHADOWY PERIOD OF THE NEW WORLD, 1497–1523

LEIF ERIKSSON was probably the first discoverer of New England. Whether the four voyages of the Greenland Vikings between the years 1003 and 1015 entered the Martha's Vineyard area or a region of Maine or Nova Scotia remains in dispute. They did winter in Vinland through three years, however, and should be honored for the most brilliant exploit in navigation of the medieval period. The Vinland discovery forms a curiously isolated chapter in the discovery of America. It was for centuries forgotten, and it made no conceivable impress upon the later colonization of New England, except in that a continuing traffic between Europe and Iceland encouraged long voyages. The Vinland voyages therefore were not the first chapter in any preliminaries of the permanent settlements which made New England. Those all followed the voyages of Columbus, who, it is true, may have heard of Vinland. We may think of the Vinland sagas as the ancient phase of New England's annals. We are here concerned only with the modern phase, which followed the voyages of Columbus and the Cabots.

The dramatic quality of the discoveries by Columbus and John Cabot is likely to obscure in our minds the extremely gradual emergence of America from the mists of the Atlantic. Even the discoveries themselves appear to have been gradual. The Vikings had discovered very early in the game that it was possible to cross the Atlantic without ever being out of sight

5

of land for longer than three or four hundred miles at a time. The Faeroes, Iceland, and Greenland made this possible. Fishermen of Brittany and the west coasts of England had been plying their trade for two centuries before Columbus' time in the waters around Iceland. Only a hundred and fifty miles away from Iceland lay Greenland. There is some evidence that a Portuguese named João Fernandez, called "Llavrador," who appears to have sailed with Cabot in 1497, had already been in Greenland. The Portuguese had previously subdued a thousand miles of open ocean in discovering the Azores in 1432, so that we must immediately dispel any remnant of our childhood notions that European sailors were afraid of losing sight of land for fear of falling off the edge of a flat earth. As early as 1488 the French Captain Cousin of Dieppe had been blown far to the west and had returned reporting a strange land out of which emerged the mouth of a great river. It was out of such facts as these, along with their theory of a round earth, that the two great Italian explorers constructed their faith in a western route to Asia. Thus there is a distinct possibility that New England Indians saw sailing vessels even before Cabot.

In any case the little ship *Mathew* sailed from Bristol in May of 1497, filled with hope aroused by reports of the two voyages of Columbus. Cabot and his eighteen men sailed westward for fifty-two days before sighting Cape Breton. They observed signs of habitation in the shape of snares and notched trees, but saw no natives. Coasting along Newfoundland the codfish were so thick they caught them in baskets. They hurried back to England in August with the news that they had found the country of the Grand Khan.

The next year Cabot, and perhaps his son Sebastian, again appeared at Newfoundland. This time they had come by way of Greenland and the adjacent American coasts, which in honor of Fernandez had been named Labrador. Still in search of Japan and the Indies, the little flotilla, this time with some three hundred men aboard, seems to have coasted Nova Scotia and New England, and to have reached the latitude of 36° in the neighborhood of Cape Hatteras before turning back to England. One can well imagine the disappointment of Henry VII at the meager cargo of furs and fish with which Cabot returned.

The immediate English result of the Cabot voyages was that merchants of Bristol in each of the years 1501, 1502, 1503, and 1504 sent vessels to the "New Founde Island." That of 1502 returned with "three men brought out of an Iland farre beyond Ireland, the which were clothed in Beestes skynnes and ate raw fflessh and were rude in their demeanure as Beestes." We have no knowledge of the destination of any of these voyages.

One or more of them appear to have been led by the same Fernandez who accompanied Cabot. J. G. Kohl states, "on Nov. 17, 1503, the King [Henry VII] paid one pound to a 'man that brought hawkes from the Newfound island'; on April 8, 1504, two pounds to a priest 'who was going to that island', and on Aug. 25, 1505 a small sum to a man who brought 'wylde cats and popyngays of the Newfound Island to Richmond.'"

Portugal, in the meantime, was turning some attention to these coasts. A nobleman named Gaspar Cortereal, whose father was a governor of Terceira in the Atlantic outpost of the Azores, set sail at his own expense to search for new lands in 1500. He likewise investigated the shores of Greenland and Labrador and returned with a description of the natives there. The next year with three vessels he again sailed "in a west-north-west direction" from Lisbon, and "at a distance of about two thousand Italian miles," he discovered land, which would seem to have been in the same general region as the preceding year. Somewhere in the Newfoundland area he apparently separated from his two accompanying vessels with the intention of exploring the coasts to the southward. At this point he disappears from history. The other ship returned without him, bringing seven kidnaped Indians and descriptions of abundant forests, large rivers, and a seacoast well stocked with codfish.

The winter passed with no word of Gaspar Cortereal. In May of 1502 his brother Miguel determined to go in search of him. Miguel's three vessels reached Newfoundland in June, and agreed to undertake the search separately and to return to St. John's on August 20th. Curiously enough, Miguel's vessel failed to meet the rendezvous, and after waiting in vain for some time, the others returned to Lisbon. Miguel Cortereal was never seen again.

The significance of the Cortereal voyages for our New England purposes has to do with the deciphering by Dr. E. B. Delabarre of Brown University of an inscription on a rock near Dighton, Massachusetts. While it is partly obliterated by later Indian pictographs, this inscription is in such abbreviated Latin as was common in those days. It reads: "M. Cortereal 1511 V. Dei Dux Ind." and is followed by an emblem which might be a simplified rendering of the seal of Portugal. A free translation of the Latin would read: "by the grace of God, Leader of the Indians." It is only fair to state that the validity of this inscription is doubted by some authorities. Dighton is at the head of Narragansett Bay, and it therefore may seem strange that Giovanni da Verrazano, who spent two weeks in that region in 1524, only thirteen years after the date of the inscription, should not have made some note of a "White Indian" legend. Inasmuch as Verrazano, however, was in the service of the King of France, one might excuse him for not establishing a prior Portuguese claim to the same region, if he did in fact hear of such a legend. We shall have to be content, I think, with allowing the Cortereal inscription to remain a mystery. It does suggest a possibility that these Indians of the Narragansett Basin knew white men intimately almost a century and a quarter before 1620. But regardless of the worth of the inscription, we may consider it entirely probable that either Gaspar Cortereal, sailing southward from Newfoundland in 1501, or his brother Miguel, searching for him in that direction in 1502, coasted along New England shores. A Portuguese chart made by Pedro Reinel about 1505 clearly indicates for the first time a part of the Nova Scotia coast that must have been explored by those who did return from these voyages. And, like the Cabot voyages, these explorations of the Cortereals were immediately followed up by a

Portuguese Fishing Company, formed in the harbors of Viana, Aveiro and Terceira. By 1506 King Emanuel ordered "that the fishermen of Portugal, at their return from Newfoundland, should pay a tenth part of their profits at his customhouses."

Meanwhile the voyages of the Cabots were being followed up by another nation. Francis Parkman says that the French Captain Denis of Honfleur explored the Bay of St. Lawrence in 1502. According to John Fiske, there were Breton, Norman and Basque fishermen at Cape Breton as early as 1504. Thomas Aubert reached the Gulf of St. Lawrence in 1504, and in 1508 brought several Indians and a map of the coast to the French port of Dieppe. In 1509 Norman vessels returned to Rouen with seven Indians and a canoe. By the year 1517 it is stated that there were fifty Castilian, French and Portuguese vessels fishing on the Newfoundland banks. One of the few of these whose name has come down to us was a Portuguese, John Fagundes of Viana. The next year, 1518, Baron de Léry made the first attempt to found a French colony, which Parkman believes was on Sable Island off Nova Scotia. The cattle which were brought with this soon abandoned colony multiplied on the island and were found there by Sir Humphrey Gilbert seventy years later.

These early fishermen and traders left no logbooks or other direct record of their voyages, and one finds mention of them only in such form as contemporary letters later collected by men like Hakluyt, Purchas, Herrera and Ramusio, who were interested in information about the new country for purposes of studying its commercial possibilities. From such evidence we can be certain that there was gradually developing around Newfoundland and Cape Breton a rather extensive fleet of fishermen, consisting of lowly English, French and Portuguese mariners who had been accustomed to fishing in the neighborhood of Iceland, and merely transferred their activities to the rich Newfoundland banks which John Cabot had found teeming with "baccalaos," or codfish. We have no way of knowing how early these men discovered the equally rich Brown's Bank and

Georges Bank off the Maine and Massachusetts coasts. The progression of fishing boats southward following the line of shoals down from the Newfoundland and Nova Scotia areas toward New England is a natural one, and it is quite probable that some of these unremembered fishermen coasted along these shores before the time of Verrazano. All this, at any rate, constitutes a background of hearsay that must have influenced King François I of France in commissioning Giovanni da Verrazano to go on a voyage of exploration in 1523. A commercial impulse undoubtedly prompted the voyage. This was the first deliberate attempt to learn what lay between Florida and Newfoundland.

Chapter Three

THE VOYAGE OF VERRAZANO, 1524

"WEIGHING ANCHOR, we sailed fifty leagues toward the East, as the coast stretched in that direction, and always in sight of it; at length we discovered an island of a triangular form, about ten leagues from the mainland, in size about equal to the island of Rhodes, having many hills covered with trees, and well peopled, judging from the great number of fires which we saw all around its shores; we gave it the name of your Majesty's illustrious mother (Louisa)."

In these words was announced the first documented discovery of New England by a modern European. The year, 1524; Giovanni da Verrazano was reporting to his patron, King François I of France, his discovery of Block Island.

"We did not land there," he goes on, "as the weather was unfavorable, but proceeded to another place, fifteen leagues distant from the island, where we found a very excellent harbor. Before entering it we saw about twenty small boats full of people, who came about our ship, uttering many cries of astonishment, but they would not approach nearer than within fifty paces; stopping, they looked at the structure of our ship, our persons and dress, afterwards they all raised a loud shout together, signifying that they were pleased."

This was Narragansett Bay, in the modern Rhode Island. Verrazano's sojourn of two weeks in that area enabled him to recount in the most fascinating detail this first certain contact of Europeans with the Algonkian Indians of New England.

Before launching into Verrazano's interesting first portrayal of the New England scene, let us take account of stock. The beginnings of New England, according to John Fiske's excellent version, were at Plymouth in 1620, or if you insist on priority, at Scrooby, England, some few years earlier. What had Verrazano to do with all that? The answer is, practically nothing. But the Indians of Narragansett Bay, about whom Verrazano will presently tell us, had a great deal to do with Plymouth. If one's memory serves, the friendship of a sachem named Massasoit was of enormous significance to the Plymouth of 1620, and of 1650; indeed the peace of Massasoit was the background of security without which Plymouth would probably have perished. On the upper shores of Narragansett Bay stood Pokanoket, which was Massasoit's later headquarters. Plymouth itself, the Patuxet of the Indians, was only forty miles away. It is entirely possible that in one of these canoes clustering around Verrazano's ship sat a grandfather of Massasoit.

This contact of Verrazano with the Indians of Narragansett Bay is an excellent example of the important effect earlier voyages could have upon the attitude of Indians who were to be neighbors of later Massachusetts colonists. The peculiar geographical characteristics of the region surrounding the Massachusetts coast make it essential that our study of these earlier European visits be not limited to Massachusetts Bay, but include also voyages to the Maine coast, to the area surrounding Martha's Vineyard, and, as we have seen, the Rhode Island region. There is sufficient evidence in the chronicles of the Pilgrims that Massasoit's people had frequent communication and dealings with the inhabitants of all these areas. Impressions gained by the natives through trade or quarrel with Europeans who touched any of these shores must have been quickly imparted to the Indians of Massachusetts. European disease, transmitted to the Indians by one or another of the later explorers, seems to have played a significant part in making Massachusetts possible. And to these Stone Age natives the more subtle disease of being presented with axes and knives of steel was probably an even more effective inducement to making colonization by the strangers tolerable. It will be of tremendous importance therefore to learn how extensively the Indians of Massachusetts were initiated into the ways of Europe before 1620.

There is a larger sense also in which a study of the preliminary investigations of the eastern coast of North America is important to New England history. In the past the root of the colonization of Massachusetts has been usually sought, as by John Fiske, in the Puritan Reformation in England. But the initial urges which made English colonization of New England inevitable had nothing to do with the Puritan movement. They arose, rather, from bitter commercial rivalries which followed Spain's discovery of the wealth of the New World. The impulse which first brought these coasts into prominence was the motive of plunder. With but one exception so far as I know the visits to these shores prior to 1620 were all motivated chiefly by the desire for economic gain. It was therefore the more remarkable that this area should finally have been settled as a refuge for religious exiles. But it must not be imagined that the economic motive which had prevailed for over a century was forthwith abandoned when New England became a Puritan refuge. The Puritan impulse was the spark which happened to ensure the persistence of colonists, but the assurance of commercial gain which the explorers had established was the bedrock on which any thought of permanent settlement had to be built. This commercial background is therefore just as essential to an understanding of the earliest days of New England as is the history of the Puritan movement. The mapping of the coast, the establishment of information about the fisheries, the fur trade and other commodities was a primary requisite to the success of the Pilgrims, and all this work was done previously by men whose steadfast struggle to plant colonies was in no way influenced by the religious movements of the period.

Thus there are two dominant ideas which we should carry along with us in examining the preliminary voyages by Europeans of the several nations who explored New England. The first of these was the preparation of the psychological environment of settlers; that is, the explorers' treatment of the natives. The second, as we have seen, concerned the settlers' livelihood; what were the prospects of trade? These, obviously, are the practical aspects of colonization; the Puritans proved themselves thoroughly competent to see to the spiritual and social phases.

Verrazano sailed in 1523 under instructions to seek a sea route to Cathay. Within two months of his setting sail on that voyage, however, he returned to France bringing with him as prizes the first Spanish treasure ships laden with gold from Mexico. Cortes had discovered the temples of the Aztecs the previous year, and these were the first fruits of the Mexican conquest. This marks the beginning of the steadily increasing hoard of treasure which from that moment flowed across the Atlantic to fill the war chest of Charles V of Spain. It also establishes the onset of the growing private warfare carried on by French privateers on Spanish shipping during the next forty years. These, for France, were perhaps her greatest years on the high seas. Not only did French ships play havoc with the West Indies colonies, but the movement included colonization efforts in Canada and Florida. It was surpassed only by later development of the English sea dogs under Sir Francis Drake. In view of all this, it was of great significance that the King of France persisted in his desire to send Verrazano on a voyage of exploration after capturing the Aztec prize. It probably meant that a project was in his mind to establish in America a base for commercial rivalry with Spain.

Verrazano sailed a second time from Madeira on January 17, 1524, and sighted land somewhere along the Carolina coast early in March. He cruised northward, anchoring his ship, the *Dauphine*, momentarily at New York Harbor, which he well describes. The passage above quoted, with which New England was discovered and a landing made at Newport, marked his first landfall after passing Long Island.

His men won the confidence of the natives by imitating their gestures and presenting them with toys and bits of bric-abrac, whereupon they came aboard without fear. Among these people were two sachems of about forty and twenty-four years, dressed in deerskin "artificially wrought in damask figures." They wore chains about their necks ornamented with stones of various colors. He was impressed with the splendid physique of the people, the elaborate ornamentation of their hair and clothes, and their pleasant manners. They painted their faces in diverse colors. The women he found very graceful and of fine countenance. They also wore ornamented deerskins, some with "very rich lynx skins upon their arms, and various ornaments upon their heads, composed of braids of hair." The older and married people of both sexes wore ornaments in their ears. Several wore pieces of wrought copper about them. Of the gifts offered them they prized ornaments above cloth, or implements of steel or iron. "When we showed them our arms they expressed no admiration, and only asked how they were made." He found them very generous and friendly and allowed the ship to be brought in close to the shore so that they could come aboard it more easily from their little boats. They guided him to the safest anchorage. He says that they were very careful of their wives, never allowing them to come aboard ship. "One of the two kings often came with his queen and many attendants, to see us for his amusement, but he always stopped at the distance of about two hundred paces, and sent a boat to inform us of his intended visit, saying that they would come and see our ship—this was done for safety, and as soon as they had an answer from us they came off, and remained a while to look around; but on hearing the annoying cries of the sailors the king sent the queen, with her attendants, in a very light boat, to wait near an island a quarter of a league distant from us, while he remained a long time on board, talking with us by signs, and expressing his fanciful notions about everything in the ship, and asking the use of all. After imitating our modes of salutation, and tasting our food, he courteously took leave of us."

Verrazano states that he and his men several times traveled

inland as far as fifteen or twenty miles and found extensive open plains suitable for cultivation; and forests sufficiently open to "be traversed by an army ever so numerous." We may note here that this was no casual landing of a ship's boat to take on wood and water, but a fairly thoroughgoing piece of exploration involving several days of investigation ashore. Oaks and cypresses were the only trees he attempted to name, the latter being probably our red cedars, which were called cypresses also by many later explorers. He speaks of "Apples, plumbs, filberts, and many other fruits, but all of a different kind from ours." The fauna included "stags, deer, lynxes," and the Indians took them "by snares and by bows, the latter being their chief implement, their arrows are wrought with great beauty and for the heads of them they use emery, jasper, hard marble and other sharp stones, in the place of iron. They also use the same kind of sharp stones in cutting down trees and with them they construct their boats of single logs, hollowed out with admirable skill, and sufficiently commodious to contain 10 or 12 persons. Their oars are short and broad at the end, and are managed in rowing by force of the arms alone, with perfect security and as nimbly as they choose." Here is one of many evidences that language difficulties are not one-sided when explorers meet a new race: European languages had not at that time acquired either the concept or a word to describe paddling. This is also the place for noting that these were dugout canoes. The canoe birch does not grow south of Cape Ann in Massachusetts. When Henry C. Murphy attempted to cast doubt on the authenticity of Verrazano's narrative he cited this description of dugouts as one of the obvious inaccuracies of Verrazano's story, saying that these canoes should have been of birch bark. On the contrary, it only serves to confirm us in the belief that this harbor was indeed as far south as Rhode Island, where canoe birch does not grow. "We saw their dwellings which are of a circular form, about 10 or 12 paces in circumference, made of logs split in half without any regularity of architecture, and covered with roofs of straw, nicely put on, which protect them from wind and rain. They change their habitations from place to place as circumstances of situation and season may require: this is easily done as they have only to take with them their mats and they have other houses prepared at once. The fathers and the whole family dwell together in one house, in great numbers, in one we saw 25 or 30 persons." These houses were of course not wigwams, but circular beehive-shaped frameworks of saplings covered with mats of cattails or other rushes.

"Their food is pulse [i.e., beans] as with the other tribes, which is here better than elsewhere, and more carefully cultivated. In the time of sowing they are governed by the moon, the sprouting of grain and many other ancient usages. They live by hunting and fishing, and they are long-lived. If they fall sick they cure themselves without medicine, by the heat of the fire, and their death at last comes from extreme old age." Perhaps this repetition of the old-age idea suggests the surprise with which a sailor accustomed to a life of violent activity and early death by war or disease confronts the peaceful existence of an agricultural society. "We judge them to be very affectionate and charitable towards their relatives, making loud lamentations in their adversity and in their misery calling to mind all their good fortune. At their departure out of life their relations mutually join in weeping, mingled with singing for a long while."

This whole account is particularly significant as a picture of the Indians unchanged by such European influences as later degenerated them. It is an honest and a human picture, and one can read evidence in it of the respect with which Verrazano regarded this people. There is no mention of the thievery which later explorers deplore. Nowhere in the account is there any suggestion that these natives were treacherous or hostile. Verrazano was plainly delighted with them, and enjoyed his stay there. It is a particularly trustworthy account, because so many of the details he describes are in accord with later chronicles of the region, and an especially valuable one because written by a man who apparently allowed no predatory or commercial

activities to interfere with his observations of the people. I think
that we may accept Verrazano's judgment of the original character of these Indians as of greater validity than the judgment
of any later explorer. His honesty is particularly well evidenced
by his later comment about the natives of the Maine coast;
"The people were entirely different from the others we had
seen, whom we had found kind and gentle, but these were so
rude and barbarous that we were unable by any signs we could
make, to hold communication with them—They have no pulse,
and we saw no signs of cultivation; the land appears sterile and
unfit for growing of fruit or grain of any kind." It seems almost
certain that those Maine Indians had seen Europeans before, for
he says of them: "If we wished at any time to traffick with
them, they came to the sea shore and stood on the rocks, from
which they lowered down by a cord to our boats beneath
whatever they had to barter, continually crying out to us not
to come nearer, and instantly demanding from us that which
was to be given in exchange, they took from us only knives,
fish hooks and sharpened steel. No regard was paid to our
courtesies; when we had nothing left to exchange with them,
the men at our departure made the most brutal signs of disdain
and contempt possible."

I quote the above at this time purely to emphasize by contrast Verrazano's appraisal of the Rhode Island Indians. This
estimate is at marked variance with our usual notion of the
Narragansetts derived from the memory of King Philip's War
a century and a half later. We have no way of ascertaining
whether the Indians whom Verrazano found about Newport
were Wampanoags or Narragansetts, but the question does not
seem particularly important when one considers that the Narragansetts before King Philip's time were the tribe who welcomed
and remained on splendid terms with kindly Roger Williams,
even as Massasoit and his Wampanoags welcomed the Pilgrims.
There is sufficient later evidence to show that both tribes were
originally industrious agricultural people, even as Verrazano
found them. There is also abundant testimony that many ele-

ments among the later white settlers supplied plenty of provocation to arouse their hostility. But in the beginning Verrazano's
peaceful picture of this people was unquestionably an accurate
one.

"This region," he continues, still speaking of Narragansett
Bay, "is situated in the parallel of Rome, being 41° 40′ of north
latitude, but much colder . . . It looks toward the south, on
which side the harbor is half a league broad; afterwards, upon
entering it, the extent between the coast and the north is twelve
leagues, and then enlarging itself it forms a very large bay, 20
leagues in circumference, in which are five small islands of great
fertility and beauty, covered with large and lofty trees. Among
these islands any fleet, however large, might ride safely, without
fear c₂ tempests or other dangers. Turning towards the south,
at the entrance of the harbor, on both sides, there are very
pleasant hills, and many streams of clear water, which flow
down to th₌ sea. In the midst of the entrance there is a rock of
freestone, formed by nature, and suitable for the construction
of any kind of machine or bulwark for the defense of the
harbor.

"Having supplied ourselves with everything necessary, on
the fifth day of May we departed from the port, and sailed
150 leagues, keeping so close to the coast as never to lose it
from our sight; the nature of the country appeared much
the same as before, but the mountains were a little higher, and
all in appearance rich in minerals. We did not stop to land as
the weather was very favorable for pursuing our voyage, and
the country presented no variety. The shore stretched to the
East, and 50 leagues beyond more to the north, where we
found a more elevated country, full of very thick woods of
fir-trees, cypresses and the like, indicative of a cold climate."

I have assumed throughout this chapter that Verrazano's
account applies to Narragansett Bay, and the preceding two
paragraphs are quoted in full as corroboration of that assumption. The latitude given corresponds well with the middle portion of Narragansett Bay. The description coincides with no

other region as well, and the general conformation of the coast line nowhere else fits as well with Verrazano's account. His failure to mention any difficulties with the renowned tide rips of Vineyard and Nantucket sounds which bothered many a later explorer suggests that he took the outside route around Nantucket. This would well account for the lack of any recognizable description of Cape Cod, especially since the two eastern promontories of Cape Cod, which Bartholomew Gosnold named Point Gilbert and Point Care, since washed away, at that time held navigators much farther off shore from the cape than at present.

And so we leave Verrazano sailing up the Maine coast, trafficking with its reluctant natives as described before. "In this region," he says, "we found nothing extraordinary except vast forests and some metalliferous hills, as we infer from seeing that many of the people wore copper earrings. Departing from thence we kept along the coast steering northeast, and found the country more pleasant and open, free from woods, and distant in the interior we saw lofty mountains, but none which extended to the shore. Within 50 leagues we discovered thirty-two islands all near the mainland, small and of pleasant appearance, but high and so disposed as to afford excellent harbors and channels, as we see in the Adriatic gulph near Illyria and Dalmatia."

One problem is raised by this voyage. Both at Newport and in Maine he found copper. So also did Gosnold among the people of Cape Cod in 1602, and Henry Hudson on Cape Cod in 1607, and Martin Pring notes "Brasse" at Plymouth in 1603. Did these Indians have sources of native copper near by? The alternatives are these: first, that they imported native copper from the great Lake Superior lodes which Indians there are known to have mined; second, that they found enough nuggets in glacial gravel here and there locally to fulfill their needs for beads and pipestems; third, that European traders carrying copper had preceded Verrazano in Rhode Island. When Gosnold asked an Indian of Cape Cod their source: "yet I was desirous to under-

stand where they had such store of this metal, and made signes
to one of them, who taking a piece of Copper in his hand
made a hole with his finger in the ground, and withall pointed
to the maine [mainland] from whence they came." Certain
statements in the report of Richard Grenville from Roanoke in
1585 correspond well with this statement of Gosnold's Indian.
Indeed, the weight of evidence leads one to the belief that Indian
trade in American copper extended from tribe to tribe for as
much as a thousand miles. Such information rightfully increases
our respect for the American Indian.

We are indebted to Verrazano for a first vivid picture of
New England that gives us considerable occasion for thought.
It presents a flattering picture of the unspoiled Indian of Rhode
Island, and a singularly unpleasant one of the trader Indian of
Maine. It shows the contentment of the Rhode Island native in
his concern over personal adornment even to the point of refus-
ing the advantages of iron and steel, but quite the contrary in
Maine. This difference was of course cultural—the peasant as
opposed to the hunter; but I think it can be argued that the
attitudes of the two peoples toward Verrazano and his men displayed more than a cultural difference. Why should the bringers
of knives and fishhooks be so unwelcome to the coast of Maine?

There is evidence enough in the Newport story that Verrazano had his men under sufficiently good control to prevent any
more serious misdemeanors than some hooting of sailors at the
Indian women. That seems to have been a prerogative of sailors
in all eras. Why, then, this manifest hostility on the part of the
Maine natives? To me it suggests some disagreeable precursors
of Verrazano on that coast. Perhaps Gosnold's Indian lied: possibly the copper evidence signifies earlier traders in the Newport
region too. It seems to me that the general tenor of Verrazano's
story opposes this conclusion. The Indian copper of 1524 probably came from American soil. Of course the Dighton Rock
inscription has never been explained away, and no other logbook
of the Cortereal voyages is likely to be discovered. This all
leaves us with the question in our minds: Did Miguel Cortereal

sail into Newport Harbor in 1501 with a cargo of copper, and did his vessel sink beneath the waves, leaving him "by the Grace of God, leader of the Indians"? Or is the inscription false and did the Indians import their copper from Michigan? I think the most logical inference to draw is that if Cortereal indeed lived for ten years among the Indians, he arrived there as an empty-handed castaway. I feel that time will prove the Indian copper of that period was of American origin. This leaves Verrazano as the first significant modern explorer of the Rhode Island region and the discoverer of New England. His splendid report sets a high standard for New England history at its very beginning.

Two final conclusions about Verrazano are the most important of all. If we may judge him on his own story of the voyage, he did nothing which could prejudice the Indians against white men, but rather showed the natives the kindlier side of European character. This is a good record for a man who just previously had indulged his taste for Spanish gold torn from the temples of the Aztec gods. But perhaps even more important to the future of French efforts in New England was his discovery that here were no Aztec treasure hoards, nor yet any of the Oriental wealth of Cibangu or Cathay. No doubt the King of France regarded this voyage with as thorough disappointment as had Henry VII the second expedition of Cabot along these shores. It was becoming apparent that nothing approaching the wealth of the Indies was to be found upon these coasts.

Chapter Four

THE STRUGGLE FOR SUPREMACY, 1525–1600

UP TO THIS point Spain had shown very little interest in northern voyages, except in so far as her diplomatic representatives in England and France were assiduously reporting the movements of her rivals' ships. Now, however, in the year immediately following Verrazano's voyage she sent Estevan Gomez along the same shores. We have already noted that there were Castilian fishermen on the Grand Banks in 1517, and fishermen were probably always a primary source of information about new regions, despite their inability to furnish written reports. But when one nation was found to have sent a formal expedition to new lands, other nations seem often to have followed it up with an immediate reconnaissance in the same area. This probably accounts for the tendency of voyages to occur in closely spaced groups.

Verrazano's report of a continuous coast stretching from Florida to Nova Scotia was certainly of such vital importance as to demand confirmation, if indeed any report of it had reached Spain.

Gomez, best known for his participation in the mutiny in the Strait of Magellan on the circumnavigation voyage five years earlier, arrived off Newfoundland in the winter of 1524-1525, only about six months after Verrazano's departure for France. Largely from evidence noted on a Diego Ribero map of 1529, and from contemporary documents, H. P. Biggar has attempted

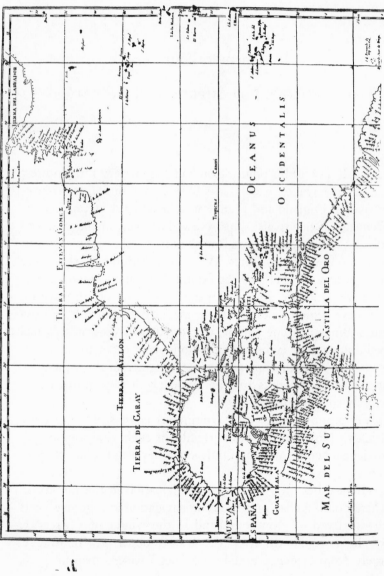

FIG. I—MAP OF THE NORTH AMERICAN COAST, A PORTION OF THE WORLD-MAP MADE BY DIEGO RIBERO, IN 1529, showing the results of the explorations of Estrevan Gomez in 1525. The Penobscot and Cape Cod are clearly indicated. (Reproduced from the copy in the Yale University Library.)

to reconstruct this voyage. After coasting Nova Scotia and the Bay of Fundy, Gomez seems to have cruised southward along the Maine coast in the months of January and February. He first clearly noted and explored broad Penobscot Bay, which from this time appeared regularly on countless maps of the New England coast. The islands of Penobscot and Casco bays he named Gomez's Archipelago. Somewhere along the Gulf of Maine he seems to have kidnaped several Indians, thus inaugurating a New England practice which became more and more frequent among explorers on this coast. He took note of the Kennebec, Saco and Merrimac rivers. Gomez apparently named certain of the landmarks along the shore for the religious holidays during which he sighted them. This affords a sort of calendar of the voyage. Biggar believes that about April 14th Boston Bay received from him the fast-day name of St. Christopher's Bay, and that he arrived in the hook of Cape Cod on May 1st, and therefore named it Cape St. James, whose festival falls on that day. After he rounded Cape Cod, the Island of Nantucket received the well-deserved name of Cape of Shoals, by which it continued to be known throughout the sixteenth century. He then apparently sailed on down the coast to Cuba.

John Fiske, writing twenty years earlier than Biggar, locates Gomez's landmarks more to the southward but agrees that the Spaniard took notice of Cape Cod and thinks that he saw Narragansett Bay and the mouths of the Connecticut and Hudson rivers. Reading between the lines, one may assume that Gomez became embayed by a headland which Biggar calls Cape Cod, and Fiske Cape Henlopen in Delaware Bay. It does seem strange that Gomez should have chosen to spend four months on the coasts of Maine and Massachusetts in the ice and sleet of a New England winter, but whether it was two months or four makes little difference for our purposes. This whole question involves a dispute which has raged for nearly a century among historians of this period, in the attempt to determine whether the deep triangular river mouth first depicted by Ribero, and later usually referred to as the River of Norumbega, was indeed the

Penobscot or, as Fiske thought, the Hudson. The weakness in Fiske's theory is in the assumption that Cape Cod, the most striking geographical object on the whole Atlantic coast, was unrecognized by Gomez, sailing as he did from north to south in the pursuit of an otherwise careful exploring voyage. If the prominent cape depicted by Ribero is not Cape Cod, one is at a loss to find anything resembling it on his map. In any case Ribero's map portrays the Land of Estevan Gomez in sufficient detail to warrant a belief that he made a deliberate study of this shore. If indeed Gomez sailed up Narragansett Bay, it would be of great interest to learn, if one could, what impression he in turn made upon those grandfathers of the Wampanoags. It seems that possibly these Rhode Islanders had an exceedingly thorough acquaintance with Portuguese, French and Spaniards almost a century before the arrival of English settlers in that region.

Only two years later the English again appeared on New England shores. Henry VIII, now on the English throne, gradually began to follow up his father's somewhat hesitant interest in the New World. In 1527 he appears to have commissioned a voyage in search of a passage to India by way of icebound Davis Strait. The *Samson* and the *Mary Guildford* set forth from Plymouth in June of that year. Three weeks later the *Samson* foundered in a storm. The *Mary Guildford* proceeded into Davis Strait, but like Cabot and Cortereal and many later navigators, the ship was forced by pack ice to turn back down the Labrador coast. In St. John's Harbor, Newfoundland they saw eleven Norman, one Breton and two Portuguese ships, "all a fishing." We know that Nicolas Don, a Breton, and the English Captain Robert Thorne were there at about this time. Obtaining no word of the *Samson*, they sailed southward along our coasts in a vain search for her. Somewhere in the course of this cruise the Italian pilot of the expedition—who, Biggar remarks, "may have been Verrazano"—was killed in a skirmish with the Indians. This ship arrived at Puerto Rico and Santo Domingo in November and eventually returned to England. We have no details of its New England travels, and indeed Williamson believes that it was not the *Mary Guildford*, but perhaps the *Samson*, that made the voyage from Newfoundland to Santo Domingo. J. G. Kohl, however, gives strong evidence for the belief that the whole voyage was made by the *Mary Guildford*.

For a reconstruction of the remainder of New England's part in the succeeding fifty years we must proceed largely by inference from what happened in adjoining areas. The reader may judge for himself whether these inferences are justifiable. The recorded history so far as it concerns this coast becomes fragmentary, for I can find only four definite records between 1527 and 1580 of voyages that clearly touched these shores.

Enough has been said up to this point to show that by 1527 the news was certainly traveling from tribe to tribe among the natives that great white ships had come and brought curious gifts to Newport and to Maine. Some tidings of the fishermen must also have reached these southern shores. For as Francis Parkman says: "From this time forth, the Newfoundland fishery was never abandoned. French, English, Spanish and Portuguese made resort of the Banks, always jealous, often quarrelling, but still drawing up treasure from those exhaustless mines, and bearing home bountiful provision against the season of Lent."

The same year that Gomez took his course southward along New England shores the Portuguese were attempting a colony on Cape Breton. These early "Colonies" were not settlements in the later sense, but were probably in the nature of trading stations with flakes erected on which to sun-dry codfish. Shelters for fishermen were undoubtedly built much earlier than this in Newfoundland. Few colonies of this earlier sort ever achieved permanence. They are to be compared with branch offices set up by agents in a new country for their temporary convenience in a new project and not to settlements of homes erected by families permanently cut loose from a home base. It was only when women migrated along with their menfolk that settlements were made. This is the distinction between these early colonies and those of Massachusetts. The French, who now came to dominate these early efforts were in this sense *colonials;*

the English, in the later phase, came as *settlers*. This difference was the distinction between failure and success. But the colonial experiment was an essential preliminary to the final settlement.

We enter now upon the period when the French were trying to challenge the supremacy of the Spanish throughout the Western world. Verrazano's capture of the Spanish treasure ship in 1523 had been an important landmark. The wealth of Mexico had just been revealed by Cortes and this shipment was the first. It was significant that François immediately sent Verrazano back to the New World. But the Italian's report was, as we have seen, probably disappointing. Europe was in a gold rush, and the rivalry of opinions about the value of the New World was intense. For many years the "southern theory," of capitalizing immediately on the discoveries of Spain, was paramount. As a consequence France now bent its strongest efforts toward breaking the Spanish power by piracy. She attacked the ports of the West Indies and played havoc with Spanish fleets. Thoughts of trade and of a Northwest Passage to Asia, which constituted the "northern theory," languished. The French were soon to return to the northern theory, but in the ten years between 1524 and 1534 the north held little interest save to the plodding fishermen who, as some surviving examples of their maps show, were extending their knowledge southward into the Bay of Fundy. But New England, falling between the two theories of commercial advantage, was to lie neglected until a later, English, day. Only a theory which should involve a medium between the two extremes of Newfoundland and Mexico could give New England any part to play.

Pursuing the northern theory came in 1534 Jacques Cartier, under a commission from the Admiral of France. He sailed north of Newfoundland through the Straits of Belle Isle and into the Gulf of St. Lawrence. Setting up a cross at Gaspé he proceeded into the St. Lawrence River along the shores of Anticosti Island, kidnaped two Indians lured by treachery aboard his ship, and sailed back to France. The next year he returned and proceeded up the St. Lawrence to Quebec and Montreal, then occupied by an Iroquois people. After wintering in misery at Quebec he again returned to France, bringing with him the shanghaied chiefs of the Quebec village.

Cartier's third voyage in 1541 was a more pretentious attempt at colonization. With five ships he sailed to a point above Quebec, where a fort was built, and Cartier himself proceeded up the river to make further exploration. But the Sieur de Roberval, who was expected to follow with three additional ships and two hundred settlers male and female, seems to have been slow to make his appearance. Roberval eventually arrived to make a settlement on Cartier's site, but after a wretched winter of suffering the colony disappeared from history. Cartier had returned to France in the meantime. The accounts of this ambitious project are unfortunately fragmentary, and the reasons for Cartier's abandonment of the attempt not altogether clear. In any case it was the first attempt at a true settlement, and it appears, had it not suffered the mischance of Roberval's delayed arrival, might conceivably have survived. The three voyages of Cartier constituted the most sustained northern effort in a single region over so short a period, since the time of Leif Eriksson. It illustrated well the fact that the kidnaping of Indians was a poor preliminary for settlement, for a tribe which had been cordial and helpful at the first visit was sullen and suspicious seven years later. Fortunately this tribe was extinct when the French again settled this region, in 1608 under Champlain.

For our New England purposes there is one interesting feature of this French endeavor. One of Roberval's pilots, Jehan Allefonsce of Saintonge, reported sailing southward in 1542 to a great bay in the latitude of 42°. Later there was published a corrupt version of his description of the coast which was rendered into French verse by one Jehan Maillard, poet royal, prior to 1547. This was the first appearance of New England in verse.

The voyage marks the first of those four recorded New England landfalls between 1527 and 1580. This "great bay" almost without question was Massachusetts Bay. The observations of these early navigators were made with the astrolabe. It is natural to question their accuracy, particularly in as ill-defined an instance as this of Allefonsce. But the more one reads of these voyages the more one is struck with the ability of their navigators not only to return repeatedly to the same region without difficulty but, what is more significant, to make a correct landfall at the end of a five to eight weeks' transatlantic voyage. A further testimony of their accuracy is the tendency for readings of latitude made by different captains at the same place at different times to agree. The general factor of error as indicated by such comparison of their journals is not often so much as half a degree, which is to say not more than thirty-five miles. Thus in this note of Jehan Allefonsce, we can safely assume that his "great bay" was somewhere between Martha's Vineyard and Salem.

In 1542, the same year that Allefonsce was investigating Massachusetts shores, John Fiske tells us that French traders had found their way up the Hudson River as far as Albany, and had there established a trading post. Here is a piece of historical irony, for if Verrazano, Gomez and now unnamed Frenchmen all found their way into the Hudson River before 1550, how is it that it was "discovered" by Henry Hudson in 1609? But here is also an observation that serves our New England interest well by indicating that the French activities were not limited to the northern coasts. Is it reasonable to suppose that French fishermen and traders were at work just outside the limits of New England on both ends of her coast without frequently trespassing on these intermediate shores? De Costa says: "In 1541 the prospect of the settlement of Canada under the French gave such a stimulus to merchants that in the months of January and February, 1541 and 1542, no less than 60 ships went to fish for cod in the new lands. Gosselin, who had examined a great number of the ancient records, says 'in 1543, 1544 and 1545 this ardor was sustained; and during the months of January and February from Havre and Rouen and from Dieppe and Honfleur about 2 ships left every day.'"

Surely it is not an unjustified inference to suppose that an occasional ship among all these hundreds of fishermen coasted New England and traded for beaver with the Indians, even as Verrazano had done twenty years earlier. Nor is it surprising that among the dusty records of this period in the western ports of France, there began to appear vague references to "Norumbega," an indefinite coast between Cape Breton and Florida out of which poured a great river. Norumbega became later identified with a small area of the New England coast, but to these early fishermen the name seems to have been applied to the whole American coast from Maine to the Carolinas.

During this period when the French were so busily occupied with the attempt to establish themselves on the great waterways of the St. Lawrence and the Hudson, the Spaniards were making an equally energetic attempt to follow up the immense valley of the Mississippi. During the years 1538-1543 Hernando De Soto, one of the conquerors of Peru, first marched from the west coast of Florida to a point on the shores of South Carolina, and then across some parts of the Appalachian range back to the coast of Mexico. Not satisfied with what he had found among the southeastern Indians, De Soto again set out northward, leaving his fleet in the Gulf of Mexico under its captain, Diego Maldonado, and after traversing a large part of the present states of Alabama and Mississippi, reached the "father of waters" and followed it northward almost to its junction with the Ohio. Here he died. A remnant of his company, after some investigations westward in the "country of the wild cows," eventually sailed down the Mississippi and reached Mexico after an absence of five years.

Meanwhile, De Soto's accomplished wife, Isabella de Bobadilla, carried on for her husband the responsibilities of governing Cuba. Increasingly anxious for the safety of her husband, she finally fitted out an expedition under the leadership of Captain Maldonado to go in search of him. Thus it came about that in 1541 Maldonado, having spent a fruitless year in search of De Soto in the Gulf of Mexico, extended his search along the eastern coast as far as the country of the Baccalaos. Not until 1543 did he return, so that we may judge that he performed a meticulous exploration of our eastern coasts. Unfortunately we have no further details about this voyage, although Dr. Kohl surmises that perhaps Maldonado's researches produced some Spanish place names on the maps of this period not previously seen after the Gomez voyage. In Spanish minds, Baccalaos was identified with Newfoundland, beyond the Tierra de Estevan Gomez. This, the second of our New England voyages in the period between 1527 and 1580, was the last known appearance of Spaniards on these northern shores.

The third of these mid-century voyages to New England was again incidental to a larger enterprise on other coasts. In 1555 that great Huguenot leader Admiral Coligny set in motion an attempt to establish in Brazil a refuge for French Protestants. Under the leadership of Durand de Villegagnon a settlement was made at Rio de Janeiro, which ended disastrously after five years through a combination of internal dissension and a naval attack by the Portuguese. Its interest for us lies in the fact that the celebrated French traveler and cosmographer André Thevet accompanied the expedition and in 1556 sailed home to France by way of the North American coast, like Maldonado, as far north as Baccalaos. In his *Cosmographie Universelle*, which he wrote after returning from this voyage, he gives the following interesting account of his visit to a river at Norumbega.

"Having left La Florida on the left hand, with all its islands, gulfs and capes, a river presents itself, which is one of the finest rivers in the whole world, which we call 'Norumbegue', and the aborigines 'Agoncy', and which is marked on some marine charts as the Grand River. Several other beautiful rivers enter into it, and upon its banks the French formerly erected a little fort about ten or twelve leagues from its mouth, which was surrounded by fresh water, and this place was named the Fort of Norumbegue.

"Some pilots would make me believe that this country is the proper country of Canada, but I told them that this was far from the truth, since this country lies in 43 N. and that of Canada is 50 or 52. Before you enter the said river appears an island surrounded by eight very small islets, which are near to the country of the green mountains and to the Cape of the islets. From there you sail all along into the mouth of the river, which is dangerous from the great number of thick and high rocks; and its entrance is wonderfully large. About three leagues into the river, an island presents itself to you, that may have four leagues in circumference, inhabited only by some fishermen and birds of different sorts, which island they call 'Aiayascon', because it has the form of a man's arm, which they call so. Its greatest length is from north to south. It would be very easy to plant on this island, and build a fortress on it to keep in check the whole surrounding country."

Nowhere south of Rhode Island is there any such accumulation of islands as this account suggests, nor is there south of the Maine coast such a group of islands made "dangerous from the great number of thick and high rocks." If we add to these requirements a river with a "wonderfully large" entrance, and in this entrance an island stretching from north to south (Islesboro), we are led inevitably to the Penobscot. A good deal of doubt exists about the authenticity of Thevet's account, and indeed as to whether he made the voyage at all. This is not the place for a discussion of these doubts, since it is of little interest to us to determine whether he was borrowing his material from someone who had visited these coasts or was reporting in fact his own experiences. We can be content here to draw from the internal evidence in the text a conclusion as to whether the general tenor of the description fits into any known geographical area with sufficient certainty to indicate that *someone* visited this area in 1556, or that the whole thing is imaginative. From this standpoint the above account seems to me to have so many resemblances to the Penobscot Bay region as to satisfy us that it is not a product of imagination.

FERNALD LIBRARY
COLBY-SAWYER COLLEGE
NEW LONDON, N.H. 0325

The latitude of 43° is in error by about a degree, which is within the factor of error of these early navigators and therefore is additional evidence to support the Maine rather than the Hudson River theory. The mention of "fresh water" surrounding the site of Fort Norumbegue is sufficient to eliminate any misapprehension as to whether we are dealing with a bay or a river. The near-by "green mountains" correspond well with the Camden Hills, the most striking coastal range in New England. The association of fishermen and birds on the island fits into no other area so well as the Maine shore, where great colonies of nesting gulls are frequent among the islands throughout the splendid codfishing area that surrounds Monhegan Island and Matinicus.

One passage in Thevet's account strikes me as of extraordinary interest. After giving the latitude of his river, he goes on to say: "before you enter the said river, appears an island surrounded by eight very small islets which are near to the country of the green mountains and to the Cape of the islets. From there you sail all along into the mouth of the river . . ." The sequence certainly suggests that he is giving sailing directions for entering the river. Any yachtsman will agree that the landmark for an approach to the Penobscot from the open sea is Matinicus Island, which is surrounded by six or eight small islets in a group farther seaward than anything else along the coast except lonely Monhegan. The westerly entrance of the Penobscot, from Matinicus, is a direct line toward the Camden Hills. Furthermore, reference to Ribero's map of 1529 will show that just to the west of his great river he has marked "Cabo de muchas yslas" and "motanos." If we may suppose that Thevet, cosmographer as he was, had with him a copy of Ribero's or a similar map, of which we know several, then what would be more natural than for Thevet to indicate in his sailing directions a reference to such a chart? It seems clear to me that in the above-quoted passage we have just that reference: his island surrounded by eight small islets is "near to the country of the green mountains and to the Cape of the islets." If this reasoning is sound, we may immediately conclude that Thevet's Norumbega River was identical with the Rio de las Gamas, or Rio Grande or Rio de Estevan Gomez of the map makers who followed Ribero and Gomez, and that this great river was unquestionably the Penobscot. Ribero's "motanos" have become Thevet's "green mountains" and Ribero's "Cabo de muchas yslas" is Thevet's "Cape of the islets." To these landmarks, I am convinced that Thevet has added Matinicus, the "island surrounded by eight very small islets." In short, the coincidences which connect Thevet's narrative with characteristics of the Penobscot region multiply themselves to such a degree that identification of the two becomes almost a mathematical certainty. Regardless of where Thevet may have obtained his information, its details ring true. And we may note in passing that, if the account in other respects is thus accurate, we have no reason to doubt his statement that at this early date French fishermen had not only found the New England fishing banks, but had even erected a "little fort" as a base for their operations in this locality.

Thevet continues from the last quoted passage: "Having landed and put our feet on the adjacent country, we perceived a great mass of people coming down upon us from all sides in such numbers that you might have supposed them to be a flight of starlings. Those which marched first were the men, which they called 'Aquelums'. After them came the women, which they called 'Peragonastas', then the 'Adegestas', being the children, and the last were the girls, called 'Aniusgestas'. And all this people was clothed in skins of wild animals, which they call 'Rabatotz.' Now considering their aspect and manner of proceeding, we mistrusted them, and went on board our vessel. But they, perceiving our fear, lifted their hands into the air, making signs that we should not mistrust them; and for making us still more sure, they sent to our vessel some of their principal men, which brought us provisions. In recompense of this, we gave them a few trinkets of a low price, by which they were highly pleased. The next morning I, with some others, was commissioned to meet them, and to know whether they would be inclined to assist us with more victuals, of which we were very much in need. But having entered into the house, which they call 'Canoque', of a certain little king of theirs, which called himself 'Peramich', we saw several killed animals hanging on the beams of the said house, which he had pre-pared (as he assured us) to send to us. This chief gave us a very hearty welcome, and to show us his affection, he ordered to kindle a fire, which they call 'Azista', on which meat was to be put and fish to be roasted. Upon this some rogues came in to bring to the king the heads of six men, which they had taken in war and massacred, which terrified us, fearing that they might treat us in the same way. But toward evening we secretly retired to our ship without bidding good-bye to our host. At this he was very much irritated, and came to us the next morning accompanied by three of his children, showing a mournful countenance, because he thought that we had been dissatisfied with him; and he said in his language: 'Coaquoca Ame Conascon Kazaconny' (Come to drink and to eat what we have): 'Arca somiopyach Quendria dangua ysmay asso-maka (we assure you upon oath by heaven, moon and stars, that you shall fare not worse than our own persons).

"Seeing the good affection and will of this old man, some twenty of us went again on land, everyone of us with his arms; and then we went to his lodgings, where we were treated, and presented with what he possessed. And meanwhile great num-bers of people arrived, caressing us and offering themselves to give us pleasure, saying that they were our friends. Late in the evening, when we were willing to retire and to take leave of the company with actions of gratitude, they would not give us leave. Men, women, children, all entreated us zealously to stay with them, crying out these words: 'Coziquo aguyda hoa' (my friends, do not start from here: you shall sleep this night with us). But they could not harangue so well as to persuade us to sleep with them. And so we retired to our vessel; and having remained in this place five full days, we weighed anchor, parting from them with a marvelous contentment of both sides, and went out to the open sea."

We note that there is no mention here of corn or squashes, or beans. The French were given only meat and fish. We know from both Verrazano and Champlain narratives that these more northern tribes carried on no agriculture, at least along the shore, and it was not until Champlain reached the area about the Saco River, and from there southward, that he found gardens. This omission again serves to confirm us in our belief that here was a people north of Portland. Champlain later cited an instance of a Passamaquoddy Indian desiring the head of a victim. The other characteristics—the haranguing, the exchange of gifts, the maneuverings of distrust and the eating of meals together—were in no way different from innumerable such encounters between explorers and Indians throughout the American continent. I am not prepared to express any opinion on the dialect reproduced by Thevet, or upon his translations of it. It is, however, characteristic of a man of learning like Thevet, a professional geographer and traveler, to attempt such a rendering of a new language, and it would seem that if all this was sheer hokum we would expect to find similar nonsense scattered through the remainder of his account. This we do not find, for the type of detail given is not of the unicorn-and-emerald variety, but rather a restrained choice of observations such as we who are more familiar with the region than he was can readily believe. This, I think, is a basis for believing that this narrative is genuine.

There remains one inconsistency. If Verrazano found the Indians of Maine so ferocious, why are the French here received so hospitably? All that can be said on this point is that the initial experiences of Champlain, George Waymouth and the Popham colonists in this area fifty years later of which more will be said in later chapters of this book, were more similar to Thevet's chronicle than to Verrazano's. Whether Verrazano ran into a different tribe of natives we can only conjecture.

We leave the consideration of Thevet's voyage with the

feeling that, after Narragansett Bay, the Penobscot was the next portion of the New England coast to become well known in Europe, and that Thevet contributed to that knowledge not only a furtherance of the Norumbega controversy, but a very definite increase in specific information about the coast of Maine. In this sense he was a worthy successor to both Gomez and Verrazano.

After 1556 impetus to French exploration of northern America was interrupted for many years by the desolate religious wars in France itself. The Huguenot impulse to colonization in exile did last a while longer and French fishermen continued to ply their trade in "those exhaustless mines" of Newfoundland, but the dominant influences in the trend toward organized ventures in the new continent began slowly to pass to the English. This was not a sudden change, but is evidenced rather by the increasing frequency of English voyages, which was in consonance with the development of the Elizabethan sea dogs. Drake and his romantic group of bold navigators early turned their attention to the rich opportunities which the French had been first to take advantage of, in privateering on the gold-laden galleons returning from Mexico and Peru to Spain. From this beginning other forms of international racketeering soon suggested themselves. Prominent in the beginning of this movement was Sir John Hawkins, who in 1562 had entered with eminent success into the illegitimate business of transporting Negroes from Africa and selling them as slaves to the Spanish colonies. On the way home from the second of these freebooting expeditions in 1565 he sailed north from Florida to Newfoundland on what William Wood calls "the first voyage ever made along the coast of the United States by an all English crew." We are inclined to give the *Mary Guildford* that priority, or perhaps even John Cabot.

In any case this voyage of Hawkins is the fourth of those New England landfalls I have spoken of above. He had stopped en route at Laudonnière's ill-fated colony in Florida, which was annihilated later in the same year by the Spaniard Menendez, and

unfortunately reports only that he came home by way of Newfoundland, the sole note being that they were running short
of provisions in the last weeks of the voyage. Here again we
are forced to resort to surmise. Would Hawkins have chosen
this long route home, short of supplies as he was, unless some
intent to investigate these unknown shores was in his mind?
Payne feels that this move was a part of an English reconnaissance of these coasts with a view to establishing a colonial
rivalry to the Spaniards.

This voyage, however, is not the only nor yet the most
significant mention of Hawkins that interests us. Three years
later he made his third, and only disastrous, voyage. With six
ships he set sail again. Young Francis Drake, then only twenty-
three, was captain of the *Judith*, one of the six. After some
vicissitudes in the slave trade, the little fleet was caught in a
storm in the Gulf of Mexico and forced to put in for shelter
at the Spanish "port that serveth the city of Mexico," which
was San Juan de Ulloa, near the present Vera Cruz. To make
matters worse, the next morning there appeared a Spanish fleet
of thirteen great vessels which soon attacked the English and
sank four of their six ships. The survivors managed to make
their escape on two small vessels. Drake, in the *Judith*, rode out
the storm at sea and sailed forthwith for England. But Hawkins
was faced with an ugly dilemma. Heavily overloaded with three
hundred men, his ship dismasted, he found shelter in the lee
of an island until the gale blew itself out, then beat about for
two weeks of starvation, hunting for some means of subsistence.
None found, at length a hundred men determined to take their
chances ashore. Landed near the modern Tampico, in Mexico,
only five are known to have survived. Two of these, Miles
Philips and Job Hortop, escaped to England after fourteen and
twenty-three years, respectively, of Spanish servitude. The
third, David Ingram, perpetrated one of the most astounding
improbabilities that history ever recorded as the truth. With
two companions, he *walked* to a point near St. John, in New
Brunswick, Canada, and was there picked up by a friendly

French trader. His account of the journey, dictated to a secretary before witnesses some fourteen years later, reads like the travels of Marco Polo, and is fully as incredible. It took him eleven months, of which he says that seven were in the region north of the River of May in Florida, where, as we know, Laudonnière's Huguenot colony had already been exterminated by the Spaniards. He apparently skirted the shores, as would be natural to one anticipating rescue. Of the text, the best that can be said of it is that there are many details which are descriptive of the American Indian in certain of the areas which he traversed. Their villages of round houses, their canoes, their weapons and social usages he describes with the undiscriminating eye of an unlettered sailor. He fails to differentiate, however, between the various regions and tribes through which he passed, and the result is a miscellaneous commentary from which one can glean something here that is true of the Iroquois, and in the next sentence a characteristic of the Aztec. The geographical descriptions are similar hodgepodge. One finds a recognizable account of buffalo, of maize and yams and some other animals and plants. But the fellow has such a nauseating obsession with gold, iron, rubies, silver and pearls that, after we have given him the benefit of the doubt by calling much of his gold, copper, and his iron swords, polished slate knives, and his pearls, wampum, we still find a great deal of marvelous residue too fantastic for plausibility. When he endows the Indian with a variety of domesticated animals, horses, swine and guinea hens, one is forced to conclude that he was wishfully hunting for a good old English barnyard. And when he describes elephants, and "a monstrous beast twice as big as a horse" with "two teeth or horns, of a foot long, growing straight forth by their nostrils," one wonders if the man was maundering still about his slave-trading in Africa. Undoubtedly Ingram did pass through New England. But we can glean no more useful information from his story than did Richard Hakluyt, of whom Purchas remarked: "As for David Ingram's perambulations to the north parts, Master Hakluyt, in his first editions, published the same; but it seemeth some incredibilities of his reports caused him to leave him out in the next impression; *the reward of lying being, not to be believed in truths.*"

Let us not belittle Ingram's exploit, however, in condemning his narrative of it. The thing happened, and is apparently attested to on good authority. It is the more unfortunate that Richard Browne and Richard Twide, his two companions, left no record of their part in the adventure. Would that some kind star would enlighten such miraculous experiences of very ordinary, ignorant men in history and present them with a gift of language sufficient to leave us with good records. Few were the sailors and fishermen in those early days who had even the gift of reading or writing. That is why we have to fill in the gaps with conjecture.

One statement of Ingram's we can well consider accurate; "Travelling towards the north, [Ingram] found the main sea, [probably the Gulf of St. Lawrence] upon the north side of America; and travelled in sight thereof the space of two whole days; where the people signified unto him that they had seen ships on the coast, and did draw upon the ground the shape and figure of ships, and of their sails and flags." The fact that the French trader who rescued Ingram and his companions must have penetrated the Bay of Fundy to its head is sufficient proof of this, nor should we forget that Bay of Fundy voyages necessarily skirted the shores of eastern Maine as well. Indeed the horizons of the Maritime Provinces, and therefore those of Maine also, must have been studded with sails. Sir Richard Whitbourne reported that in 1578 there were a hundred Spanish, fifty English, one hundred and fifty French and fifty Portuguese ships on the Newfoundland banks. Quarreling was almost the rule among the different nationalities. Hakluyt is filled with references to marooned crews, confiscated cargoes, and freebooting of all kinds. The habit which in southern waters had grown to the proportions of a major industry since the Spanish treasure ships first began their heavy-laden homeward voyages was spreading to other areas. It was easier to be a pirate than to fish. Both Verrazano and Cartier had won their spurs as corsairs before they were explorers. And now it was the turn of the English. During the summer of 1563 four hundred privateering vessels, English and Huguenot, had captured seven hundred Spanish prizes. It is not strange, therefore, that we begin to hear of privateering on the Newfoundland banks. About 1570 Sir Bernard Drake began to appear and seize Portuguese vessels there. Almost every voyage we read of in these closing years of the century refers at some stage to the heightening of the international rivalries on the fishing banks. The English were making a great bid for supremacy in every sort of activity on the high seas. From 1576 to 1578 Martin Frobisher was exploring the northern seas in an attempt to find a passage between Greenland and North America. He was followed by John Davis ten years later. Walter Raleigh was founding his colony at Roanoke, off the Carolinas. English ships were attacking the Portuguese in Brazil and making inroads in Guiana. Drake was harrying the Spaniards at Panama and Cartagena, and in 1577 surprised them from the rear in the Pacific on Magellan's circumnavigation route. That defeat of Hawkins at Vera Cruz was being avenged in a manner that was beyond anyone's wildest fancies. The culmination in the Armada victory in 1588 was all that was needed to place England at the very peak of her supremacy. The universal English purpose was to displace Spanish dominance of the New World.

We do not know that the New England coasts played any part in this widespread movement of the English. The only voyages that certainly touched her coasts in the last quarter of the century were of such minor importance that they secured only fragmentary mention even by so ardent an annalist as Richard Hakluyt. One Simon Ferdinando, a Portuguese sailing a "little ffrigate" in the service of the Earl of Walsingham, made a very swift voyage of only three months in 1579 to an unrecorded portion of Norumbega, which at that time could mean anything from the mouth of the Penobscot River to the whole New England coast. In the next year, 1580, Sir Humphrey Gilbert sent John Wallace to Norumbega also, and this time there is sufficient evidence to identify the region definitely as the Penobscot area. Wallace stayed only long enough to learn that there was an abundance of furs thereabout, and a silver mine, and then returned to France, where he sold his furs at forty shillings apiece (De Costa). This voyage was perhaps the genesis of English commerce in New England, but it seems to have attracted little notice. Three years later Sir Humphrey Gilbert, after having taken possession of Newfoundland in the name of Elizabeth, himself headed for Norumbega, perhaps in search of the land Wallace had visited, but his great ship *Admiral* was wrecked in Nova Scotia on the way and Gilbert was drowned in a shipwreck off the Azores on his way home. So ended, tragically, the first English attempt at a northern colony. In the same year one Stephen Bellinger is said to have sailed along Cape Breton "and the coasts to the south," but again with no particular contributions to our zealous interest in New England. The same applies to Richard Fisher and Richard Strong of Apsham, who in 1593 met trading boats "up and down the coast of Arembec to the west and southwest of Cape Breton" in the latitude of 44°. Arembec was evidently that shadowy coast of Maine appearing under a new corruption of the Norumbega name.

No discussion of these closing years of the sixteenth century would be adequate without some account of Sir Walter Raleigh. He more than any other man came to personalize the English challenge of the Spanish claim to the New World. At the age of twenty-six he was commanding the *Falcon* in the fleet of his half brother, Humphrey Gilbert, setting out to occupy American soil, but ending up, as so often, in fights with Spanish ships. From this time on, English colonization of America became his passion. He furnished one of the five ships with which Gilbert attempted so disastrously to settle Newfoundland in 1583. Nothing daunted by this defeat, he secured a new charter, and in 1584 sent Captains Amadas and Barlowe to explore for a site north of Florida. These reconnoiterers returned with a glowing account of the Carolina coast. The next spring he sent seven ships under command of his cousin, Sir Richard Grenville, with Ralph Lane as colonial governor. About a hundred men, left on Roanoke Island for a year, unwisely antagonized the natives, fell short of supplies, and were in 1586 finally rescued by Sir Francis Drake and his fleet of twenty-three vessels, and returned to England. Meanwhile an overdue supply ship had landed fifteen more men at Roanoke, and these were soon massacred by the Indians. In 1587 Raleigh sent another party of one hundred and twenty colonists with the intention of trying a new site in Chesapeake Bay, but by the duplicity of Simon Ferdinando, he of the "little ffrigate" at Norumbega a few years earlier, the colony was left again at Roanoke Island. During the next three years Raleigh made two futile attempts to send relief expeditions, but they were turned back by the Armada crisis in England and by Spanish pirates. Finally in 1590 an expedition reached Roanoke, to find the colony in ruins and uninhabited. Two more voyages failed to turn up evidence of its fate. Only in 1607 did the Jamestown settlers learn some hints of the massacre and intermarriage of a few pitiful survivors of Roanoke with the Hatteras Indians. Raleigh spent more than forty thousand pounds in his attempts to establish and maintain his colony, but was at last forced to abandon the attempt. The war with Spain at home had wrecked all hopes of supporting the venture. On the death of Elizabeth, Raleigh was imprisoned and after another disastrous attempt to colonize in Guiana he was beheaded at the request of Spain, to the dishonor and shame of the civilized world.

The forces which shortly were to put New England on the map in large letters were conceived beforehand in all this feverish marine activity of the English nation. Hawkins and Drake had built an English navy and established its prestige on the high seas. Spain had been forced to relinquish hundreds of her treasure ships, which served to build yet more of England's fleet. Elizabeth fought Philip with every maritime weapon she could command. A merchant tradition which for centuries had grown strong in the Flanders wool trade now expanded to cover the seven seas. Adventurers of Bristol and Plymouth and Devon began to compete with the great old London companies for profits overseas. If Spain grew fat on America, why, so could England. Others took up the cry of Gilbert and of Raleigh and of Hakluyt: "Make of America an English nation." Gilbert had failed in the north, and Raleigh in the south. Frobisher and Davis had been thwarted in the Northwest Passage search. But the triumphs of Drake and the Armada victory consolidated English nationalism and laid the foundation for building an empire. And the defeat of Raleigh's hopes served only to strengthen the idea he preached.

Much of this maritime enthusiasm was now to be converged on the intensive development of a few hundred miles of the eastern coast line of North America. The coincident phenomenon of a Puritan exodus served only to sustain all that had gone before, and resulted from chance. The real basis of New England's success was grounded in the hard-won inheritance by the Elizabethan sea dogs of the merchant traditions of Spain, France and Portugal. All the preliminary work of the other nations on these shores was now to be turned to the English purpose. The almost forgotten enterprise of John Cabot and those early Bristol merchants was now at long last to be crowned with an English empire. Her way at last cleared by her hard-bitten freebooters, it was now to be determined what England could derive from the new continent.

Part Two

PRECURSORS OF THE PILGRIMS

Calendar of Voyages

1602   Bartholomew Gosnold, Casco Bay to Martha's Vineyard

1603   Martin Pring, Casco Bay to Plymouth

1604   Samuel de Champlain, Penobscot Bay and Mount Desert

1605   George Waymouth, Monhegan and St. Georges River

1605   Samuel de Champlain, Kennebec, Saco, Plymouth and Cape Cod

1606   Samuel de Champlain, Gloucester to Woods Hole

1606   Thomas Hanham and Martin Pring, Maine Coast

1607–1608   Popham or Sagadahoc Colony, Kennebec River

1609   Henry Hudson, Penobscot Bay and Cape Cod

1610   Samuel Argall, Penobscot Bay and Cape Cod

1611   Pierre Biard and Biencourt, Kennebec and Penobscot

1611   Edward Harlow, Monhegan to Cape Cod

1611   Captain Plastrier, Passamaquoddy to Monhegan

1613   Jesuit Colony and Samuel Argall, Mount Desert

1614   Adriaen Block, Manhattan, Connecticut, Rhode Island and Massachusetts

1614   John Smith, Monhegan, Massachusetts Bay

1614   Francis Popham, Kennebec

1614   French traders, Boston Harbor

1614   Thomas Hunt, Monhegan, Plymouth and Eastham

1614   Nicholas Hobson, Martha's Vineyard

1614 Humphrey Damerill, Damariscove
1615 Richard Hawkins, Monhegan
1615 Thomas Dermer, New England Coast
1615 Richard Vines, Saco Bay
1616 Edward Brande, Monhegan
1616 French vessel burned, Peddocks Island, Boston
      Harbor
1618 Edward Rocroft, Monhegan
1618 French traders, Monhegan
1619 Thomas Dermer, Monhegan, Cape Cod, Buz-
      zards Bay and Long Island Sound
1619 Sampson from Virginia, Monhegan
1620 Thomas Dermer, Nantucket
1620 Pilgrims, Cape Cod to Plymouth

Chapter One

THE MERCHANT ADVENTURERS

THE MARITIME supremacy of England had one important influence on her colonies that has sometimes been overlooked. We usually trace the lineage of American democracy and its representative forms too credulously to the justly famous governments established in the Plymouth and Massachusetts Bay colonies. Those governments were indeed important as milestones among the precedents that eventually established our free institutions. But they were only two in a long line of such illustrious precedents. The Spanish colonies were as a rule directly controlled in all their activities by the Spanish crown. But in the case of English enterprises there was a difference. They were, it is true, founded under charters from the crown, but between the settlers and the crown there existed a business organization, the "company." This company was in the nature of a private owner, who secured a patent or monopoly from the king to occupy certain territory and derive whatever profits he could from its exploitation. The company was usually empowered to set up its own forms of government within the colony, and here is the enormous distinction between the English colonial system and those of other nations. It was by virtue of such a charter, that of the English Plymouth Company, that the Pilgrims were allowed to persist in their government. Thus it becomes immediately evident that the roots of such governmental freedom as the Massachusetts colonies exemplified go farther back into the history of the English companies.

If Spain had founded Plymouth, it would have been governed by a royal viceroy whose decrees would have been absolute. All profits from the enterprise would have gone into the royal treasury. If France had sent out the Pilgrims, they would have been governed by a "company" instigated by the king and his ministers only thinly disguising the royal absolutism. In either case, whether Spanish or French, the colonists would normally have consisted of soldiers, convicts and exiles ruled by a few nobles. But since Plymouth was English, it followed the tradition of English patents, which sent out a group of self-governing free men whose only responsibility was to return a profit to a self-sustaining group of English investors. All that the king insisted on was that the settlers' government should not be inconsistent with the laws of England. Thus once the charter was granted there was no marriage of the project to any royal pleasure, to any majority in Parliament or political party, but only to a group of merchants expecting a profit. The significance of all this to the happiness of settlers and to their cooperation in the commercial effort for which any colony was primarily founded is obvious, particularly if, as sometimes happened, settlers were themselves shareholders in the venture. We all recognize the historic importance of this type of colonization to later American institutions and traditions, and the development of the British Empire. But let us be clear as to where it all started. It was certainly not original in the cabin of the *Mayflower*.

For indeed an examination of the charters of Virginia, of Raleigh's Roanoke, of Gilbert's empire in Newfoundland, and indeed of Cabot's projected claims in the country of the Grand Khan shows that something of the elements of this peculiar English view of overseas government was common to them all. Even the earliest charter of the Merchant Adventurers who conducted the English wool trade with Holland in 1406 "was not a charter to give a trade monopoly," says Lucas. "It was a charter to grant a constitution, a charter to enable Englishmen sojourning in foreign parts to govern themselves. . . . The one and only object of the charter is better government and the way in which better government is to be attained is by granting self-government. The King knew well, and the merchants knew well, that, given law and order, English trade would prosper without government assistance. . . . The king knew well, and the merchants knew well, that among English the golden road to law and order is to give them definite authority to govern themselves, to choose their own rulers and make their own laws. Exactly two hundred years later, in 1606, the continuous history of the British Empire beyond the seas began with the granting of a royal charter to the Virginia Company; the charter which was given to the English Merchants in the Low Countries for their better government in 1407 might almost have been a model for the founding of English colonies in America." Thus it is unfair to urge that the concept of self-government was the peculiar invention of the Pilgrims. It arose, rather, in the genesis of the English mercantile system.

While many of the privateering fleets of England had been instigated and subsidized by the queen, they were likewise organized as private companies who invested funds in the venture and collected shares of the plunder they reaped. The royal treasury never could have afforded such a fleet as this system produced. For private enterprise here went hand in hand with patriotism, and the stimulus of private profit kept the enterprises going regardless of the tendency of royal interest to become distracted by other national problems. The capriciousness of government in the Spanish and early French colonies is well known. But in the English enterprises, whether in privateering, trade or settlement, the controlling interest was so tempered by the continuous desire for private profit that things tended, on the whole, to go more smoothly. Privateering was a wildcat speculation, in which either profits or losses were enormous, depending on whose ships won. Elizabeth herself took shares in some of these projects. Fishing and trading were moderate investments which paid more moderate dividends. It was only gradually realized that permanent settlement might be the greatest guarantee of profits from trade. Even Raleigh, idealist that he was, looked on colonies for the commercial advantage that would come from them fully as much as for the glory of England. Most of the colonial enterprises which now began, in the early years of the seventeenth century, to burst upon the eastern shores of North America were motivated by the desire for trade. As Spain learned to protect her West Indies more successfully through better ordnance and more soldiers, the English speculation was forced more and more to seek new channels of commercial enterprise. Drake's death at Panama in 1596 marked the end of the great period of the freebooters. Merchant adventurers began to look to the northern coasts of America for plunder. Raleigh's ideas of settlement began to take hold of their imagination. The result was a whole new series of companies organized for the purpose of investigating and exploiting these northern coasts. The first of these to get under way was an independent group who were not above suspicion of deliberately seeking a contraband cargo within the territory granted as a monopoly to Sir Walter Raleigh. But whatever the motives of Gosnold's voyage in 1602, it was destined to influence greatly the exploration of New England that soon followed. Gosnold himself, a captain formerly in the employ of Raleigh, was later to become a founder of the Jamestown Colony in which he died.

Chapter Two

BARTHOLOMEW GOSNOLD
IN NANTUCKET SOUND, 1602

BARTHOLOMEW GOSNOLD was the first skipper to sail directly to the New England coast from Europe. Raleigh had tried the southern coast. His colony there had succumbed to the weapons of mistreated Indians. New England perhaps would offer a more friendly reception. In any case in a small bark, the *Concord*, with 32 men among whom was Sir Humphrey Gilbert's son, Bartholomew Gilbert, Gosnold sailed from Falmouth in the end of March, 1602, and touched the Azores on April 14th. The next land sighted was in southern Maine, near Portland. He immediately began to cruise southward toward the short New Hampshire shore, to be met with the following amazing welcome: "Our going upon an unknown coast," writes John Brereton, one of the crew, "made us not over-bolde to stand in with the shore, but in open weather; which caused us to be certain daies in sounding, before we discovered the coast, the weather being by chance somewhat foggie. But on Friday the 14th of May, early in the morning, we made the land, being full of faire trees, the land somewhat low, certaine hummocks, or hills lying into the land, the shore ful of white sand but very stony or rocky. And standing faire alongst by the shore, about twelve of the clocke the same day, we came to an anker, where six Indians in a Baske-shallop with mast and saile, an iron grapple, and a kettle of copper, came boldly aboard us, one of them apparelled with a waist-coat and breaches of blacke serdge, made after our sea-fashion, hose and shoes on his feet; all the rest (saving one that had a paire of breeches of blue cloth) were all naked. These people are of tall stature, broad and grim visage, of a blacke swart complexion, their eie-browes painted white, their weapons are bowes and arrows; it seemed by some words and signs they made, that some Baskes or [men] of S. John de Luz, have fished or traded in this place, being in the latitude of 43 degrees."

Gabriel Archer, a "gentleman in the said voyage," later a leader of the Jamestown Colony, described the event as follows: "The fourteenth, about six in the morning, we descried land that lay north, the northerly part we called the north land, which to another rock upon the same lying twelve leagues west, that we called Savage Rock, [Cape Neddick] (because the savages first showed themselves there); five leagues towards the said rock is an out point of woody ground [Cape Porpoise at Kennebunkport], the trees thereof very high and straight, from the rock east-north-east. From the said rock came toward us a Biscay Shallop with sail and oars having eight persons in it, whom we supposed at first to be Christians distressed. But approaching us nearer we perceived them to be savages. These coming within call, hailed us, and we answered. Then after signs of peace, and a long speech by one of them made, they came boldly aboard us, being all naked, saving about their shoulders certain loose deer skins, and near their wastes seal skins tied fast like to Irish dimmie trousers. One that seemed to be their commander wore a waistcoat of black work, a pair of breeches, cloth stockings, shoes, hat and band, one or two more had also a few things made by some Christians; these with a piece of chalk described the coast thereabouts, and could name Placentia of the Newfoundland; they spoke divers Christian words, and seemed to understand much more than we, for want of language could comprehend. These much desired our longer stay, but finding ourselves short of our purposed place, we set sail westward, leaving them and their coast. About sixteen leagues from thence we perceived in that course two small islands, the one lying eastward from Savage Rock, the other to the southward of it." These were probably Boone Island and the Isles of Shoals.

What an astonishing difference between this welcome and the one accorded Verrazano seventy-eight years earlier at Newport and in Maine! What dark chapter of shipwreck and massacre does this strange tale leave unrecorded? Are these the unsophisticated savages with which tradition has surrounded our Pilgrims in an untouched wilderness? Where had they got their "Christian words," their clothes, their boat, and strangest of all, their knowledge of sailing and of Newfoundland? The recorded travels of John Hawkins, David Ingram, Bellinger, Ferdinando, Wallace, and Fisher, on these coasts could never have brought all this to pass. How long a time must we suppose Biscayan fishermen had needed to teach these Indians to draw maps with a piece of chalk, to speak the French of Saint-Jean-de-Luz, and to wear a hat? Surely all these circumstances did not come about at the first visit. Certainly a considerable number of those 350 fishing vessels that from 1578 on plied increasingly their quiet trade at Newfoundland must have strayed upon these shores. This incident is the first proof of that theory that one can offer since Thevet's voyage. Would that one could name, and immortalize, those unremembered fishermen.

"About three of the clocke the same day in the afternoon we weighed," continues Brereton, "and standing southerly off into the sea the rest of that day and night following, with a fresh gale of winde, in the morning we found ourselves imbayed with a mightie headland; but coming to anker about 9 of the clocke the same day, within a league of the shore, we hoised out the one halfe of our shallop and Captain Bartholomew Gosnold, myself and three others went ashore, being a white sandie and very bolde shore; and marching all that afternoon with our muskets on our necks, on the highest hills which we saw (the weather very hot) at length we perceived this headland to be parcell of the maine, and sundrie Islands lying almost around it—and returned to our ship where in five or sixe hours absence we had pestered our ship so with Cod fish that we threw numbers of them overboard againe, and surely, I am persuaded that in the months of March, April and May, there is upon this coast better fishing, and in as great plentie, as in Newfoundland; for the sculles of Mackerell, herrings, cod and other fish that we daily saw as we went and came from the shore were wonderfull; and besides the places where we tooke these cods, (and might in a few daies have laden our ship) were but in seven faddome water and within lesse than a league of the shore; where in Newfoundland they fish in forty or fiftie fadome water, and farre off." The party had on their first arrival named this place "Shoal Hope," but now "altered the name and called it Cape Cod." Here for the first time a Massachusetts landmark received its modern name. One can still stand on the dunes of Race Point, Provincetown, and watch a little fleet of fishing boats, many of them manned by descendants of those Portuguese who in all probability first fished here, still in this twentieth century hauling up fish within a mile or two of shore. Captain John Smith says that it was this account of Brereton's which first interested him in similar American adventures, and he also was to spend some time fishing on New England shoals. It is possible that never a year has gone by since this visit of Gosnold's when vessels have not fished along this Cape Cod shore. New England fishermen were later on to fight the War of 1812 and to lay the foundations of the American clipper trade: here in Provincetown harbor, in the year 1602, is the first recorded beginning of that age-long uninterrupted procession of the New England fisheries. Archer agreed with Brereton that the fishing here was better than in Newfoundland. Can anyone deny that here was a motive of major importance for the colonization of this region?

The next day the *Concord* proceeded "round about this headland almost all the points of the compasse," and came upon the two easterly prolongations of Cape Cod, named by Gosnold Point Gilbert (for his cocaptain Bartholomew Gilbert) and Point Care. These promontories have in succeeding years gradually eroded away, but parts of them are remembered by men who are still living. Tree stumps and peat still thrown up by storms on Nauset Beach are their only remnants today. Shoal water delayed the party for several days, and they spent a good deal of time bartering with the Indians. At Provincetown the landing party had been approached by a lone young Indian who, Archer remarks, "showed a willingness to help us in our occasions." He says that these Indians of the more southerly coast, whom we may suppose were the Nauset tribe of Eastham and Chatham, were "more timorous than those of the Savage Rock, yet very thievish." They came in canoes, had "Tobacco, and pipes steeled with copper," and skins. One had hanging about his neck "a plate of rich copper, in length a foot, in breadth half a foot, for a breastplate, the ears of all the rest had pendants of copper. Also one of them had his face painted over and head stuck with feathers in manner of a turkey cock's train." And to the southward of Point Gilbert, which would agree with the Chatham shore, he again notes: "This coast is very full of people, for that as we trended the same savages still run along the shore, as men much admiring at us."

From the story of this voyage along the exposed eastern shore of Cape Cod, we can get no real testimony as to whether or not these Indians had seen white men before. Brereton's narrative is no more helpful than Archer's. We know that the Nausets were a peaceful agricultural people, despite the fact that Champlain came in conflict with them four years afterward. Eighteeen years later the Pilgrims on their first landing "borrowed" a cache of corn from these Nausets, and later repaid the debt. In a still later phase, many of the Plymouth settlers emigrated to this region of Cape Cod, and lived on friendly terms with the Nausets.

We can have little doubt that Indians of Cape Cod had seen the ships of Verrazano, Gomez, and Allefonsce, but Gosnold's is the first landing of which we have any record. Probably Sebastian Cabot, the Cortereals, the *Mary Guildford* and John Hawkins all sighted Cape Cod. But there was no Biscay shallop or European clothing here in 1602 to argue a closer contact, despite the presumptive visits of the fishermen. For all we know exactly, Gosnold may have been the first to trade with these natives, though their "thievishness" would suggest the contrary. In the light of what we know of the prevalence of fishing and trading all the way from Newfoundland to the Hudson during the preceding seventy-five years I prefer to believe that Gosnold's was the first recorded landing among a series of such incidents.

A week of reconnoitering south of Cape Cod brought Gosnold to Martha's Vineyard and the Elizabeth Islands, to both of which he gave their modern names. Gosnold seems to have determined on the island of Cuttyhunk in the Elizabeth group as a site for settlement. The expedition found on this island a "pond of fresh water, in circuit two miles, on the one side not distant from the sea thirty yards, in the centre whereof is a rocky islet, containing near an acre of ground full of wood, on which we began our fort and place of abode." They now settled down for three weeks, employing their time in a variety of occupations that give us good insight into the region. Some of the geographical details are sufficiently ambiguous to make one uncertain which side of Buzzards Bay is called the mainland and which of several islands is being referred to in specific instances. The characteristics of the area in general are unmistakable, however, and nothing more concerns us for the New England purpose.

In the course of the three weeks some of the men accompanied Captain Gosnold in the shallop on exploring expeditions, while Captain Gilbert remained aboard ship and a work party of ten men built a sedge-thatched house "sufficient to harbor twenty persons at least with their necessary provisions." A flat-bottomed punt was built to ferry men and materials across the pond to the little island. The exploring expeditions found game, in the shape of hundreds of nesting shore birds and numerous deer. They planted on Martha's Vineyard wheat, barley, oats, and peas "which in fourteen daies were sprung up nine inches

and more," if Brereton can be believed. They, like the Vinland
Vikings centuries before, were struck by the profusion of grapevines, which is still a characteristic of those islands. On the shore
of one island they found "many huge bones and ribbes of
Whales." They saw strawberries, raspberries, tansy, gooseberries, and "great store of ground nuts, fortie together on a string
some of them as big as hennes eggs; they grow not two inches
under ground; the which nuts we found to be as good as Pota-
toes." All these plants are still common in that region. "Also
divers sorts of shellfish, as Scollops, Muscles, Cockles, Lobsters,
Crabs, Oisters and Wilks, exceeding good and very great."
These men probably here inaugurated the clambake and the
shore dinner. But the commodity which they valued most was
sassafras, which had attained in the England of that day a great
popularity as a supposed remedy for plague, smallpox and many
other diseases. Archer testifies to this: "the powder of sassafras,
in twelve hours cured one of our company that had taken a
great surfeit by eating the bellies of dog fish." Finding much
sassafras here, Gosnold's crew occupied several days in cutting
and loading it aboard ship as the principal source of revenue
from the voyage. Cedar wood also was cut and included in the
cargo.

The reports of all these commodities as enumerated by
Archer and Brereton were no doubt perused in the greatest
detail by the merchants who had sent Gosnold on this expedition, as well as by later adventurers like Ferdinando Gorges,
who was soon to enter this area of enterprise. Gosnold set out on
this voyage, according to his letter to his father, with Verrazano's report of the near-by Rhode Island region in his hand.
One may gather that the Italian's narrative had at least in part
accounted for this later expedition. The merchant adventurers
of 1602 were seeking for more prosaic plunder than had Verrazano's patron of 1524. The reports of Brereton and Archer gave
promise not only of such shellfish, game and native fruits as
would sustain prospective colonists, but also merchantable fish,
sassafras, cedar wood and, as we shall soon see, furs. These

matters are not so carefully included in the narratives without good reason. They were to arouse increasing interest among many groups of investors. These things were possible substitutes for Spanish gold. Time was to prove them powerful enough to colonize New England.

But one more significant phase needed investigation. Roanoke had fallen victim of the Indian. What of the Indians of Vineyard Sound? On the first island, perhaps Nantucket or Chappaquiddick, which Gosnold explored after leaving Chatham, the only evidences of habitation were an abandoned lean-to, the charcoal of extinct fires, and an old fish weir. He found no villages, and only an occasional house on the islands; indeed most of the Indians he saw arrived in canoes from the mainland.

On Martha's Vineyard thirteen Indians came running and brought with them a basket of boiled fish, deerskins, and some "Tobacco, which they drinke [smoke] greene, but dried into powder, very strong, and pleasant and much better than any I have tasted in England" (Brereton). "We gave unto them certain trifles, as knives, points, and such-like which they much esteemed."

Four days later, which was May 25th, Archer, now installed on Cuttyhunk, notes that an Indian with his wife and daughter arrived, and that the native showed the same concern for the welfare of the women that Verrazano had noted at Newport.

"The thirtieth, Captain Gosnold, with divers of his company, went upon pleasure in the shallop towards Hills Hap [an island near the mainland] to view it and the sandy cove, and returning brought with him a canoe that four Indians had there left, being fled away for fear of our English, which we brought into England." We shall consider whether this stolen canoe had anything to do with later events.

The next day Gosnold and a party went to the mainland, and came upon "men, women, and children." Brereton says that "at first they expressed some feare," but, Archer continues, they "with all courteous kindness entertained him, giving him certain skins of wild beasts, which may be rich furs, tobacco, turtles, hemp, artificial strings colored, chains, and such like things as that instant they had about them."

Several days later, while the crew worked on the thatched house, there appeared from the mainland nine canoes containing fifty Indians with their sachem. After an exchange of gifts the English entertained the Indians at a fish dinner, "whereof they misliked nothing but our mustard, whereat they made many a sowre face." In the course of this first New England banquet, one of the Indians stole a shield from the English and surreptitiously deposited it in a canoe. Brereton's story of this incident is so pithy that it cries out to be quoted: "while wee were thus merry, one of them had conveyed a target of ours into one of their canowes, which we suffered, only to trie whether they were in subjection to this leader [the sachem], to whom we made signs (by showing him another of the same likeness and pointing to the canowe) what one of his companie had done; who suddenly expressed some feare, and speaking angerly to one about him (as we perceived by his countenance) caused it presently to be brought backe again." Archer adds this: "Seeing our familiarity to continue they fell afresh to roasting of crabs, red herrings, which were exceedingly great, ground nuts etc., as before." For the rest of that day the English traded with the Indians, securing a great variety of furs, including beaver, otter, marten, wildcat, black fox, rabbit, deer, and seal skins. Archer says that the Indians marveled greatly at the knives which they received, that they were so bright and sharp. This in spite of the fact that they had a great variety of copper implements of their own, "all of which they so little esteeme, as they offered their fairest collars or chains, for a knife or such-like trifle." It is at this point in Brereton's narrative that he cites the origin of their copper which we quoted in the chapter on Verrazano.

These Indians did not differ in dress from those of Cape Cod, or the Newport of 1524. Brereton says: "They strike fire in this manner: every one carrieth about him in a purse of tewed leather, a Minerall stone (which I take to be their copper) [this was iron pyrites] and with a flat Emery stone (wherewith Glasiers cut glass, and Cutlers glase blades) tied fast to the end of a little sticke, gently he striketh upon the Minerall stone, and within a stroke or two, a sparke falleth upon a piece of Touchwood (much like our Sponge in England) and with the least sparke he maketh a fire presently. We had also of their Flaxe, wherewith they make many strings and cords, but it is not so bright of color as ours in England." These details are of interest to us in bearing out an impression that one gains the more one reads these narratives, namely that these Indians south of Cape Cod were probably, contrary to those of the Maine coast, about as uninfluenced by European customs as they had been at Newport in 1524. They seem to have shown a childish delight in the gifts the English brought to them, and there is nowhere in these narratives, detailed as they are, any indication that they possessed any articles of European manufacture, with the possible exception of their copper. It seems hardly conceivable that they should have had European copper without some other European articles along with it. The contrast between these Vineyard Sound Indians and those of Maine seems just as striking as it was in Verrazano's chronicle. Gosnold's island, of course, was only twenty miles from Newport. To me, this is as good evidence as we have available of the location of earlier European contacts between traders and Indians, namely, that they were for the most part confined to the Maine coast.

After two or three days of trading with the English, all except six or seven of the Indians returned to the mainland. These few, Brereton says, "remained with us behinde, bearing us company every day into the woods, and helpt us to cut and carie our sassafras, and some of them lay aboard our ship." In describing them further, he says that "some of them are blacke thin-bearded; they make beards of the hair of beasts; and one of them offered a beard of their making to one of our sailors, for his that grew on his face, which because it was of a red color, they judged to be none of his own!" He also remarks that "they pronounce our language with great facilitie; for one of them one day sitting by me, upon occasion I spake smiling to him these words; 'How now (sirha) are you so saucie with my tobacco,' which words (without any further repetition) he suddenly spake so plaine and distinctly, as if he had been a long scholar in the language."

We now come to the series of incidents which seem to have accounted for the failure of Gosnold's rather feeble attempt to found a colony. "The eighth," writes Archer, "we divided the victuals, namely, the ship's stores for England, and that of the planters, which by Captain Gilbert's allowance could be but six weeks for six months, whereby there fell out a controversy, the rather, for that some seemed secretly to understand of a purpose Captain Gilbert had, not to return with supply of the issue. Those goods should make by him to be carried home." The next day an Indian arrived who apparently acted so suspiciously that many decided he was a spy sent to watch the movements of the English.

On June 10th Gosnold went on another expedition for cedar wood to an island some distance away. A garrison of ten men were left at Cuttyhunk. Apparently owing to short rations, the men on the island had to forage for food, and while doing so two of them were "assaulted by four Indians, who with arrows did shoot and hurt one of the two in his side, the other, a lusty and nimble felow, leaped in and cut their bow strings, whereupon they fled" [Archer]. We can imagine that this incident did nothing to improve the courage of the mere twenty men who proposed staying on to found a colony! It is therefore not surprising to learn that "The thirteenth, began some of our company that before vowed to stay, to make a revolt: whereupon the planters diminishing, all was given over." Four days later the entire company set sail for England. On July 23rd they "came to anchor at Exmouth."

The significance of the Gosnold voyage was not the failure of this attempt at colonization, as often represented. That is putting the cart before the horse. The colonization attempt was obviously ill prepared and halfhearted. The meaning of the voyage was, rather, that here for the first time was a forthright expedition to America which returned to England with a paying cargo of something besides fish or furs, and a trustworthy description of a commercially attractive coast. It is said that the sassafras cargo of the *Concord* was confiscated by Raleigh because of his royal monopoly through the queen's patent. But it is also said that the cargo influenced the market sufficiently to produce a sudden drop in price of that product. Richard Hakluyt certainly thought it worth his while to fit out two vessels under Martin Pring to revisit the sassafras forests only eight months later. There is evidence enough in the Gosnold cargo therefore as to the importance of the voyage.

From the historical standpoint there is another interesting observation to be made about the expedition. Ignoring for the moment the Biscay shallop episode, consider the train of events between the explorers and the Indians. Both on Cape Cod and among the islands, the first stray natives encountered were friendly, consumed with curiosity, and once their fears were overcome, inclined to offer gifts. This seems to have been their usual approach to strangers. From this beginning, trade was easily established, apparently to the mutual pleasure and advantage of each group. This did not proceed very far before the acquisitive instincts of certain individuals, native or white, brought about "thievish" incidents: the English stole a canoe, an Indian stole a shield. The Indian was forced to return the shield under humiliating circumstances. But it is recorded that the canoe was "brought into England."

Now when a group of Indians have at great pains chopped down a huge tree with stone axes and, by dint of two or three weeks of firing and scraping, have hollowed it out to make a boat big enough to carry five or six men safely across the tide rips of Buzzards Bay, can anyone suppose that they should accept the theft of it lightly? These Indians obviously did not, for within three or four days they appeared in force with their sachem to investigate matters. They were met with public humiliation over the shield. Trading proceeded in the normal way for a few days, then the main body of Indians returned home, leaving certain of their number among the whites, probably to keep in touch with their movements. At the first opportunity, which came a week later, four of these natives attacked two stray Englishmen. The amusing defense of the uninjured Englishman, by cutting the natives' bowstrings, should not blind us to the fact that, judging even from the Englishmen's own account of their experiences, this attack was in no sense unprovoked treachery. The Indians undoubtedly considered it a just repayment for the theft of their canoe.

This is a characteristic pattern of what almost invariably happened when a European merchant traded with natives. Monotonously this process was going on throughout North and South America—a friendly greeting, a pleasant exchange of gifts, a few days of bartering under increasing tension, then a robbery or kidnaping, culminating in open conflict, and the white men sailed away. Certainly this was no planting of a colony. This was, rather, the typical trading venture of men trained as privateers. The "colony" of Cuttyhunk thus went the way of Roanoke, but in three weeks instead of six years. As with the early attempts of the French in Newfoundland, it was hard to colonize a savage country solely on the profit motive basis. But from the standpoint of profit, and that of awakening an interest in New England, Gosnold's voyage was a striking achievement.

Chapter Three

Martin Pring
Explores New Plymouth, 1603

The attractive description of "Northern Virginia" which Gosnold and his men brought back with them was widely disseminated in England among men interested in the new continent. Second only to Raleigh in his enthusiasm for exploration was Richard Hakluyt, whose published collections of *"Divers Voyages Touching the Discovery of America, etc."* had appeared in 1589. Hakluyt now approached a group of merchants of Bristol, that port which had given us John and Sebastian Cabot, a host of fishermen and many unnamed sea dogs, and quickly arranged for a second voyage. Martin Pring, a Devon skipper, was placed in charge of the two ships, *Speedwell* and *Discoverer*, with forty-four men and boys. Robert Salterne, who had been Gosnold's pilot, was Pring's assistant on the voyage. Setting sail from England on April 10, 1603, they arrived early in June among the islands of Casco Bay within a few miles of the landfall of Gosnold the year before. They had come by way of Gosnold's new short route; here was one of those striking examples of navigational skill referred to in a previous chapter.

Among the Maine islands Pring's company "found an excellent fishing for Cods, which are better than those of Newfoundland," and he also wrote that "salt may be made in these parts, a matter of no small importance." Such remarks as this and the similar one already cited in reference to Gosnold's naming of Cape Cod suggest how important the Newfoundland fishing had become among seafaring men. Apparently there were men in the crews of both these voyages who had fished at Newfoundland and could thus make the comparison between the two areas. In 1607 a French mariner named Savalet, who frequented the fishing grounds about Cape Breton, stated that he had then made forty-two voyages to that region. It is not surprising therefore that almost any crew, particularly out of Bristol as in this case, should include men familiar with the fishing banks.

Exploring southwestward from these islands, Pring's vessels entered in succession "foure Inlets, the most Easterly whereof was barred at the mouth, but having passed over the barre, wee ran up into it five miles. In all these places we found no people, but signs of fires where they had beene." "But meeting with no Sassafras," Pring continues, "we left these places with all the aforesaid Ilands, shaping our course for Savage Rock, discovered the yeere before by Captain Gosnold, where going upon the Mayne we found people, with whom we had no long conversations, because here also we could find no Sassafras." Savage Rock is generally supposed to be Cape Neddick. This cape is the most dramatic, exposed ledge on that coast. Pring does not reward us with any further mention of the Biscay shallop and its extraordinary native proprietors.

"Departing hence we bare into that great Gulfe, which Captain Gosnold over-shot the yeere before, coasting and finding people on the north side thereof. Not yet satisfied in our expectation, we left them and sailed over, and came to an anchor on the South side in the latitude of 41 degrees and odde minutes." The "great Gulfe" was of course Massachusetts Bay, and the above note is the first record in the annals of Cape Ann. Gosnold had passed it during the night the year before. Jehan Allefonsce had undoubtedly seen it in 1542, but left us no recognizable mention of the fact. Sassafras is still uncommon in that area.

The story continues: "in the latitude of 41 degrees and

odde minutes: where we went on land in a certain Bay, which
we called Whitson Bay, by the name of the worshipfull Master John Whitson, then Maior of the Citie of Bristoll, and one
of the chiefe Adventurers, and finding a pleasant Hill there-
unto adjoining, we called it Mount Aldworth, for Master
Robert Aldworth's sake a chiefe furtherer of the Voyage, as
well with his purse as with his travail. Here we had a sufficient
quantitie of Sassafras." Near the end of Pring's narrative there
is a further description of "this excellent Haven at the entrance
whereof we found twentie fathomes water and rode at our
ease in seven fathomes being Land-locked, the Haven winding
in compasse like the Shell of a Snaile, and it is in latitude of one
and forty degrees and five and twentie minutes."

To anyone familiar with the Massachusetts coast this
description leaves little doubt as to the identity of "Whitson
Bay." The latitude is indeed about half a degree in error, but in
most other details the account perfectly conforms with the
Plymouth of the Pilgrim fathers. So here were English vessels
riding at ease in Plymouth Harbor seventeen years before those
wanderers set foot on Plymouth Rock! As we shall later observe, a French vessel of Samuel de Champlain, a ship from
Dutch Manhattan, a pinnace of Captain John Smith, a ship of
one Thomas Hunt, and the pinnace of Thomas Dermer were
also to enter this port before the justly memorable year of
1620. No injury can possibly be done to the glory of the Pilgrim
achievement by a frank recognition that there were precursors
to the *Mayflower* in Plymouth Harbor, particularly as no serious attempt at colonization of Massachusetts was made by any
of these men. It seems that some injustice has been done to the
memory of these earlier navigators, however, by the manner
in which overwhelming popular interest in the Pilgrim story
has submerged these preliminary reconnaissances of the region. Let us see what the Plymouth of 1603 looked like. The
text of Pring requires little comment; let him tell the story:

"At our going on shore, upon view of the people and
sight of the place, wee thought it convenient to make a small

baricado to keepe diligent watch and ward in, for the advertize-
ment and succor of our men, while they shoulde work in the
woods. During our abode on shore the people of the country
came to our men sometimes ten, twentie, fortie, or threescore,
and at one time one hundred and twentie at once. We used them
kindly, and gave them divers sorts of our meanest merchandize.
They did eat Pease and Beanes with our men. Their owne victuals were most of fish.

"We had a youth in our company that could play upon
a Gitterne [guitar], in whose homely Musicke they took great
delight, and would give him many things, as Tobacco, Tobacco-
pipes, Snakes skinnes of sixe foot long, which they use for
Girdles, Fawnes skinnes, and such-like, and danced twentie in
a Ring, and the Gitterne in the middle of them using many
Savage gestures, singing Lo, la, lo, la, la, lo: him that first broke
the ring the rest would knocke and cry out upon. Some few
of them had plates of Brasse a foot long, and halfe a foote broad
before their breasts. Their weapons are Bows of five or sixe
foote broad of wich-hasell, painted blacke and yellow, the
strings of three twists of sinewes, bigger than our Bow-strings.
Their arrows are of a yard and an handfull long not made
of reeds, but of a fine light wood, very smooth and round with
three long and deepe blacke feathers of some Eagle, Vulture or
Kite, as closely fastened with some binding matter as any
Fletcher of ours can glue them on. Their quivers are full a yard
long, made of long dried Rushes wrought about two handfuls
broad above, and one handful beneath with prettie workes and
compartiments, Diamant wise of red and other colours.

"We carried with us from Bristoll two excellent Mastives,
of whom the Indians were more afraid then of twentie of our
men. One of these Mastives would carrie a halfe Pike in his
mouth. And one Master Thomas Bridges a gentleman of our
company accompanied only with one of these dogs, and passed
sixe miles alone in the Country having lost his fellowes and
returned safely. And when we would be rid of the Savages company wee would let loose the Mastives, and suddenly with out-

cryes they would flee away. These people in colour are inclined to a swart, tawnie, Chestnut colour, not by nature but
accidently, and doe weare their haire brayded in foure parts,
and trussed up about their heads with a small knot behind in
which haire of theirs they sticke many feathers and toyes for
braverie and pleasure. They cover their privities only with a
piece of leather drawne betwixt their twists and fastened to
their Girdles behind and before; whereunto they hang their
bags of Tobacco. They seeme to bee somewhat jealous of their
women, for we saw not past two of them, who weare Aprons
of Leather skins before them downe to the knees, and a Bears
skinne like an Irish Mantle over one shoulder. The men are of
stature somewhat taller than our ordinary people, strong, swift,
well proportioned and given to treacherie, as in the end we
perceived.

"Their boats, where of we brought one to Bristoll, were in
proportion like a wherrie of the River of Thames, seventeene
foot long and four foot broad, made of the Barke of a Birch-
tree farre exceeding in bignesse those of England: it was sowed
together with strong and tough Oziers or twigs and the seams
covered over with Rozen or Turpentine little inferior in sweet-
ness to Frankincense, as we made triall by burning a little
thereof on the coales at sundry times after our coming home;
it was also open like a wherrie and sharpe at both ends, save
that the beake was a little bending roundly upward. And though
it carried nine men standing upright yet it weighed not at the
most above sixtie pounds in weight, a thing almost incredible in
regard of the largenesse and capacitie thereof. Their oares were
flat at the end like an Oven peele, made of Ash or Maple very
light and strong, about two yards long, wherewith they row
very swiftly." These Plymouth Indians seem to have imported
birch canoes from farther north. Champlain found dugouts
in this region three years later. "Passing up a river we saw
certaine Cottages together abandoned by the Savages, and not
farre off we beheld their Gardens, and one among the rest of an
Acre of Ground. And in the same was sowne Tobacco, Pum-

pions, Cowcumbers and such like; and some of the people had Maiz or Indian wheate among them. In the fields we found wild Pease, strawberries very faire and bigge, Gooseberries, Raspices Hurts and other wild fruits.

"Having spent three weeks upon the coast before we came to this place where we meant to stay and take in our lading, according to our instructions given us in charge before our setting forth, we pared and digged up the Earth with shovels, and sowed Wheate, Barley Oats, Pease, and sundry sorts of garden seeds, which for the time of our abode there, being about seven weeks, although they were late sowne, came up very well giving certaine testimonie of the goodness of the Climate and the Soyle. And it seemeth that Oade, Hempe, Flaxe, Rape-seed and such-like which require a rich and fat grounde, would prosper excellently in these parts. For in divers places have we found grasse above knee deepe.

"As for Trees the Country yeeldeth Sassafras, a plant of sovereigne vertue for the French Poxe, and as some of late have learnedly written, good against the Plague and many other maladies; Vines, Cedars, Oakes, Ashes, beeches, Birch trees, Cherrie trees bearing fruit whereof we did eate, Hasel, Wich-Hasels, the best wood of all others to make Sope-ashes withall, Walnut trees, Maples, holy to make bird-lime with, and a kind of tree bearing a fruit like a small red peare-plum with a crowne or knop on the top (a plant whereof carefully wrapped up in earth, Master Robert Salterne, brought to Bristoll). We also found low trees bearing faire Cherries. There were likewise a white kind of Plums which were growne to their perfect ripe-nesse. With divers other sorts of trees to us unknowne.

"The Beasts here are Stags, fallow Deere in abundance, Beares, Wolves, Foxes, Lusernes, and (some say) Tygres, Porcu-pines, and Dogges with sharpe and long noses, with many other sorts of wild beasts, whose Cases and Furres being hereafter purchased by exchange may yield no smal gaine to us. Since as we are certainly informed, the Frenchmen brought from Canada the value of thirtie thousand Crownes in the yeare 1604.

Almost in Bevers and Otters skinnes only. The most usuall
Fowles are Eagles, Vultures, Hawkes, Cranes, Herons, Crowes,
Gulls and great store of other River and Sea Fowles." This is
the only note in all the New England narratives prior to 1614
indicating that the English were familiar with the profitableness
of the French fur trade.

"By the end of July we had laded our small Barke called
the Discoverer with as much Sassafras as we thought sufficient,
and sent her home into England before, to give some speedie
contentment to the Adventurers; who arrived safely in King-
rode about a fortnight before us. After their departure we so
bestirred ourselves, that our shippe also had gotten in her lading,
during which time there fell out this accident. On a day about
noone tide while our men which used to cut down Sassafras
in the woods were asleep, as they used to do for two houres in
the heat of the day, there came down about seven score Savages armed with their Bowes and Arrowes, and environed our
House or Barricado, wherein were foure of our men alone with
their Muskets to keepe Centinell, whom they sought to have
come down unto them, which they utterly refused, and stood
upon their guard. Our Master like-wise being very carefull
and circumspect having not past two with him in the shippe
put the same in the best defence he could, lest they should
have invaded the same, and caused a piece of great Ordnance
to bee shot off to give terrour to the Indians, and warning to
our men which were fast asleepe in the woods: at the noyse
of which peece they were a little awaked, and beganne a little
to call for Foole and Gallant, their great and faithful Mastives,
and full quietly laid themselves down againe, but being quick-
ened up eftsoones againe with a second shot they rowsed up
themselves, betooke them to their weapons, and with their
Mastives, great Foole with an halfe Pike in his mouth drew
down to their ship; whom when the Indians beheld afarre off
with the Mastive which they most feared, in dissembling manner
they turned all to a jest and sport and departed away in friendly
manner, yet not long after, even the day before our departure,

they set fire on the woods where wee wrought, which wee did behold to burne for a mile space, and the very same day that wee weighed Anchor, they came down to the shore in greater number, to wit, very neere two hundred by our estimation, and some of them came in theire Boates to our ship, and would have had us come in againe, but we sent them backe, and would none of their entertainment." And so ended the first known contact of Englishmen with the Plymouth Indians, just short of open conflict.

"About the 8th or 9th of August, wee left this excellent haven . . ." There follows the description of Plymouth Harbor already quoted. The *Speedwell* reached England early in October.

Before leaving Martin Pring, let us take note of his further career. As we shall later discuss in greater detail, one Captain George Waymouth in 1605 sailed from England to the Maine shores around Musongus Bay and returned with five kidnaped natives, who, wrote Sir Ferdinando Gorges, became the means "under God, of putting on foot and giving life to all our plantations." These Indians were trained in England, apparently to be pilots for new expeditions. Meantime Gorges had sent out a ship under a Captain Challons, but it seems to have been captured by Spaniards; at any rate, it disappeared. Martin Pring was therefore sent again, in 1606, to go in search of Challons, with Dehanada, one of the kidnaped Pemaquid natives, as his pilot. Pring found no evidence of Challons, but, partly of course with the help of Dehanada, "after he had made a perfect discovery of all those Rivers and Harbors," wrote Gorges, ". . . he brings with him the most exact discovery of that coast that ever came into my hands, and indeed he was the best able to perform it of any I met withall to this present." Thus Pring seems to have made himself an authority on the geography of Maine, but as we have no copy of his "most exact discovery," we must remain content with the good estimate which Sir Ferdinando Gorges wrote of him. He later acquired fame in the East Indies for his defeat of the Dutch at Batavia.

Little need be added in commentary on Martin Pring's discovery of Plymouth. This, like Gosnold's, was a successful commercial voyage. Gosnold's reports of merchantable commodities were confirmed. Again a canoe was stolen. The description of birch canoes argues that these people had dealings with the natives north of Cape Ann, and if we required further proof of this we would have only to remember that Samoset, of the "Welcome, Englishmen" episode in 1621, was a native of Pemaquid in Maine. These Indians had almost unquestionably learned of previous Europeans on the coast. A bare seven weeks of association with the Englishmen brought them to the verge of open hostility. How long may we suppose the Pilgrims could have defended themselves against these natives, mobilizing as they did in those short weeks to a force of two hundred? How providentially this number was reduced by disease before 1620 we shall shortly learn.

One of the most amiable characteristics of these explorers' narratives, well instanced in Brereton and here by Martin Pring, is the good humor which seems often to have prevailed in the relationship of whites and Indians. Their earnest concern over their own affairs and their religious convictions seem to have prevented the Pilgrims from enjoying any such easy familiarity with the Indians as did these earlier navigators and their crews of men and boys. One may well speculate on what might have been William Bradford's consternation could he have seen the youth playing his guitar for the leaping savages here at Plymouth in 1603. It inevitably brings up comparisons with the Pilgrim attitude toward dancing about the Merrymount Maypole which jovial Thomas Morton set up at Quincy in 1625. These explorers of 1603 were men of a different stamp from the Pilgrims, and more akin, probably, to Thomas Morton himself, whose chief crimes seem to have been that he used the Anglican Book of Common Prayer and sold muskets to the Indians. The familiarity and good humor of these English crews must in all fairness soften somewhat our judgment of the scandalous cruelty with which, in their commercial capacity, they often treated the Indians. "They did eat Pease and Beans with our men," writes Pring, and here, I suppose, the English had their first baked beans, roasted in original Indian fashion, in a hole in the ground. Surely Gosnold's shore dinner and Pring's baked bean roast deserve to be remembered in the same breath with that first Thanksgiving dinner of turkey which we annually celebrate. The Indians, indeed, must have returned often to their villages thoroughly perplexed that a people who could be so pleasant and convivial at one moment could steal and kidnap in the next.

Chapter Four

CHAMPLAIN ON THE PENOBSCOT, 1604

IN THE INTEREST of chronological sequence we must at this point interrupt the progress of English explorations of New England in order to note the appearance of the French on the coast of Maine. During the same summer that Martin Pring spent in Massachusetts Bay, a distinguished French fur trader and merchant. named Pont Gravé, who had previously made several voyages to the New World, set out to explore the St. Lawrence River region. This enterprise was set in motion by the venerable Amyar de Chastes, governor of Dieppe, who succeeded in organizing a group of merchants to back the venture, and in securing a commission from Henri IV to choose a suitable place for a French settlement. Historically the great significance of the voyage was that it marked the first appearance in those waters of Samuel de Champlain, who was specifically commissioned by the king to bring back a careful and detailed report of the discoveries. The expedition repeated much of the work of Cartier's three expeditions of sixty years earlier, and in addition explored the Saguenay River. It returned with a valuable cargo of furs. To Champlain's great disappointment, de Chastes had died in their absence, and his colonial project was therefore abandoned. But Champlain wrote such a vigorous and hopeful account of the expedition that it was published under the king's auspices and became sufficiently widely read to influence many merchants in supporting a continuation of the enterprise. Ac-

cordingly, under a new commission granted to the Sieur de
Monts, giving him a monopoly on all fur trading north of Philadelphia, a second expedition of 120 men set out in 1604, about
two-thirds of whom, including laborers and artisans, planned
to settle in the new colony. De Monts and Pont Gravé were in
command of the two ships, and Champlain was again royal
geographer. De Monts this time decided on a region of milder
climate, and began his explorations along the Nova Scotia coast,
leaving Pont Gravé to assure the expedition of financial success
by pursuing the fur trade in the Gulf of St. Lawrence. We
have already learned that the results of Pont Gravé's previous
work were known to Martin Pring. Champlain and de Monts
made a thorough reconnaissance of the Bay of Fundy coast, and
determined on a settlement in Passamaquoddy Bay, on Dochet
Island at the mouth of the St. Croix River. This was only
about forty miles from the St. John River where David Ingram
emerged from his overland trip in 1567. Champlain seems to have
directed the construction of buildings on this site, this occupy-
ing until September of 1604. Then he started his series of three
annual voyages down the New England coast, which were so
thorough that he produced the first reasonably clear maps of
the region ever made.

The first of these surveys, which, because it did occur in
1604, we are mentioning here, was really a continuation of the
mapping of the Bay of Fundy coast. In a small bark with twelve
sailors and two Indian guides Champlain skirted the northern
portion of the Maine coast as far as the Penobscot. "Continuing
from the St. Croix River," he says, "along the coast about 25
leagues, we passed a great quantity of islands, banks, reefs and
rocks, which project more than four leagues into the sea in
some places. I called them the Ranges. Most of them are covered with Pines and Firs and other poor kinds of wood. Among
these Islands there are a great many fine harbors, but they are
not attractive. I went near an island about four or five leagues
long. The distance from this island to the mainland on the north
is not a hundred paces. It is very high with notches here and

there so that it appears when one is at sea, like seven or eight mountains rising close together. The tops of most of them are without trees because they are nothing but rocks. The only trees are pines, firs, and birches. I called it the Isle Des Monts Deserts. It is in latitude 44½°." This is still a good description of Mount Desert Island, as we have come to know it. Here began the modern nomenclature of the Maine coast.

"The Savages of this place, having made an alliance with us, guided us on the Pemetigoit River [Penobscot], so called by them, and told us that their captain, named Bessabez, was the chief of the river. I think that this river is the one which several pilots and historians call Norumbegue—It has been said also that there is a large city, well populated with savages who are so skilful and expert making use of cotton thread. I am confident that most of those who mention them did not see them, and speak from what they heard from those who knew no more about them than they did. I know very well that there are some people who may have seen the mouth of it, because, as a matter of fact, there are a quantity of islands and it is in latitude 44° at its mouth, as they say. But there is nothing to show that any one ever entered it, for they would have described it in a different way, so that so many people would not doubt it. I shall state then what I discovered and saw from the beginning as far as I went."

In these words Champlain well summarized the peculiar exaggerations about Norumbega and its city and river which had grown in France ever since the corrupt versions of Jehan Allefonsce's travels and those of Thevet had been published fifty years before. Champlain's was the first detailed investigation of the Norumbega legends, and he therefore deserves credit for being the first accurate explorer of this region of Maine, although many less literate navigators had probably seen the coast. He described well the islands in Penobscot Bay, one of which "is so high and striking that I named it Isle Haute," by which name it is still known. He gave explicit directions for entering the mouth of the Penobscot, taking sights of the Camden Hills and Mount Desert, thus improving on Thevet. He made notes of how the river narrows above Castine and he described the waterfall which impeded his progress at Bangor: "If we had wished to go farther, it would have been impossible to make half a league on account of a waterfall there, which came down a slope seven or eight feet. I saw it from a canoe with the savages that we had with us, and found only enough water there for a canoe. But beyond the falls, which are about two hundred paces wide, the River is beautiful and delightful as far as the place where we anchored. I went ashore to see the country, and, as far as I went, going hunting, I found it pleasant and agreeable. From the entrance to where I went which was about 25 leagues, I did not see any city, or village, or appearance of there having been any, although there were one or two cabins of the savages, with no one in them, which were made in the same way as those of the Souriquois [Micmacs, of Nova Scotia], covered with the bark of trees; and, as far as I could judge, there are not many savages on this river. . . . They do not come there any more than to the islands except some months in summer, during the season for fishing and hunting which are very good there. They are a people who have no fixed habitation as far as I have found out and learned from them, for they winter sometimes in one place, sometimes in another, where they see that the hunting for wild beasts is better; for they live from it as necessity compels, without having anything in reserve for times of scarcity, which is sometimes very great." This account compares closely with that of Thevet half a century before.

"On the sixteenth of the month, about thirty savages came to us, on the assurance of those who had served as guides. This Bessabez came also to find us that same day, with six canoes. As soon as the savages who were on land saw him coming they fell to singing, dancing and jumping until he was ashore; then afterward they all sat down on the ground in a circle, according to their custom when they wish to make a speech, or have a feast. Soon after Cabahis, the other chief, arrived also with

20 or 30 of his companions, who withdrew to one side and greatly enjoyed looking at us, for it was the first time they had seen Christians. Some time afterward I went ashore with two of my companions and two of our savages, who served as interpreters, and ordered those on our boat to approach the savages and have their arms ready for use if they noticed any movements among these people against us. Bessabez, seeing us ashore, had us sit down, and began to smoke with his companions as they usually do before making their speeches, and made us presents of venison and game. All the rest of the day and night following they did nothing but sing, dance and make good cheer, until the dawn. Then each one returned, Bessabez with his companions on his side, and we on ours, well satisfied at having made the acquaintance of these people."

The courage which marked this undertaking of Champlain's is patent. What is not always so obvious is the tact with which he must have treated these Indians, in order to have gone with his little company of a dozen men a full sixty miles into unexplored territory. Three factors aside from Champlain's powers of diplomacy seem to me significant in explaining the friendliness of these savages. The first is the small show of force with which his little party could have threatened the natives. The second is that we are dealing here with a geographer whose commercial motives were held in abeyance when display of trickery might have antagonized the Indians. Finally, Champlain had discovered the value of taking along with him a friendly Indian as interpreter. The less subtle English rarely mastered the art of winning an Indian's confidence, and chose usually to kidnap their native pilots.

The account concludes as follows: "On the seventeenth of the month I took the altitude and found the latitude was 45° 25'. This done I departed, to go to another river called Quinibequy [Kennebec] 35 leagues away from this place and almost 15 from Bedabedec. This tribe of savages of Quinibequy is called Etechemins as well as those of Norumbegue.

"The eighteenth of the month I went near a little river

where Cabahis was. He came with us in our boat about 12 leagues, I asked him where the River Norumbegue came from, and he told me that it comes from beyond the fall which I have mentioned above, and that after going some distance on it one enters a lake, by way of which they go to the St. Croix River [Matawamkeag, or east branch of the Penobscot]. Besides, another river flows into the lake, and on it they go several days and then enter another lake, and they go through the middle of this, and, when they reach the end, they go some distance by land, and afterward enter a little river which flows into the great St. Lawrence River. . . .

"This is an exact statement of all that I observed, whether of the coasts, the people, or the River Norumbegue, and not of the marvels that any one has written about them. I believe that this place is as agreeable in winter as St. Croix."

The knowledge of distant geography which the Indians of the eastern seaboard often displayed is at times somewhat breath-taking. That this instance in Champlain's account is not exceptional is attested by the fact that Thomas Morton found the Massachuset Indians in possession of information not only about Lake Champlain but about the St. Lawrence as well. And Sir Richard Grenville, writing from Raleigh's Roanoke Colony, speaks of the Indians there obtaining their copper from a place twenty days' journey inland.

Champlain now returned to St. Croix, there to spend a miserable winter of hardship, during which half the colony died. Before taking up his further investigations of the New England coast, we must return to consideration of another English expedition, which preceded by a few weeks Champlain's second expedition on the coast of Maine.

Chapter Five

GEORGE WAYMOUTH INVESTIGATES
THE MONHEGAN AREA, 1605

AMONG THE adventurers who had fostered the expedition of Gosnold in 1602 was Henry Wriothesley, Earl of Southampton, Shakespeare's good friend. Implicated in the Essex conspiracy against the queen, he had in the meantime been thrown into prison and his estates seized. But with the death of Elizabeth and the accession of James I, he was freed and his lands restored. This occurred just before the return of Martin Pring from New England, and coincident with the tragic imprisonment of Sir Walter Raleigh, who thereby lost the charter to exploit his territories in Virginia and New England. The opportunity which this latter circumstance presented was only accentuated by the promising fruits of Pring's voyage. Southampton was not slow to act, and immediately arranged with his son-in-law, Thomas Arundel, and Sir Ferdinando Gorges, whose name was now to be extensively associated with the colonization of New England, to fit out a new expedition to America. Captain George Waymouth had returned a year before from yet another futile attempt to find a Northwest Passage to the Indies in icebound Davis Strait, this time under the aegis of the newly formed East India Company. He it was who was chosen to captain the new venture to New England. Owing apparently to a difference of opinion between the Muscovia Company and the East India Fellowship as to who now possessed the monopoly of navigating in the northern seas, these two groups did not participate or invest in the enterprise. This, like the expeditions of Gosnold and Pring, was therefore the project of an independent group of adventurers. Along with Waymouth, Arundel sent James Rosier, "To take due notice and make true reports of the discovery therein performed." Arundel and Rosier were both Roman Catholics, and there is considerable reason to believe that one of the purposes of this voyage was to search for a colonial refuge for oppressed English papists. A document in the Roman Archives says that a priest accompanied the expedition, and this priest is usually held to have been Rosier. It is from Rosier's narrative that we learn the events of the voyage. Rosier tells us in his preface that he purposely omits the latitudes and some other identifying details of the regions explored "because some forrein Nation (being fully assured of the fruitfullnesse of the countrie) have hoped hereby to give some knowledge of the place." Whether this was France we can only speculate, but it gives some indication of the awakening international rivalries that from this time began to be a prominent phase of the New England developments.

On March 31, 1605, the ship, named the *Archangel,* put to sea from Dartmouth. Rosier says it was "Well victualed and furnished with munitions and all necessaries. Our whole Company being but 29 persons; of whom I may boldly say few voyages have been manned forth with better Sea-men generally in respect of our small number." They sighted the Azores two weeks later, and on May 14th they came into shoal water off a "whitish sandy cliffe," which is generally supposed to have been Sankaty Head, Nantucket. The ship became involved in treacherous shoals in a southwest wind, which prevented them from entering Nantucket Sound, and since their water and fuel were running low, they extricated themselves as best they could by sailing out to the northward. Waymouth has been charged by some writers with irresolution for thus easily abandoning his apparent intention to settle in Gosnold's territory. The limitations of the square-rigged ships of that period, however, included their complete inability to sail in any direction except with the wind astern or abeam. The art of tacking had been discovered in 1539 by Fletcher of Rye, but there were still no fore-and-aft sails. This same ship of Waymouth's had beaten up and down for six days on the south coast of England, and then lain at anchor at Dartmouth for two weeks waiting for the southwest wind to change so that they could put out to sea. One can well imagine that they were heartily sick of waiting for the wind, especially in uncharted shoal water with a shortage of provisions. This sort of incident is illuminating when we come to consider how much of the coastwise exploration by Gosnold, Champlain, Captain John Smith and many others was done in pinnaces or shallops, whose unwieldy oars were an attempt to remedy the deficiencies of square sails. At least they could travel against the wind. What would not these men have given for a modern sloop or a schooner!

Waymouth must have veered far to the eastward from his northerly departure from Nantucket, for it took him two days to find land again, and this time Monhegan Island off the Maine shore loomed ahead. Waymouth was its discoverer. "About two a clocke our Captaine with twelve men rowed in his ship boat to the shore where we made no long stay, but laded our boat with dry wood of olde trees upon the shore side, and returned to our ship where we rode that night.

"This Iland is woody, growen with Firre, Birch, Oke, and Beach, as farre as we saw along the shore; and so likely to be within. On the verge grow Gooseberries, strawberries, wild pease and wild rose bushes. The water issued forth down the Rocky Cliffes in many places; and much fowle of divers kinds breed upon the shore and rocks." Monhegan has changed little in appearance from this description of Waymouth's first discovery of it in 1605.

"While we were at shore, our men aboard with a few hooks got above thirty great cods and haddocks, which gave us a taste of the great plenty of fish which we found afterward wheresoever we went upon the coast.

"From hence we might discerne the maine land from the West-south-West to the East-North-East and a great way (as it then seemed, and as we after found it) up into the maine we might discerne very high mountains, though the maine seemed but low land which gave us hope that it would please God to direct us to the discoverie of some good; although we were driven by winds farre from that place, whither (both by our direction and desire) we ever intended to shape the course of our voyage." Here is suggestive evidence that the expedition had been instructed to visit the regions previously explored by Pring and Gosnold. The mountains were the Camden Hills. There has been a great deal of controversy among Maine historians as to the precise locations of the places Rosier describes, which at times has been so energetic as to obscure the more interesting phases of the narrative. I shall be content here to accept what seem to be the prevailing ideas as to locality in the references at my command. It is of little moment for the New England purpose whether the harbor which Waymouth now entered was at the mouth of the Kennebec or in Muscongus Bay. It was almost undoubtedly the latter.

"The next day being whit-sunday; because we rode too much open to the sea and windes, we weyed anker about twelve a'clocke, and came along to the other Islands more adjoining to the maine, and in the rode directly with the mountaines, about three leagues from the first Island where we had ankered." These were the Georges Islands.

"When we came neere unto them (sounding all along in a good depth) our Captaine manned his ship-boat and sent her before with Thomas Cam one of his Mates, whom he knew to be of good experience, to sound a search betweene the Islands for a place safe for our shippe to ride in; in the meane while we kept alloofe at sea. . . . it pleased God to send us, farre beyond our expectation, in a most safe birth defended from all windes in an excellent depth of water for ships of any burthen, in six, seven, eight, nine, ten fathoms upon a clay ooze very tough.

"We all with great joy praised God for his unspeakable goodness, who had from so apparent danger delivered us, and directed us upon this day into so secure an Harbor; in remembrance whereof we named it Pentecost Harbour." This anchorage is now known as St. Georges Harbor, off Port Clyde, and a great stone cross on the shore commemorates Waymouth's visit.

They went ashore on Allen's Island [Burrage] and secured fresh water. "Upon this Island, as also upon the former [Monhegan], we found (at our first coming to shore) where fire had beene made, and about the place were very great egge shelles bigger than goose egges, fish bones, and also as we judged, the bones of some beast. . . .

"Whitson-monday, the 20th of May, very early in the morning, our Captaine caused the pieces of the pinnesse to be carried a shore, where while some were busied about her, others digged welles to receive the fresh water. . . . In digging we found excellent clay for bricke or tile. The next day we finished a well of good and holesome cleere water in a great empty caske, which we left there. We cut yards, waste trees, and many necessaries for our ship, while our Carpenter and Cooper labored to fit and furnish forth the shallop."

The company spent the next ten days in fishing and exploring the neighboring islands. They secured thirty lobsters and numerous flounders with a net, which is to us amusing evidence of their abundance. They planted "peaze and barley which in sixteen days grew eight inches above ground." They were impressed by the quantities of spruce gum they found. "This would be a great benefit for making Tarre and Pitch." Many mussel beds were found and apparently a pearl hunt was instituted, not without success. Also "we set up a crosse on the shore side upon the rockes."

On May 30th Captain Waymouth with thirteen men set out on a tour of exploration in the shallop, leaving fourteen men with the ship, moored as it was in a safe harbor. Later the same day, "about five a'clocke in the afternoone, we in the shippe espied three Canoas comming towards us, which went to the Iland adjoining, where they went a shore, and very quickly had made a fire, about which they stood beholding our ship; to whom we made signes with our hands and hats, weffing unto them to come to us, because we had not seene any of the people yet. They sent one Canoa with three men, one of which, when they came neere unto us, spake in his language very loud and very boldly; seeming as though he would know why we were there, and by pointing with his oare towards the sea, we conjectured he meant we should be gone. But when we showed them knives and their use, by cutting of sticks, and other trifles, as combs and glasses, they came close aboard our ship, as desirous to entertain our friendship. To these we gave such things as we perceived they liked, when we showed them the use; bracelets, rings, peacocke feathers, which they stucke in their haire, and tobacco pipes. After their departure to their company on the shore; presently came foure others in another Canoa, to whom we gave as to the former, using them with as much kindness as we could."

Rosier describes these people in much the same terms as had Gosnold and Verrazano, with but few added details: "Their clothing is Beavers skins or Deares skins, cast over them like a mantle and hanging downe to their knees, made fast together upon the shoulders with leather; some of them had sleeves, most had none; some had buskins of such leather tewed. . . . They seemed all very civill and merrie, showing tokens of much thankfullnesse for those things we gave them. We found them (as after) a people of exceeding good invention, quicke understanding and readie capacitie." Rosier, like everyone else, was impressed with their birch canoes.

"The next morning very early, came one Canoa aboard us againe with three Salvages, whom we easily then enticed into our ship, and under the decke, where we gave them porke, fish, bread and pease, all which they did eat; and this I noted, they would eat nothing raw, either fish or flesh. They marvelled much and much looked upon the making of our canne and kettle, so they did at a head-geare and at our guns, of which they are most fearfull, and would fall flat downe at the report of them. At their departure I signed unto them, that if they would bring me such skins as they wore I would give them knives, and such things as I saw they most liked, which the chiefe of them promised to do by that time the Sunne should be beyond the middest of the firmament; this I did to bring them to an understanding of exchange, that they might conceive the intent of our comming to them to be for no other end."

Later that morning Waymouth unexpectedly returned, having found the mouth of a great river up which he intended to explore. Before proceeding to do so, he thought it expedient to "flanke his light horsman for arrowes, least it might happen that the further part of the river should be narrow, and by that means subject to the volley of Salvages on either side out of the woods." This precaution of Waymouth's presents a striking contrast with the attitude of Champlain on the neighboring Penobscot, only eight months previously. The river was the St. Georges.

The Indians who had promised to return "by that time the Sunne should be beyond the middest of the firmament" were as good as their word. About one o'clock four canoes arrived at the near-by island, and one of the craft, containing a chief and two others, approached somewhat hesitantly and then left, its occupants promising to return shortly. Despite a hard rainstorm they soon did return. The English presented them with some clothing to protect them from the rain. Rosier says that the chief never seemed to have seen such clothing before. The chief seemed delighted with gifts of "a brooch to hang about his neck," a large knife, a comb, and various articles of food and a mirror. The type of these gifts was doubtless suggested by the observations made in the Gosnold and Verrazano voyages; yet we recall the peculiar fact that the Maine natives whom Verrazano had seen wanted only "knives, fish hookes, and sharpened steel." These Indians whom Rosier describes were akin to Verrazano's in the absence of any evidences of agriculture other than tobacco but obviously dissimilar in their attitude toward Europeans and in their regard for adornment. The only conclusion one can draw on the scanty evidence is that there were indeed quite distinct types of natives on the coast of Maine. But there is also an extremely suggestive explanation offered in Rosier's remark: "Thus because we found the land a place answerable to the intent of our discovery, viz. fit for any nation to inhabit, we used the people with as great kindness as we could devise, or found them capable of." Sometimes the mercenary motive served a humanitarian purpose. The reward of this kindness was immediately evident, for Rosier the next day traded with these natives, and "for knives, glasses, combes, and other trifles to the valew of foure or five shillings we had 40 good Beavers skins, Otters skins, Sables, and other small skins which we knew not how to call."

Such friendly intercourse between the two races always brought out interesting bits of lore of various kinds. The natives marveled greatly to see Captain Waymouth catch fish with a net. "Most of that we caught we gave them and their company," says Rosier in an excess of generous spirit. It is a little surprising to find these Indians unfamiliar with nets, for in many areas farther south they seem to have used fish weirs before the arrival of Europeans.

Rosier went ashore and "learned the names of divers things of them; and when they perceived me to write them downe, they would of themselves fetch fishes and fruit bushes and stand by me to see me write their names." Waymouth amusingly magnetized his sword with a lodestone and showed the Indians how it would then pick up a knife or a needle. "This we did," writes Rosier, "to cause them to imagine some great power in us and for that to love and feare us." He examined their bows and arrows, the latter of which were headed with "the long shanke bone of a Deere, made very sharpe with two fangs in manner of a harping iron. They have likewise Darts, headed with like bone, one of which I darted among the rockes, and it brake not. These they use very cunningly, to kill fish, fowle and beasts." Such bone artifacts are often found in shell heaps in this region today.

He found their tobacco excellent. He saw a few of the Indian women of which characteristically the native men were very jealous, and two small children "which they love tenderly." The children, judged to be only a year and a half old, "wore thin leather buskins on their legs attached to girdles decked round about with little round pieces of red copper; to these I gave chaines and bracelets, glasses and other trifles, which the Salvages seemed to accept in great kindness."

At night the English sent Owen Griffin ashore as a hostage, and several Indians thereupon came and slept aboard ship. Griffin was "one of two we were to leave in the country if we had thought it needful or convenient." Whenever the Indians were aboard, the European dogs were tied up, as the natives here suffered the same terror of these animals that the natives of Plymouth had manifested two years before on Martin Pring's visit there.

Owen Griffin, ashore, had the unique experience that night of observing a circle dance of the natives around the fire, lasting about two hours. Who would choose to be a hostage in such circumstances?

Two days after this, the English having exhausted the natives' supply of merchandise to trade, the Indians desired that the white men accompany them to the mainland where their chief had more furs and tobacco. Accordingly, Captain Waymouth fitted out the pinnace and with fifteen men accompanied the canoes to a point of land which was probably the eastern shore of Pemaquid Point. There, after an exchange of hostages, the English became convinced that the great body of natives at Pemaquid, numbering about 280, not only had no merchandise to trade but were plotting to lure the English into a little river the better to fall on them and exterminate the party. This is the same curious reversal of attitude which had come over Gosnold's party as soon as the trading was done and natives appeared in superior numbers. It is identical also with the experience of Pring in Plymouth Harbor. These English of Waymouth's crew, hitherto so kindly toward the Indians, seem overnight to have grown fearful and suspicious to a degree that they now became concerned only with means of kidnapping a number of the Indians to take back to England with them. "These things considered," says Rosier, "we began to joyne them in the ranks of other Salvages, who have beene by travellers in most discoveries found very treacherous; never attempting mischiefe, untill by some remisnesse, fit opportunity affordeth them certaine ability to execute the same. Wherefore, after good advice taken, we determined so soone as we could to take some of them, least (being suspitious we had discovered their plots) they should absent themselves from us."

It seems to me at least a matter open to discussion, whether it was not the English, becoming overawed by their own weakness in the face of an imagined enemy, who conjured up these alleged plots. Once their trading venture had been accomplished, what was there left to maintain their friendly relationship with the savages? Perhaps indeed Owen Griffin's account of two hours of dancing around a fire had struck fear into their hearts, for this seems to have been a sort of turning point in their attitude. Certainly Rosier's abrupt change of front in his narrative looks suspiciously like an attempt to produce an apologia.

In any event, the next two days were spent in preparing the ship for departure from this harbor and with the sordid matter of bringing three Indians by virtue of kindly treatment aboard the ship, where they were promptly imprisoned. Not satisfied with these, a shore party enticed two more of the natives with gifts of food, and set upon them. "It was as much as five or sixe of us could doe to get them into the light horsman," says Rosier, "For they were so strong as our best hold was by their long haire in their heads; and we would have beene very loathe to have done them any hurt . . . being a matter of great importance for the full accomplement of our voyage.

"Thus we shipped five Salvages, two Canoas, with all their bowes and arrowes."

During the last days of their stay at the Georges, the captain made very careful soundings in the vicinity, and must have collected a great deal of navigational information, which, we have seen, Rosier deliberately omitted from his narrative. Also two canoes came from the east containing natives they had not seen before, elaborately painted and wearing feathered head-dresses and sculptured bone ornaments. These "came sent by the Bashabes and . . . his desire was that we would bring up our ship to his house, being as they pointed, upon the main towards the East from whence they came, and that he would exchange with us for Furres and Tobacco. But because our Company was but small, and now our desire was with speed to discover up the river, we let them understand, that if their Bashabes would come to us, he should be welcome, but we would not remove to him. Which when they understood (receiving of us bread and fish, and every one of them a knife) they departed; for we had then no will to stay them long aboard, least they should discover the other Salvages which we had stowed below." This "Bashabes" was without question the "Bessabez" whom Champlain had visited the year before on the Penobscot. Waymouth would have been astounded to learn that these Indians had traveled sixty miles to bring their message.

"Tuesday, the 11th of June, we passed up into the river with our ship, about six and twenty miles." This, as I have said above, was the St. Georges River below Thomaston. The river is described as varying in width from half a mile to a mile, bordered in places by open low plains and in others by tall forest. Various members of the crew compared it with the Orinoco in Raleigh's ill-fated Guiana colony, and with the Rio Grande, and some with the Loire and the Seine in France. It is interesting to find that there were in this crew sailors who had been with Raleigh in 1596, and others apparently who had been on sea-dog voyages to Mexico. Waymouth seems to have anchored the *Archangel* a few miles below the present site of Thomaston, and to have gone farther up the river in the pinnace, from which a shore party of ten "marched up into the country towards the mountains . . . about foure miles into the Maine and passed over three hilles; and because the weather was parching hot, and our men in their armour not able to travel farre and returne that night to our ship, we resolved not to passe any further, being all very weary of so tedious and laboursome a travell." A memorial erected by the town of Thomaston in 1905 celebrates this event and the planting of a cross by Waymouth as "The earliest known claim of right of possession by Englishmen on New England soil."

On the way back to the ship they were met by a canoe whose occupants they recognized. These natives entreated them to return and trade with the "Bashabes for many Furres and Tabacco. This we purceived," says Rosier, "to be only a meere device to get possession of any of our men to ransome all those which we had taken." Apparently one of these Indians was a kinsman of one of the prisoners.

The country delighted the Englishmen. Rosier spends several pages in describing the open, pasturelike land along the river and the opportunities for farming and grazing which it afforded. Salmon were plentiful. Of special interest to us is his comment: "We diligently observed, that in no place, either about the Islands, or up in the Maine, or alongst the river we could discerne any token or signe that ever any Christian had been before; of which either by cutting wood, digging for water or setting up Crosses—we should have received some mention left." Scarcely could he know that the French had been only a few miles away on the Penobscot the previous autumn, had wintered at St. Croix, and that Champlain was even now about to set out on a voyage down this coast on his way to Cape Cod.

After setting up the cross at Thomaston, Waymouth proceeded down the river. He spent, as before at the Georges Islands, several days in taking soundings and making observations. On Sunday, June 16th, he set sail for England, and stopping only to try the fishing on Brown's Bank when two days out, arrived in the Harbor of Dartmouth on July 14th.

Sir Ferdinando Gorges must have come over from Plymouth to greet him, for we learn that Gorges took three of the captive Indians into his own family, where their information greatly stimulated his interest in New England. He later wrote that these savages manifested "shows of great civility far from the rudeness of our common people."

Waymouth's men brought back with them the first accurate English knowledge of the coast of Maine, which was to be responsible for the first English attempt, in the Popham Colony, to establish a plantation in that region. They secured the first written rudiments of the Indians' language, and many observations of their way of living. In his summary Rosier tells of how they hunted whales, made bread of their Indian corn, and had names for the constellations. He even claims that they made butter and cheese from milk of fallow deer, which we may regard as a bit of fantasy worthy of David Ingram. On the whole Rosier's narrative is sound, and was a useful addition to the now rapidly growing bibliography of the New England scene. Waymouth's voyage is to be regarded as a rounding out of the New England discoveries, a worthy successor in the same group with Gosnold and Pring, of the voyages primarily for trade, whose secondary fruits in the form of explorations were far more significant than the cargo of furs he obtained. The coast was now for the first time well enough known among the English to provide a sound basis for serious colonial projects. That he kidnaped Indians was unfortunate from the human standpoint, but, as Gorges afterward said, those same five natives were put to the practical use of providing the means "under God, of putting on foot and giving life to all our plantations." With this perhaps justifiable exception, Waymouth treated the Indians well. We may question whether there was not some faintheartedness among the party in its latter days. It was an intelligently planned and well-executed piece of exploration, though in a very small area. It is a bit difficult to understand why Waymouth did not extend his investigation farther, even as Champlain was so splendidly doing in that same year, for the season was only half advanced when the ship returned to England. But the discovery of Monhegan alone should be considered an important achievement, since it soon became, as a harbor of refuge free from the threat of Indians, an habitual rendezvous for English fishermen and trading ships. Captain John Smith and Gorges referred to it in subsequent years as "the usual place" for English ships to go.

Chapter Six

CHAMPLAIN IN MASSACHUSETTS, 1605–1606

1. The Voyage of 1605

THE SITE which the French had chosen for their settlement in Passamaquoddy Bay in 1604 was singularly unfortunate. Champlain returned to it from his Penobscot investigations on October 2nd. Four days later it began to snow. On the six- or seven-acre island the colonists had built a secure enough quadrangle of buildings. It must have looked like a welcome refuge to Champlain, on his return from his voyage. He doubtless anticipated a winter similar to those in the same latitudes in sunny France. Apparently no firewood was laid by. There was little on the island, nor was much fresh water available. By December ice cakes began to appear in the tidal currents that surrounded the island. Soon it was impossible to traverse the shifting floes between the colony and the mainland. Fresh game and fish disappeared from the larder. Shrieking blizzards buried the inadequately heated houses. Even the cider the French had brought with them froze and was dispensed in solid blocks. With the seventy-nine men subsisting almost wholly on salted meats, it was little wonder that death claimed thirty-five of their number during the winter. A down-East island might be ample protection against Indians or privateers, but few would choose one even in this twentieth century as a place for winter refuge.

Thawed out by spring, the unhappy survivors began to build two small boats with the idea of migrating northward, where they might perhaps be able to hail a passing vessel and secure passage home to France. But on June 15th Pont Gravé arrived from France with a supply ship, and immediately Champlain changed his plans. Three days later he and de Monts set out with twenty men and several Indians to search for a kindlier place for settlement, farther south. So quickly, sometimes, do projects of empire shift from despair to hope. The date, June 12, 1605, is of interest—it was only two days after George Waymouth's departure to England from Muscongus Bay, a hundred and forty miles south of the French colony. Nine days later Champlain was himself in Muscongus Bay, having by that time shown to Sieur de Monts the previously explored shore around Mount Desert and the Penobscot. By this short interval did the French and English avoid an encounter precisely in the area where the two nations were to be in incessant conflict between 1689 and 1763.

Champlain headed for the Kennebec, which he had almost reached when he ran short of supplies in the previous September. The party anchored near Seguin Island on July 1st and were there delayed by fog. They had brought with them an Indian named Panounias from the Passamaquoddy area, and his wife whom the native had been unwilling to leave behind, and during this foggy interval these Indians now brought the Frenchmen into friendly relationship with the local savages. This facilitated Champlain's intention to explore the river, which he proceeded to do, probably by way of the Back River and Hockomock Bay as far up as Wiscasset. There he and de Monts presented gifts to the local sachem and then under the guidance of the Indians sailed through the curious upper Hell Gate rapids of the Sasanoa, into the Kennebec itself, and thence up into Merrymeeting Bay, the junction of the Androscoggin with the Kennebec. Returning down the main channel of the Kennebec, he comments that this was a "much safer and better" route. Most of Champlain's account of this sojourn of a week on the Kennebec is concerned with geography. His final comments form an interesting summary of his impressions: "The land, so far as I have seen it along the shores of the river is very poor, for there are only rocks on all sides. There are a great many small oaks, and very little arable land. Fish abound here, as in the other rivers which I have mentioned. The people live like those in the neighborhood of our settlement; and they told us that the savages who plant the Indian corn dwelt very far in the interior, and that they have given up planting it on the coasts on account of the war they had with others who came and took it away." This is probably a reference to the annual custom of the Massachuset Indians, who regularly seem to have made raids on the Indians of Maine during late summer.

"The savages that live on all these shores are very few in number. During the winter, if there is a great deal of snow, they hunt the moose and other animals upon which they live most of the time, and if there is not much snow it is not to their advantage, inasmuch as they cannot get anything without excessive labor, which causes them to endure and suffer a great deal. When they do not hunt they live on a shellfish, which is called the clam. They dress themselves in winter in good furs of the beaver and the moose. The women make all the clothes, but not so neatly but that one sees the flesh under the arms, for they are not skillful enough to make them fit better. When they go hunting they take a kind of racket, twice as big as those on our side of the water, which they attach to their feet, and they can go on the snow in this way without sinking in, the women and children as well as the men, looking for the tracks of animals. Then when they have found them, they follow them until they see the beast and then they shoot at it with their bows or kill it with stabs of swords fastened to the end of a short pike staff, which is easily done, since these animals cannot walk on the snow without sinking into it. Then the women and children come to the place and make a hut there, and give themselves a feast."

Leaving the Kennebec area about July 10th, the Frenchmen sailed southwestward into waters visited all unknown to them by both Gosnold and Pring during the previous three years. Like them, Champlain and de Monts missed the fine harbor of Portland, and noticing only the islands and the White Mountains far inland, sailed across Casco Bay to make a landing at the mouth of the Saco River near Biddeford, which was called Chouacoet. Here they found an entirely different people from the Etechemins they had encountered farther north. These he calls the Almouchiquois. His Passamaquoddy guide who had accompanied them from St. Croix was now of little use, for he and his wife could understand only a few words of what these people spoke. "We sent some articles of merchandise on shore to barter with them; but they had nothing but their robes to give in exchange, for they preserve only such furs as they need for their garments." They "shave off the hair far up on the head, and wear what remains very long, which they comb and twist behind in various ways very neatly intertwined with feathers which they attach to the head." He notes that some used the tail of the horseshoe crab, which they called the "signoc," as a point for their arrows. But, most significant difference of all: "They till and cultivate the soil, something which we have not hitherto observed. In the place of ploughs, they use an instrument of very hard wood, shaped like a spade . . . We saw their Indian corn, which they raise in gardens. Planting three or four kernels in one place, they then heap up about it a quantity of earth with shells of the signoc before mentioned. Then three feet distant they plant as much more, and thus in succession. With this corn they put in each hill three or four Brazilian beans, which are of different colors. When they grow up, they interlace with the corn, which reaches to the height of from five to six feet; and they keep the ground very free from weeds. We saw there many squashes and pumpkins, and tobacco, which they likewise cultivate.

"The Indian corn which we saw was at that time about two feet high, some of it as high as three. The beans were beginning to flower as also the pumpkins and squashes. They plant their corn in May, and gather it in September. We saw also a great many nuts, which are small and have several divisions. There were as yet none on the trees, but we found plenty under them from the preceding year. We saw also many grapevines on which there was a remarkable fine berry, from which we made some very good verjuice. The savages dwell permanently in this place, and have a large cabin surrounded by palisades made of rather large trees placed by the side of each other, in which they take refuge when their enemies make war upon them. They cover their cabins with oak bark. This place is very pleasant and as agreeable as any to be seen. The river is very abundant in fish, and is bordered by meadows. At the mouth there is a small island adapted for the construction of a good fortress, where one could be in security."

Champlain produced and published with his book a very good map of this area which indicates that the Indians inhabited the whole region from Biddeford Pool to Prout's Neck, and had their palisaded village on the south bank of the Saco River, near its mouth. The enthusiastic detail with which he describes the natives and their agricultural technique leads one to feel that these more southerly latitudes appealed to him as a more suitable area for settlement. Champlain was an excellent chronicler of these voyages—the reader of his journals is made to feel like an eyewitness, for the observations are keen and have the feel of accuracy, without that tone of commercial bias and personal apology that runs through the annals of Archer and Rosier. Champlain unvarnishes his conclusions and is no whit afraid to call a territory "very poor." He nowhere gives you a sensation of wishing to sell you a stake in this new country. When therefore he says that a place is "very pleasant" and "agreeable" one may take it for gospel. The thousands who in succeeding generations have enjoyed Biddeford and Prout's Neck confirm us in this judgment of Champlain.

He was a discriminating journalist. In both his written and his graphic representations of what he observed he was by all odds the most intelligent and thorough explorer ever to chart these coasts. He had a knack of summing up not only the geography, but also the ethnology and climatology of these areas in a way that would have been very useful to the later English settlers had they been familiar with his writings. There is no evidence that they ever read them—they had to repeat his work in their own cruder ways.

The explorers spent two days in Saco Bay and then sailed on, July 12th, to a landing in the neighborhood of Wells, where they saw in the marshes "some little birds which sing like blackbirds, and are black excepting the ends of the wings, which are orange-colored." Delayed by contrary winds, they sailed back a few miles to Cape Porpoise, which they explored and named "Island Harbor." Here they saw many currants growing, and "an infinite number of pigeons, of which we took a great quantity."

On the 15th they proceeded and soon sighted Cape Ann ahead, with the Isles of Shoals to the eastward and Portsmouth Bay indenting the shore to the west. They had now passed Gosnold's "Savage Rock," of which of course they knew nothing. There is nothing in Champlain's account to indicate that he was aware that any previous explorer had ever touched these coasts, until on his return voyage in the fall he ran across information about George Waymouth from Indians at the mouth of the Kennebec.

"On the next day we went to the above mentioned Cape [Ann] where there are three islands near the mainland, full of wood of different kinds, as at Chouacoet [Saco] and all along the coast, and still another flat one where there are breakers, and which extends a little farther out to sea than the others, on which there is no wood at all. We named this place Island Cape, near which we saw a canoe containing five or six savages, who came out near our barque, and then went back and danced on the beach. Sieur de Monts sent me on shore to observe them, and to give each one of them a knife and some biscuit, which caused them to dance again better than before. This over, I made them understand, as well as I could, that I desired them to show me the course of the shore. After I had drawn with a crayon the bay [Ipswich Bay], and the Island Cape, where we were, with the same they drew the outline of another bay, which they represented as very large [Massachusetts Bay]; here they placed six pebbles at equal distances apart, giving me to understand by this that these signs represented as many chiefs and tribes. Then they drew within the first mentioned bay a river which we had passed, which has shoals and is very long [Merrimac]. We found in this place a great many vines, the green grapes on which were a little larger than peas, also many nut trees, the nuts on which were no larger than musket-balls. The savages told us that all those inhabiting this country cultivated the land and sowed seeds like the others, whom we had before seen. The latitude of this place is 43° and some minutes. Sailing half a league farther, we observed several savages on a rocky point, who ran along the shore dancing as they went, to their companions to inform them of our coming. After pointing out to us the direction of their abode, they made a signal with smoke to show us the place of their settlement. We anchored near a small island [Thatcher's] and sent our canoe with knives and cakes to the savages. From the large number of those we saw we concluded that these places were better inhabited than the others we had seen. After a stay of some two hours for the sake of observing these people, whose canoes are made of birch bark like those of the Canadians, Souriquois and Etechemins, we weighed anchor and set sail with a promise of fine weather."

We have already learned that this was not the first visit of white men to Cape Ann. Martin Pring had coasted this shore two years before. But the above is the first description of Rockport and the outer shore of Gloucester. The episode of the natives completing Champlain's map of the shore with a crayon reminds us of Gosnold's experience with the Biscay shallop Indians at Savage Rock. Edmund Slafter notes that the six pebbles "representing as many chiefs and tribes" around Massachusetts Bay corresponds very well with the statement of the Indian historian, Gookin, who wrote that there had been indeed six tribes in the Massachusetts area: the "Weechagaskas, Nepon-

sitt, Punkapoag, Nonantum, Nashaway and some of the Nip-
muck people," all of whom were under the dominion of the
Massachusets, whose sachem lived on the southern shores of
Boston Harbor. We shall have further opportunity to mention
Gloucester and its people when we discuss Champlain's return
there a year later. He now proceeded along the North Shore and
into Boston Harbor.

"Continuing our course to the west-south-west, we saw
numerous islands on one side and the other. Having sailed seven
or eight leagues we anchored near an island whence we observed many smokes along the shore, and many savages running
up to see us. Sieur de Monts sent two or three men in a canoe
to them, to whom he gave some knives and paternosters to present to them; with which they were greatly pleased, and danced
several times in acknowledgment. We could not ascertain the
name of their chief, as we did not know their language. All
along the shore there is a great deal of land cleared up and
planted with Indian corn. The country is very pleasant and
agreeable, and there is no lack of fine trees. The canoes of
those who live there are made of a single piece, and are very
liable to turn over if one is not skilful in managing them. We
had not before seen any of this kind. They are made in the following manner. After cutting down at a cost of much labor and
time, the largest and tallest tree they can find, by means of stone
hatchets (for they have no others except some few which they
received from the savages on the coasts of La Cadie, who obtained them in exchange for furs) they remove the bark, and
round off the tree except on one side, where they apply fire
gradually along its entire length, and sometimes they put red-
hot pebble-stones on top. When the fire is too fierce, they ex-
tinguish it with a little water, not entirely, but so that the edge
of the boat may not be burnt. It being hollowed out as much as
they wish, they scrape it all over with stones, which they use
instead of knives. These stones resemble our musket flints.

"On the next day, the 17th of the month, we weighed
anchor to go to a cape we had seen the day before, which

FIG. 2—CHAMPLAIN'S MAP OF NEW FRANCE, 1606. (Reproduced from the
LXXX, portfolio of

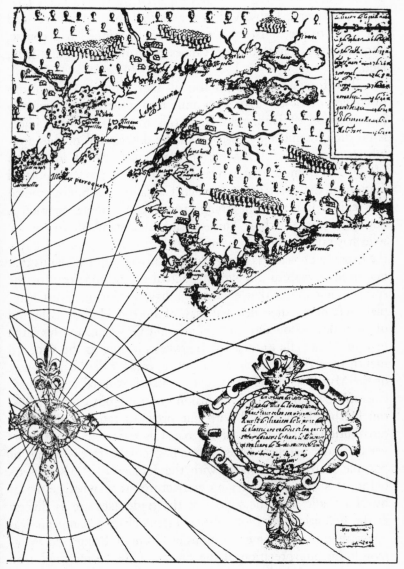

Champlain Society edition of *The Works of Samuel de Champlain*, Plate
plates and maps.)

seemeth to lie on our south-south-west. This day we were able
to make only five leagues, and we passed by some islands covered with wood. I observed in the bay all that the savages had
described to me at Island Cape. As we continued our course,
large numbers came to us in canoes from the islands and main
land."

The foregoing description is all that exists of Champlain's
discovery of Boston Bay. It is unfair to insist on too accurate
identification of landmarks from this meager account. There
is no such assemblage of islands as the description implies anywhere else on the Massachusetts Bay coast except in Boston
Harbor. We know that it was the most extensively populated
section of the coast in 1614 when Captain John Smith studied
the region. It may seem strange to some that more mention is
not made of the harbor. This is easily understandable to anyone
who has sailed a small boat among the islands of Boston Bay—
the expanse of water is everywhere so broken up by islands that
one needs a map to discover the actual extent and form of the
surrounding shores that enclose the bay. Unfortunately Champlain left us no such detailed map of Boston Harbor as he did
of Saco Bay, Gloucester, Plymouth and Chatham. On his large
map of "Nouvelle France" he represents it only as the widened
mouth of a river, which we might as easily call the Neponset
or the Mystic as the Charles, with which it is usually identified.
Champlain's portrayal of the making of a dugout canoe in Boston Harbor is in accord with our previous remarks about the
distribution of the canoe birch tree. His statement about stone
versus trader hatchets gives us our first clue as to the extent of
possible European contacts with the Indians of Massachusetts
before this time. The varying conjectures as to what he meant
by "La Cadie" for the source of the trade axes are as diverse
as the definitions of Norumbega. Inasmuch as Champlain was
unaware of the known expeditions of Gosnold, Pring, and Waymouth, his interpretation of the source of the "some few" iron
hatchets is to be taken as scarcely excluding the possibility of
earlier unknown voyages into Massachusetts Bay. The signifi-

cant thing is that there were *any* trader hatchets in so unfre-
quented a region as Boston. It is equally important that stone
hatchets and knives were still being used, for it establishes for
us that the Stone Age of the Indian in Massachusetts did not end
until after the year 1605. Nor should we fail to note that French
Catholic paternosters preceded the Puritan theology in Boston
by a quarter century.

"We anchored a league from a cape," he goes on, "which
we named St. Louis, where we noticed smoke in several places.
While in the act of going there our barque grounded on a rock,
where we were in great danger, for, if we had not speedily got
it off, it would have overturned in the sea, since the tide was
falling all around, and there were five or six fathoms of water.
But God preserved us, and we anchored near the above named
Cape, when there came to us fifteen or sixteen canoes of savages. In some of them there were fifteen or sixteen, who began
to manifest great signs of joy, and made various harangues, which
we could not in the least understand. Sieur de Monts sent three
or four in our canoe, not only to get water but to see their chief,
whose name was Honabetha. The latter had a number of knives
and other trifles which Sieur de Monts gave him when he came
alongside to see us, together with some of his companions, who
were present both along the shore and in their canoes. We
received the chief very cordially and made him welcome; who
after remaining some time, went back. Those whom we had sent
to them brought us some little squashes as big as the fist, which
we ate as a salad like cucumbers, and which we found very
good. They brought also some purslane, which grows in large
quantities among the Indian corn, and of which they make no
more account than of weeds. We saw here a great many little
houses, scattered over the fields where they plant their Indian
corn.

"There is, moreover in this bay a very broad river, which
we named River du Guast. It stretches as it seemed to me,
towards the Iroquois, a nation in open warfare with the Montagnais, who live on the great river St. Lawrence."

So ends the description of the South Shore of Massachusetts Bay.

From our standpoint they had covered a great deal of coast in a short time, and it is not surprising therefore that we identify their landmarks with difficulty. On July 16th they had rounded Cape Ann and reached Boston Harbor for the night. On the 17th they ran out of Boston Harbor and down the South Shore as far as Marshfield. The Cape of St. Louis which they had seen across the bay from the North Shore the day before probably included the whole South Shore and can be thought of as terminating at Brant Rock in Marshfield, beyond which the coast indents to make Plymouth Harbor. It is a striking confirmation of Champlain's observations that there are today in plain sight of the shore line the evidences of many sites of Indian summer villages along this stretch of coast, in Scituate, Cohasset and Marshfield. Whether the great "River du Guast" refers to the North River in Marshfield, later famous for its shipbuilding, or to one of the rivers in Boston Harbor is debatable, depending on the interpretation one gives to the bay in which he locates it. The rock upon which the expedition almost foundered may have been one of those about Minot's Ledge off Cohasset, or Brant Rock. This coast has been noted for its shipwrecks, and Champlain seems to have inaugurated the practice. The Frenchmen seem to have maintained as uniformly pleasant relations with the Indians here as in Maine, possibly because of the presence of Panounias and his wife in the party.

The expedition now proceeded southward into Plymouth Harbor. "The next day we doubled Cap St. Louis, so named by Sieur de Monts, a land rather low, and in latitude 42° 45′. The same day we sailed two leagues along a sandy coast [Humarock and Green Harbor] as we passed along which we saw a great many cabins and gardens. The wind being contrary we entered a little bay [Plymouth] to await a time favorable for proceeding. There came to us two or three canoes, which had just been fishing for cod and other fish, which are found there in large numbers. These they catch with hooks made of a piece of wood,

FIGS. 3A AND 3B.

CHAMPLAIN'S MAP OF PLYMOUTH HARBOR, 1605

with modern map and notes adapted from Professor W. F.
Ganong. Reproduced from the Champlain Society edition of
The Works of Samuel de Champlain. (Plate LXXIV)

* * *

Legends on Champlain's Map of Port St. Louis with Comments

The figures show the fathoms of water

A.—SHOWS THE PLACE WHERE VESSELS ANCHOR

The depths are now much less than those indicated on the map, and the
difference may represent an actual change.

B.—THE CHANNEL

C.—TWO ISLANDS

Clarks Island, a low swell of upland occupied by farms, and Saquish Head,
likewise low upland occupied by a few buildings and some bushes.

D.—SAND DUNES

The long line of dune beaches, collectively called Duxbury Beach, connecting Brant and Gurnet points.

E.—SHOALS

A prominent feature of this part of Plymouth Harbor and of Duxbury
Bay. As Champlain states, they are largely bare at low tide.

Continued on page 114

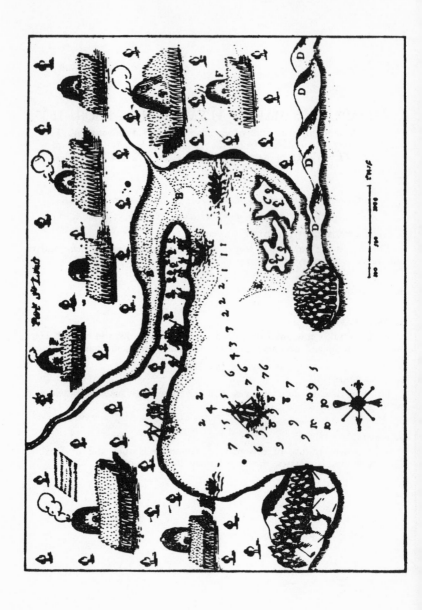

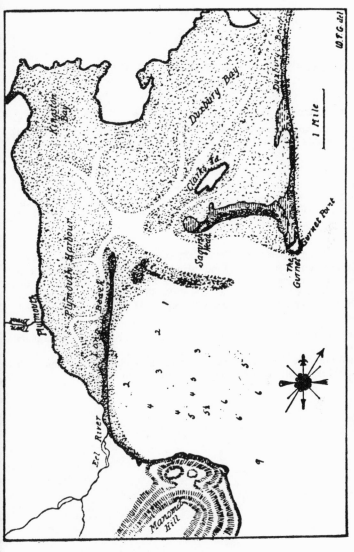

MAP OF PLYMOUTH HARBOR, MASSACHUSETTS
Adapted from the latest chart

For comparison with Champlain's map of *Port St. Louis*, to which it is adjusted as nearly as possible in scale, extent, and meridian.

The compass is Champlain's, which is supposed to be set to the magnetic meridian, but the true north is shown by the arrow.

CHAMPLAIN'S MAP OF PLYMOUTH HARBOR, 1605
—*Continued*

F.—WIGWAMS WHERE THE INDIANS CULTIVATE THE LAND

A number are situated on the slope where now stands the historic city of Plymouth founded by the Pilgrim Fathers fifteen years after this visit of Champlain.

G.—THE SPOT WHERE WE RAN OUR PINNACE AGROUND

Browns Bank, still an impediment to the navigation of the harbor. Apparently it was while their pinnace was aground that Champlain landed on the north end of Long Beach, where he sketched this map.

H.—A KIND OF ISLAND COVERED WITH TREES, AND CONNECTED WITH THE SAND DUNES

The Gurnet, a low-swelling upland island, ending in a low bluff; it is largely bare of trees and occupied by a group of buildings belonging to the light station. It was thickly wooded when the Pilgrim Fathers settled here in 1620. Slafter's contention that this was Saquish Head he later abandoned.

I.—A FAIRLY HIGH PROMONTORY, WHICH IS VISIBLE FROM FOUR TO FIVE LEAGUES
OUT TO SEA

Manomet Hill, 360 feet in height, a plateau ridge cut to an abrupt bluff where it reaches the sea, thus forming a conspicuous landmark.

to which they attach a bone in the shape of a spear, and fasten it very securely. The whole thing has a fang-shape, and the line attached to it is made out of the bark of a tree. They gave me one of their hooks, which I took as a curiosity. In it the bone was fastened on by hemp, like that in France, as it seemed to me. And they told me that they gathered this plant without being obliged to cultivate it; and indicated that it grew to the height of four or five feet." The plant here referred to was the common Indian hemp, or dogbane. "This canoe went back on shore to give notice to their fellow inhabitants, who caused columns of smoke to arise on our account. We saw eighteen or twenty savages, who came to the shore and began to dance. Our canoe landed in order to give them some bagatelles, at which they were greatly pleased. Some of them came to us and begged us to go to their river. We weighed anchor to do so, but were unable to enter on account of the small amount of water, it being low tide, and were accordingly obliged to anchor at the mouth. I went ashore where I saw many others who received us very cordially. I made also an examination of the river but saw only an arm of water extending a short distance inland, where the land is only in part cleared up. Running into this is merely a brook not deep enough for boats except at full tide. The circuit of the Bay is about a league. On one side of the entrance to this Bay there is a point which is almost an island, covered with wood, principally pines, and adjoins sand-banks which are very extensive. On the other side the land is high. There are two islets in this bay, which are not seen until one has entered and around which it is almost dry at low tide. This place is very conspicuous from the sea, for the coast is very low excepting the cape at the entrance to the bay. We named it the Port du Cap St. Louis, distant two leagues from the above cape and ten from the Island Cape. It is in about the same latitude as Cap St. Louis."

It seems remarkable that there is here no slightest mention of the visit of Martin Pring. We remember that he stayed for seven weeks in this harbor of Plymouth only two years before, and nearly came into conflict with these Indians; yet they welcomed de Monts and Champlain unreservedly. Champlain left us a good map of Plymouth Harbor on which the snail-shell channel is well marked. It is interesting to observe that according to this map there were at that time two islands, the first being of course the Clark's Island of the Pilgrims. It also indicates that the Indians tilled the land on all sides of the harbor from Duxbury around to Manomet Hill. All this tillage had disappeared by 1620. Yachtsmen will readily understand Champlain's reference to the condition of Duxbury flats at low tide.

After staying in Plymouth Harbor over one night, the French bark coasted the inner shore of Cape Cod Bay, passing near one of the rocks at the mouth of Wellfleet Harbor or perhaps at Rock Harbor. They doubled Cape Cod that day, naming it Cap Blanc, and on July 20th made Nauset Harbor in Eastham on the southeast shore of the outer side of the cape. "It was almost low tide when we entered, and there were only four feet of water in the northern passage; at high tide there are two fathoms. After we had entered, we found the place very spacious, being perhaps three or four leagues in circuit, entirely surrounded by little houses around each one of which there was so much land as the occupant needed for his support. A small river enters here, which is very pretty and in which at low tide there are some three and a half feet of water. There are also two or three brooks bordered by meadows. It would be a very fine place if the harbor were good. We named this place Port de Mallebarre.

"The next day, the 21st of the month, Sieur de Monts determined to go and see their habitation. Nine or ten of us accompanied him with our arms; the rest remained to guard the barque. We went about a league along the coast. Before reaching their cabins, we entered a field planted with Indian corn in the manner before described. The corn was in flower and five and a half feet high. There was some less advanced, which they plant later. We saw many Brazilian beans and many squashes of various sizes, very good for eating; some tobacco, and roots which they cultivated, the latter having the taste of an artichoke. The woods are filled with oaks, nut-trees, and beautiful cypresses, which are of a reddish color and have a very pleasant odor. There were also several fields entirely uncultivated, the land being allowed to remain fallow." Here is a very significant indication that these Indians knew the value of rotation of crops in keeping land fertile. "When they wish to plant it, they set fire to the weeds, and then work it over with their wooden spades. Their cabins are round, and covered with heavy thatch made of reeds. In the roof there is an opening of about a foot and a half whence the smoke from the fire passes out. We asked them if they had a permanent abode in this place, and whether there was much snow. But we were unable to ascertain this fully from them, not understanding their language, although they made an attempt to inform us by signs, by taking some sand in their hands, spreading it over the ground and indicating that it was the color of our collars, and that it reached the depth of a foot. Others made signs that there was less, and gave us to understand also that the harbor never froze; but we were unable to ascertain whether the snow lasted long. I conclude, however that this region is of moderate temperature and the winter not severe. While we were there, there was a north east storm which lasted four days; the sky being so overcast that the sun hardly shone at all. It was very cold, and we were obliged to put on our great-coats which we had entirely left off. Yet I think the cold was accidental, as it is often experienced elsewhere out of season.

"On the 23rd of July, four or five seamen having gone on shore with some kettles to get fresh water, which was to be found on one of the sandbanks a short distance from our barque, some of the savages, coveting them, watched the time when our men went to the spring, and then seized one out of the hands of a sailor, who was first to dip and who had no weapons. One of his companions starting to run after him, soon returned as he could not catch him since he ran much faster than himself. The other savages of whom there were a large number, seeing our sailors running to our barque, and at the same time shouting to us to fire at them, took to flight. At the time there were some of them in our barque, who threw themselves into the sea, only one of whom we were able to seize. Those on the land who had taken to flight, seeing them swimming, returned straight to the sailor from whom they had taken the kettle, hurled several arrows at him from behind and brought him down. Seeing this, they ran at once to him and despatched him with their knives. Meanwhile haste was made to go on shore, and muskets were fired from our barque, mine bursting in my hands, came near killing me. The savages hearing this discharge of fire arms took to flight and with redoubled speed when they saw that we had landed, for they were afraid when they saw us running after them. There was no likelihood of our catching them, for they are as swift as horses. We brought in the murdered man and he was buried some hours later. Meanwhile we kept the prisoner bound by the feet and hands on board of our barque, fearing that he might escape. But Sieur de Monts resolved to let him go, being persuaded that he was not to blame, and that he had no previous knowledge of what had transpired, as also those who at the time were in and about our barque. Some hours later there came some savages to us, to excuse themselves, indicating by signs and demonstrations that it was not they who had committed this malicious act, but others farther off in the woods. We did not wish to harm them although it was in our power to avenge ourselves."

The deliberate forbearance of the French toward this first recorded instance of a European death at the hands of New England Indians deserves notice. It is good testimony to the self-control and discipline of the men and to the sound judgment of their leaders. These Frenchmen were unwilling to incur the enmity of natives who might next year or the year after be neighbors to colonists. Better one murder than a war. Gosnold abandoned all idea of settlement after one arrow wound. Pring was happy to escape from Plymouth at the first hint of treachery. Waymouth threw caution to the winds before any crime had been committed, and displayed to the Indians how gratuitous European barbarism could be. But here, at Nauset in 1605, the Sieur de Monts conducted himself with dignity, releasing innocent natives after their compatriots had committed a crime.

That the French were not so tenderhearted in the following year at Chatham should not blind us to the fact that in this first instance in 1605 they gave the Indians the benefit of the doubt. They were willing to accept this death as murder in the act of theft, which it was. It was no occasion for warfare. In similar situations in Pilgrim Plymouth, Indians were later brought to justice and punished. But in all too many of the early quarrels casual native crime or imagined crime was punished by warfare. Credit the French with the ability to make this distinction.

It is not surprising, after this experience, that Champlain adopted a somewhat disagreeable opinion of these natives. But even in expressing this opinion he is charitable. "It would seem from their appearance that they have a good disposition," he says, "better than those of the north, but they are all in fact of no great worth. Even a slight intercourse with them gives you at once a knowledge of them. They are great thieves, and if they cannot lay hold of anything with their hands, they try to do so with their feet, as we have oftentimes learned by experience." In this observation he concurs, we remember, with the Gosnold chronicles. But Champlain adds this: "I am confident that if they had anything to exchange with us, they would not give themselves to thieving. They bartered away to us their bows, arrows and quivers, for pins and buttons; and if they had anything else better they would have done the same with it. It is necessary to be on one's guard against this people, and live in a state of distrust of them, yet without letting them perceive it." One wonders whether, if we could know more details of Gosnold's treatment of the Cape Cod Indians three summers before, we might not have a more adequate explanation of their treachery toward Champlain's men.

Here at Cape Cod Champlain again evidences his amusing fascination with the horseshoe crab, and his description of it is worthy of quotation. "In this place and along the whole coast from Quinibequy there are a great many siguenocs, which is a fish with a shell on its back like the tortoise, yet different, there being in the middle a row of little prickles, of the color of a dead leaf, like the rest of the fish. At the end of this shell there is another still smaller, bordered by very sharp points. The length of the tail varies according to their size. With the end of it these people point their arrows, and it contains also a row of prickles like the large shell in which are the eyes. There are eight small feet like those of the crab, and two behind longer and flatter, which they use in swimming. There are also in front two other very small ones with which they eat. When walking, all the feet are concealed excepting the two hindermost, which are slightly visible. Under the small shell there are membranes which swell up, and beat like the throat of a frog, and rest upon each other like the folds of a waistcoat. The largest specimen of this fish that I saw was a foot broad and a foot and a half long." Certainly this is a bit of biological observation worthy of the nineteenth century. Champlain gives a likewise detailed account of the turkey, which seems to have pestered the cornfields at harvest time. The Indians told him that the turkeys "come in flocks in summer and at the beginning of winter go away to warmer countries, their natural dwelling-place." What would we not give to have back our great flocks of that tragically extinct wildfowl that blessed the Thanksgiving table of the Pilgrims?

"We had spent more than five weeks going over more than three degrees of latitude," continues our chronicle, "and our voyage was limited to six, since we had not taken provisions for a longer time. In consequence of fogs and storms we had not been able to go farther than Mallebarre, where we waited several days for fair weather in order to sail. Finding ourselves accordingly pressed by the scantiness of provisions, Sieur de Monts determined to return to the Island of St. Croix, in order to find another place more favorable for our settlement, *as we had not been able to do on any of the coasts which we had explored on this voyage.*"

To a New Englander that last statement is like a red rag to the proverbial bull. Five weeks of cruising from Eastport to Cape Cod, and no place more favorable for settlement than Passamaquoddy Bay! No doubt the winter at St. Croix had made these men cautious. It remains at least in part mysterious as to why they moved from St. Croix to more northerly Annapolis instead of into Massachusetts. History might have been quite different had they chosen the latter course. One can only speculate as to whether the density of the Indian population or the distance from the fishing fleet may have deterred them from the move southward which they had certainly contemplated at the start of this voyage. Champlain often took care to note the character of harbors, the ease with which they could be defended and the amount of snow in winter. But he gives us few amplifications of his ideas of the requirements necessary for a site. Since we are forced into surmise, I cannot find any more convincing reason for his rejection of New England than the first one mentioned above, the populousness of the Massachusetts Indians.

Marc Lescarbot, who wrote a parallel chronicle to Champlain's, but who did not accompany these expeditions southward, records that in Massachusetts "the country is very thickly settled." To men in the position of these explorers, few in number, and at times naturally appalled at the dangers confronting them, the natives, no matter how kindly their response to kindly treatment, were their likeliest means of death. We think of Massachusetts Bay today as by all odds the best gamble as a site for their colony of all the regions they had explored. History has confirmed us in that choice. We would unerringly pick some site on the shores of Boston Harbor. But these Frenchmen entered that harbor one evening and left it the next morning. It was swarming with dugout canoes full of Indians. Can we not safely read between the lines that competition with the

populous Massachusetts natives appeared to them utterly impracticable? What chance had fifty or a hundred Frenchmen
in that environment whenever the inevitable hostility arose?
Better the snows of bleak St. Croix than the arrows of a thousand painted savages. How meet the challenge of encroached-on
cornfields, disputed ownership and the certainty of theft? Yes,
comes your question, but how did the English manage it
twenty-five years later? A later chapter will give us the answer
to that question. Suffice it to say here that disease had by then
subdued the Massachusets. Only a pitiful remnant of these
flourishing savages remained.

"Accordingly," goes on Champlain, "on the 25th of July
we set sail out from this Harbor [Mallebarre] in order to make
observations elsewhere. In going out, we came near being lost
on the bar at the entrance, from the mistake of our pilots,
Cramolet and Champdoré, masters of the barque, who had im-
perfectly marked out the entrance to the channel, on the southern side, where we were to go. Having escaped this danger, we
headed north-east for six leagues, until we reached Cap Blanc,
a distance of fifteen leagues, with the same wind. Then we
headed east-north-east sixteen leagues, as far as Chouacoet,
where we saw the savage chief, Marchin, whom we had expected to see at Lake Quinibequy. He had the reputation of
being one of the valiant ones of his people. He had a fine appearance; all his motions were dignified, savage as he was.
Sieur de Monts gave him many presents, with which he was
greatly pleased; and in return Marchin gave him a young
Etechemin boy, whom he had captured in war, and whom we
took away with us; and thus we set out, mutually good friends.
We headed north-east a quarter east for fifteen leagues, as far as
Quinibequy, where we arrived on the 29th of the month, and
where we were expecting to find a savage named Sasinou of
whom I spoke before. Thinking that he would come we waited
some time for him, in order to recover from him an Etechemin
young man and girl whom he was holding as prisoners. While
waiting, there came to us a captain called Anassou, who traf-

ficked a little in furs, and with whom we made an alliance. He told us that there was a ship, ten leagues off the harbor, which was engaged in fishing and that those on board had killed five savages of this river under cover of friendship. From his description of the men on the vessel, we concluded that they were English, and we named the island where they were [Monhegan] La Nef; for at a distance it had the appearance of a ship. Finding that the above mentioned Sasinou did not come, we headed east-south-east, for twenty leagues to Isle Haute, where we anchored for the night.

"On the next day, the 1st of August, we sailed east some twenty leagues to Cap Corneille [Machias] where we spent the night. On the 2nd of the month we sailed northeast seven leagues to the mouth of the river St. Croix, on the western shore. Having anchored between the two first islands [Eastport], Sieur de Monts embarked in a canoe at a distance of six leagues from the settlement of St. Croix where we arrived the next day with our barque. We found there Sieur des Antons of St. Malo, who had come in one of the vessels of Sieur de Monts to bring provisions and also other supplies for those who were to winter in this country."

II. The Voyage of 1606

During the autumn of 1605 the equipment and supplies of the little French settlement were transshipped from bleak St. Croix to a much better site called Port Royal near Annapolis in Nova Scotia. De Monts departed for France, leaving Pont Gravé in charge. The winter was a mild one, and friendly Indians helped to keep the kitchen supplied with game. In spite of this, twelve of the forty-five colonists died in the course of the winter.

In March and April of 1606 Pont Gravé and Champlain made two attempts to set out on exploring voyages farther south, "toward Florida," but both attempts ended in shipwreck before they emerged from the Bay of Fundy. Champdoré, the master of their little bark, was held responsible for the loss of the vessel in the second of these accidents, and was punished by being put in irons. Inasmuch as he was the only man capable of building a new vessel, however, his imprisonment was brief. By the middle of July he had completed another boat. Again as in 1605 supply ships failed to put in an appearance, and this time the colony was actually abandoned for a few days while the settlers set out in their little ship to head for Newfoundland and passage home. But once more a delayed supply ship in charge of the Sieur de Poutrincourt met them in the nick of time to turn them back while still on the Nova Scotia coast. The coincidence of these repeated eleventh-hour rescues of the colony is worthy of the most incredible brand of fiction. Yet it brings home to us with peculiar force how dependent these infant ventures were on home support during their first precarious years. For the lack of supply ships Roanoke had succumbed. How often did the Pilgrims bitterly complain of the failure of their backers to send them adequate supplies? Only with time did Europe learn that the slender thread of shipping which planted colonies must be maintained to keep them alive. One voyage could destroy half a dozen settlements, but it took a dozen voyages to plant one settlement permanently.

The Sieur de Poutrincourt brought from France instructions from de Monts to seek a new site for the colony south of Mallebarre, as he was not satisfied with either St. Croix or Port Royal. But in view of the fact that July was already far spent, there was obviously not time both to explore and to move the settlement that year. They must stay at Port Royal through another winter. Accordingly, some late planting was done in an attempt to prepare for the winter. Considerable time was spent in outfitting an expedition by Pont Gravé to confiscate the booty of certain Cape Breton fur traders who were known to be poaching within the area of the colony's monopoly. It was therefore September 5th before the exploring party, under Poutrincourt and Champlain, finally got away from Port Royal. Much against Champlain's judgment, Poutrincourt decided to

CHAMPLAIN'S MAP OF GLOUCESTER HARBOR, 1606

with modern map and notes adapted from Professor W. F.
Ganong. Reproduced from the Champlain Society edition of
The Works of Samuel de Champlain. (Plate LXXVII)

* * *

Legends on Champlain's Map of Le Beau Port, with Comments
The figures indicate the fathoms of water

A.—THE PLACE WHERE OUR PINNACE LAY

Behind Ten Pound Island, approximately as indicated on our modern map
by the anchor, and still a favorite anchorage for summer small craft. Champlain probably sketched his map of the harbor from this spot.

B.—MARSHES

These salt marshes are still a prominent feature of this part of Gloucester.

C.—A SMALL ISLAND

Ten Pound Island, now cleared, and occupied by buildings belonging to
the lighthouse, and by a fish hatchery.

D.—A ROCKY CAPE

The extremity of Eastern Point, well characterized by Champlain. The
ledges just within the harbor are those of Black Bess Point, though Champlain greatly exaggerates them, doubtless as a warning to mariners.

Continued on page 128

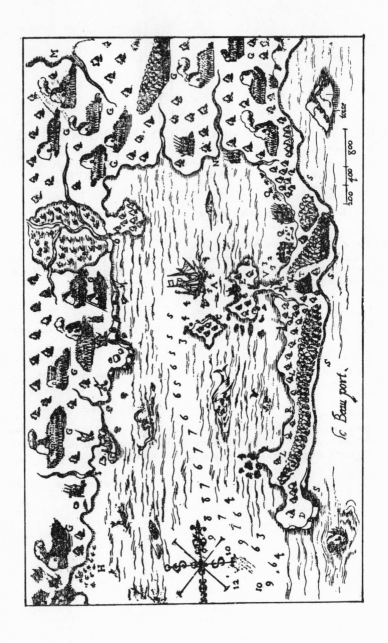

le Beau port.

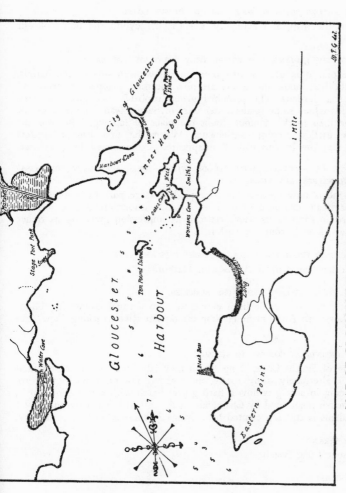

MAP OF GLOUCESTER HARBOR, MASSACHUSETTS

Adapted from the latest chart

For comparison with Champlain's map of *Le Beau Port*, to which it is adjusted as nearly as possible in scale, extent, and meridian.

The compass is Champlain's, supposed to be adjusted to the magnetic meridian, but the true north is shown by the arrow.

E.—THE PLACE WHERE OUR SHALLOP WAS CAULKED

Oakes Cove, on the northwest side of Rocky Neck.

F.—A SMALL RATHER ELEVATED ROCKY ISLAND ON THE COAST

It is *f* on the map, and evidently Salt Island, beyond the limits of our modern map.

G.—LODGES OF THE INDIANS, AND WHERE THEY CULTIVATE THE LAND

They are placed in greatest profusion on the western side of the harbor, where lie the best lands, and where are now the most prosperous farms and the pleasantest gardens. The principal group probably occupied the very pleasant fields which slope to the water west of Stage Head. The boat shown here on the map marks without doubt the place of landing. This was the site of the earliest English settlements. When the first English settlers arrived in 1623 the Indians had all disappeared, exterminated by pestilence.

L.—TONGUE OF LAND COVERED WITH WOODS, WHERE THERE ARE PLENTY OF SASSA-
FRAS, NUT-TREES, AND VINES

This tongue is now cleared, and occupied in large part by summer residences. Champlain saw it only on both coasts, without crossing it, and his great underestimation of its width reflects the impression given by its rather low relief as viewed from the harbor.

M.—A BAY CLOSED FROM THE SEA AFTER PASSING ISLAND CAPE

This represents an arm of Annisquam Harbor.

O.—A SMALL BROOK ISSUING FROM THE MARSHES

This brook has long since been converted into a canal connecting Gloucester Harbor with Annisquam Harbor *via* Squam River, making Cape Ann an island.

Q.—A TROOP OF INDIANS COMING TO SURPRISE US

The shore of Smiths Cove, along which they [the Indians] are represented as coming, is alternately sandy, rocky, and marshy. The place where they are shown dancing in a ring is now a hard gravel beach with a fringe of marsh; while the marsh mentioned by Champlain in the text as lying between himself and the Indians is still represented by a fringe in the angle of the causeway.

R.—A SANDY STRAND

The present Long Beach.

S.—THE SEA-COAST

T.—THE SIEUR DE POUTRINCOURT IN AMBUSH WITH SOME SEVEN OR EIGHT MUSKETEERS

V.—THE SIEUR DE CHAMPLAIN CATCHING SIGHT OF THE INDIANS

proceed along the Maine coast instead of sailing straight to Mallebarre. More than two weeks was spent in reinvestigating St. Croix and the coast southward to Saco Bay. Lescarbot says that this expedition went in to Casco Bay, where Marchin was sachem. Ripe grapes were found on Richmond Island. The first events that add color to our New England narrative occurred at Gloucester about September 25th.

"Continuing our course we proceeded to the Island Cape, where we encountered rather bad weather and fogs, and saw little prospect of being able to spend the night under shelter, since the locality was not favorable for this. While we were thus in perplexity, it occurred to me that while coasting along with Sieur de Monts [in 1605] I had noted on my map at a distance of a league from here a place which seemed suitable for vessels, but which we did not enter because when we passed it, the wind was favorable for continuing on our course. This place we had already passed, which led me to suggest to Sieur de Poutrincourt that we should stand in for a point in sight, where the place in question was which seemed to me favorable for passing the night. We proceeded to anchor at the mouth, and went in the next day.

"Sieur de Poutrincourt landed with eight or ten of our company. We saw some very fine grapes just ripe, Brazilian peas, pumpkins, squashes, and a very good root which the savages cultivate, having a taste similar to that of chards. They made us presents of some of these, in exchange for trifles which we gave them. They had already finished their harvest. We saw two hundred savages in this very pleasant place, and there are here a large number of very fine walnut trees, cypresses, sassafras, oaks, ashes, and beeches. The chief of this place is named Quiouhamenec, who came to see us with a neighbor of his named Cohouepech, whom we entertained sumptuously. Onemechin, chief of Chouacoet [Saco], came also to see us, to whom we gave a coat which he, however, did not keep a long time, but made a present of it to another since he was uneasy in it and could not adapt himself to it. We saw also a savage here, who had so wounded himself in the foot, and lost so much blood, that he fell down in a swoon. Many others surrounded him, and sang some time before touching him. Afterwards, they made some motions with feet and hands, shook his head and breathed upon him, when he came to himself. Our surgeon dressed his wounds, when he went off in good spirits.

"The next day, as we were calking our shallop, Sieur de Poutrincourt in the woods noticed a number of savages who were going, with the intention of doing us some mischief, to a little stream, where a neck [Rocky Neck] connects with the mainland, at which our party were doing their washing. As I was walking along this neck, these savages noticed me, and in order to put a good face on it, since they saw that I had discovered them thus seasonably, they began to shout and dance, and then came towards me with their bows, arrows, quivers and other arms. And inasmuch as there was a meadow between them and myself, I made a sign to them to dance again. This they did in a circle, putting all their arms in the middle. But they had hardly commenced when they observed Sieur de Poutrincourt in the wood with eight musketeers, which frightened them. Yet they did not stop until they had finished their dance, when they withdrew in all directions, fearing lest some unpleasant turn might be served them. We said nothing to them, however, and showed them only demonstrations of gladness. Then we returned to launch our shallop and take our departure. They entreated us to wait a day, saying that more than two thousand of them would come to see us. But unable to lose any time, we were unwilling to stay longer. I am of the opinion that their object was to surprise us. Some of the land was already cleared up and they were constantly making clearings. Their mode of doing it is as follows: after cutting down the trees at a distance of three feet from the ground, they burn the branches upon the trunk and then plant their corn between these stumps, in course of time tearing up also the roots. There are likewise fine meadows here, capable of supporting a large number of cattle. This harbor is very fine, containing water enough for vessels and affording shelter from the weather behind the islands. It is in latitude 43°, and we gave it the name of Le Beauport."

Again there is no suggestion of the possibility of settlement here, despite the combination of available land, fodder for cattle and an excellent harbor. The only obstacle would seem to be the two thousand Indians. Champlain's fine map of Beauport indicates that the present sites of Gloucester, Annisquam, and the Magnolia shore were thickly populated with Indians. The near encounter with the armed band of natives took place, according to this map, near the narrow isthmus of what is now Rocky Neck. It is interesting to compare this episode with the similar experiences of Gosnold, Pring, and Waymouth. In each case the maneuverings of the savages were observed and given a treacherous interpretation before bloodshed occurred. In each instance these maneuvers came about when the Europeans were greatly outnumbered, and when therefore the white men were strictly alert about remaining on their guard. And in each of these situations the natives are represented as responding in dissembling manner to the discovery of their intentions. It is not to be wondered at that the Indians should resent the intrusion of these portentous strangers, particularly on such a second visit. Neither is the fear of treachery aroused in the breasts of the white man surprising. These were touch-and-go meetings, in which it was extraordinarily hard for the Europeans to get or maintain any friendly foothold on the continent. Even the presence of the Frenchmen's friend Onemechin from the Saco area among these Indians could not persuade them that the French were without evil intent. Indeed they were not, for any European group was a frank menace to the rights of the Indian to the soil and its advantages. Let us make no mistake about it— the American Indian was not unintelligent, and as early in the game as in these opening years of the seventeenth century he undoubtedly appreciated fully the implications of these increasingly frequent European visits to the red man's continent. His just resentment was increasingly aroused as time went on. The stark tragedy of his inevitable fate was not yet apparent, but it no longer required individual provocation on the part of particular white men to arouse the native's antagonism to the whole race. He looked on Europeans in general with foreboding. The significance of these episodes of large numbers of Indians conspiring to attack small groups of whites can only mean that a public opinion had by this period developed among large bodies of the natives, prejudicial to all Europeans without respect to kindly treatment. Champlain and his men were usually exemplary in their treatment of the natives, but that fact did not exempt them from the general onus of their being white. And the observation of this fact must have borne great weight among the French in their deliberations as to whether Massachusetts was a fit place for settlement. Why, on any other reasoning, should these explorers have proceeded any farther than Gloucester in their quest of a place for habitation?

And so, on the last day of September, apparently late in the day, they set out for Cape Cod. They seem to have misjudged its position, for after sailing all night they found themselves in the morning embayed by Cape Cod in the vicinity of Barnstable Harbor, which they named Oyster Harbor. After investigating this port, they turned back and redoubled Cape Cod and on October 2nd reached Mallebarre, or Nauset Harbor, where they put in for shelter from a spell of bad weather. Despite the bloodshed of the previous year, a hundred and fifty natives received the Sieur de Poutrincourt, and the twelve or fifteen men who went ashore with him, with singing and dancing. The Frenchmen did not tarry here for long.

After being in difficulties among the shoals around Monomoy Island, Poutrincourt finally extricated himself and with the aid of diligent sounding and the piloting of a friendly Indian made his way into Stage Harbor, at Chatham, with no more damage than a broken rudder, which they had mended with ropes. "Within this harbor there is only a fathom of water and two at full tide. On the east there is an island and two other little bays which adorn the landscape where there is a considerable quantity of land cleared up, and many little hills, where they cultivate corn and the various grains on which they live. There are also very fine vines, many walnut-trees, oaks, cypresses, but only a few pines. All the inhabitants of this place are very fond of agriculture and provide themselves with Indian corn for the winter, which they store in the following manner:

"They make trenches in the sand on the slope of the hills, some five or six feet deep, more or less. Putting their corn and other grains into large grass sacks, they throw them into these trenches, and cover them with sand three or four feet above the surface of the earth, taking it out as their needs require. In this way it is preserved as well as it would be possible to do in our granaries."

Here at Chatham there were five to six hundred Indians. "They are not so much great hunters as good fishermen and tillers of the land. In regard to their police, government and belief, we have been unable to form a judgment; but I suppose that they are not different in this respect from our savages, the Souriquois and Canadians, who worship neither the moon or the sun, nor anything else, and pray no more than the beasts. There are however among them some persons who, as they say are in concert with the devil, in whom they have great faith. They tell them all that is to happen to them, but in so doing lie for the most part. Sometimes they succeed in hitting the mark very well, and tell them things similar to those which actually happen to them. For this reason they have faith in them, as if they were prophets; while they are only impostors who delude them, as the Egyptians and Bohemians do simple villagers. They have chiefs whom they obey in matters of war, but not otherwise, and who engage in labor, and hold no higher rank than their companions. Each one has only so much land as he needs for his support.

"Their dwellings are separate from each other, according to the land which each one occupies. They are large, of a circular shape, and covered with thatch made of grasses or the husks of Indian corn. They are furnished only with a bed or two raised a foot from the ground, made of a number of little pieces of wood pressed against each other, on which they arrange a reed mat after the Spanish style, which is a kind of matting two or three fingers thick; on these they sleep. They have a great many fleas in summer, even in the fields. One day as we went out walking we were beset by so many of them that we were obliged to change our clothes."

The explorers stayed at Chatham for ten days, the men spending this interval ashore in making needed repairs to the rudder of the bark and in baking sufficient bread to last them another two weeks. Champlain thus had leisure to make such observations of the people as those in the foregoing paragraphs. He concludes: "It would be an excellent place to erect buildings and lay the foundations of a State, if the harbor were somewhat deeper and the entrance safer."

"Meanwhile," the narrative continues, "Sieur de Poutrincourt, accompanied by ten or twelve arquebusiers, visited all the neighboring country. Some eight or nine days later while Sieur de Poutrincourt was walking out, as he had previously done, we observed the savages taking down their cabins and sending their women, children, provisions and other necessaries of life into the woods. This made us suspect some evil intention and that they purposed to attack those of our company who were working on shore, where they stayed at night in order to guard that which could not be embarked at evening except with trouble. This proved to be true, for they determined among themselves after all their effects had been put in a place of security, to come and surprise those on land, taking advantage of them as much as possible, and to carry off all they had. But if by chance they should find them on their guard they resolved to come with signs of friendship as they were wont to do, leaving behind their bows and arrows. . . .

"We returned very quietly to our barque accompanied by some of the savages. On the way, we met several small troups of them who gradually gathered with their arms, and were greatly

CHAMPLAIN'S MAP OF STAGE HARBOR, CHATHAM, 1606

with modern map and notes adapted from Professor W. F. Ganong. Reproduced from the Champlain Society edition of *The Works of Samuel de Champlain*. (Plate LXXVIII)

* * *

Legends on Champlain's Map of Port Fortuné, with Comments
The figures show the fathoms of water

A.—POND OF SALT WATER

The present Oyster Pond, the erroneous position and form of which imply that Champlain added it from observations made during his walk with the Sieur de Poutrincourt, along their route V.

B.—THE LODGES OF THE INDIANS, AND THEIR FIELDS WHICH THEY CULTIVATE

In a general way, these occupied the sites of the best farms of the present day.

D.—SMALL HILLOCKS ON THE ISLAND, COVERED WITH WOODS, VINES, AND PLUM-TREES

This characterization of Morris Island is very expressive, for it does present to this day a series of abrupt hills covered with woods. The way in which on the map these hills overlap implies, as comparison with our modern map will show, that this part of the map at least was sketched from Champlain's prominent hill R, the Sand Bluff of our map. As to the plants on the island, it is said in Smith's *History of Chatham* that "the island is still noted for Beach plums."

E.—POND OF FRESH WATER, WHERE THERE IS PLENTY OF WATERFOWL

Evidently Island Pond, on Morris Island, now open to the sea, and salt, but known locally to have been fresh, even in recent times (*cf. Report of the United States Coast Survey for 1873, 106*). It can be seen from the hills in Chatham.

G.—ISLAND COVERED WITH TREES LYING IN A LARGE CLOSED BAY

This island, called Ram Island, has disappeared, having been destroyed by a great gale in 1851, and only a shoal remains to mark its site. Its form and location on the accompanying map are taken from a chart of 1847.

H.—A KIND OF POND OF SALT WATER, WHERE THERE ARE A GREAT MANY SHELL-FISH, INCLUDING, AMONG OTHER, NUMBERS OF OYSTERS

The pretty little pond, now called the Mill Pond. Champlain apparently sketched it from his hill R.

I.—SAND DUNES ON A SMALL TONGUE OF LAND

Obviously just such a dune beach as still borders this coast, but which in Champlain's day was evidently much outside its present position. I [Professor Ganong] have indicated its probable position by the dotted lines on the modern map. Aside from the direct testimony of Champlain's map, such an inward movement is wholly in accord with our knowledge of the history

Continued on page 138

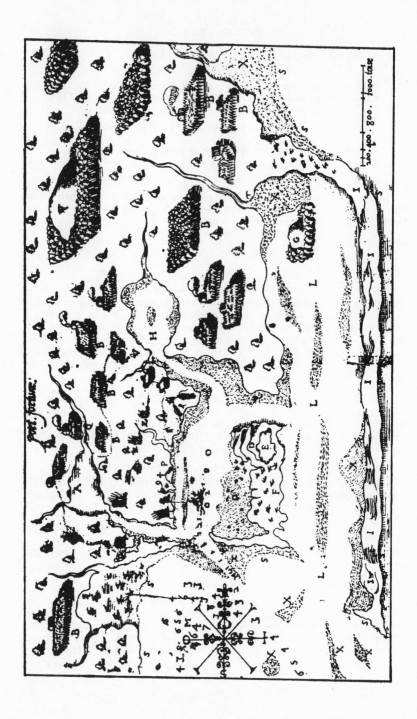

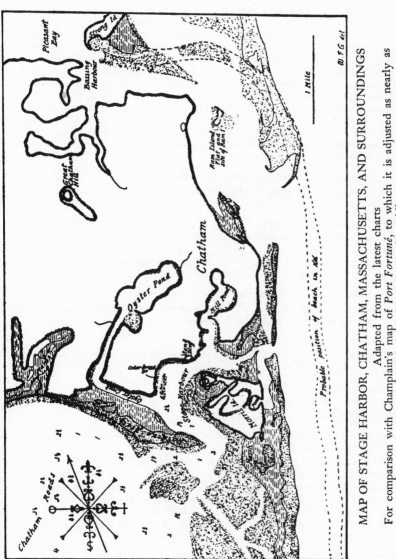

MAP OF STAGE HARBOR, CHATHAM, MASSACHUSETTS, AND SURROUNDINGS

Adapted from the latest charts

For comparison with Champlain's map of *Port Fortuné*, to which it is adjusted as nearly as possible in scale, extent, and meridian.

The compass is Champlain's, which is supposed to be set to the magnetic meridian, but the true north is shown by the arrow.

CHAMPLAIN'S MAP OF STAGE HARBOR, CHATHAM, 1606—
Continued

of this kind of beach, which is always beaten in upon the land as the sea erodes the upland points which form its natural anchorage. In its inward movement the beach has experienced many minor changes, and these are still incessant, to such a degree that it is hardly the same in two successive years. Champlain makes it end opposite Stage Harbor, but this was merely a cartographical convenience, in order to bring it within the limits of his map; for in the text he states that this point extended out three leagues, which is not far from its present length. The turn shoreward given to its northern end may represent an illusion caused by the foreshortening of more distant beaches; but the relation of this beach to the island G makes it more probable that it represents actual fact. Of this beach the great shoals extending out southeast from Strong Island would be remnants. In this case the Nauset Beach of our [modern] map would not then have had its present extent; and Pleasant Bay, east of Strong Island, would then have been open, as Champlain represents it.

M.—ROADSTEAD WHERE WE ANCHORED OFF THE HARBOR

The head of the present Chatham Roads, with ample water and good anchorage.

N.—ENTRANCE TO THE HARBOR

This entrance has shifted considerably to the eastward, in consequence, evidently, of the growth of Harding Beach. In Champlain's day, apparently, the channel continued through the straight passage shown on our modern map. Another beach, now vanished, then extended out from Morris Island.

O.—THE HARBOR, AND PLACE WHERE OUR PINNACE LAY

Now called Stage Harbor. The shoals shown between the anchorage and the western shore appear also on the modern charts.

P.—THE CROSS THAT WAS SET UP

It stood on the open raised sandy plain between the two little brooks on the western side of the harbor.

T.—SMALL RIVER

The passage south of Strong Island leading up to Bassing Harbor. Champlain probably saw only its entrance.

V.—ROUTE WE FOLLOWED THROUGH THEIR COUNTRY AMONG THEIR LODGES. IT IS
    INDICATED BY SMALL DOTS

Presumably they were taken in the boat to the bend of Oyster Creek, whence they followed the indicated route back to the beach opposite their pinnace. Their approximate route can be followed easily on the modern map. Another V, also accompanying a dotted line, is placed on the extreme northern margin of the map, and it is possible that on the way home some days later they landed on the northern side of Pleasant Bay. Otherwise, we have here an error on the part of the engraver.

Y.—SMALL MOUNTAIN WHICH SHOWS UP INLAND

Now Great Chatham Hill, said to form a prominent landmark.

9.—THE PLACE WHERE OUR MEN WERE KILLED BY THE INDIANS NEAR THE CROSS astonished to see us so far in the interior, and did not suppose that we had just made a circuit of nearly four or five leagues about their territory. Passing near us, they trembled with fear lest harm should be done them, as it was in our power to do. But we did them none, although we knew their evil intentions. Having arrived where our men were working, Sieur de Poutrincourt inquired if everything was in readiness to resist the designs of this rabble.

"He ordered everything on shore to be embarked. This was done, except that he who was making the bread stayed to finish a baking, and two others with him. They were told that the savages had some evil intent and that they should make haste to embark the coming evening, since they carried their plans into execution only at night or at daybreak, which in their plots is generally the hour for making a surprise.

"Evening having come, Sieur de Poutrincourt gave orders that the shallop should be sent ashore to get the men who remained. This was done as soon as the tide would permit, and those on shore were told that they must embark for the reason assigned. This they refused, in spite of the remonstrances that were made setting forth the risks that they ran and the disobedience to their chief. They paid no attention to it, with the exception of a servant of Sieur de Poutrincourt, who embarked. Two others disembarked from the shallop and went to the three on shore, who had stayed to eat some cakes made at the same time with the bread.

"But as they were unwilling to do as they were told, the shallop returned to the vessel. It was not mentioned to Sieur de Poutrincourt, who had returned, thinking that all were on board." Lescarbot, the other historian of the Port Royal group, tells us that some days before, these men who stayed ashore "had twice fired on the savages because one of them had stolen a hatchet."

"The next day in the morning the 15th of October, the savages did not fail to come and see in what condition our men were, whom they found asleep, except one who lay near the fire.

When they saw them in this condition they came, to the number of four hundred, softly over a little hill, and sent them such a volley of arrows that to rise up was death. Fleeing the best they could towards our barque, shouting 'help! They are killing us!' a part fell dead in the water, the others were all pierced with arrows and one died in consequence a short time after. The savages made a desperate noise with roarings, which it was terrible to hear." Lescarbot says that four Frenchmen were killed and a fifth wounded.

"Upon the occurrence of this noise and that of our men, the sentinel on our vessel exclaimed: 'To arms! They are killing our men!' Consequently each one immediately seized his arms, and we embarked in the shallop, some fifteen or sixteen of us, in order to go ashore. But being unable to get there on account of a sand bank between us and the land, we threw ourselves into the water and waded from this bank to the shore, the distance of a musket shot. As soon as we were there, the savages seeing us within arrow range, fled into the interior. To pursue them was fruitless, for they are marvellously swift. All that we could do was to carry away the dead bodies and bury them near a cross which had been set up the day before, and then to go here and there to see if we could sight any of them. But it was time wasted, therefore we came back. Three hours afterwards they returned to us on the sea-shore. We discharged at them several shots from our little brass cannon; and when they heard the noise they crouched down on the ground to avoid the fire. In mockery of us they beat down the cross and disinterred the dead, which displeased us greatly, and caused us to go for them a second time, but they fled as they had done before. We set up again the cross and reinterred the dead, whom they had thrown here and there amid the heath where they kindled a fire to burn them. We returned without any result, as we had done before, well aware that there was scarcely any hope of avenging ourselves this time, and that we should have to renew the undertaking when it should please God.

"On the 16th of the month we set out from Port Fortune, to which we had given this name on account of the misfortune which happened to us there. This place is in latitude 41° 20', and some twelve or thirteen leagues from Mallebarre."

Here at long last was the first pitched battle in the Indian annals of New England. Possibly it was the first instance in which a considerable body of Indians discovered that it was possible to escape unscathed from the gunfire of Europeans. At Mallebarre the year before we have been content to consider that the episode was murder in the act of theft. But here at Port Fortune it was a matter of a small army of Indians deliberately attacking a party of whites. This was the incident which all explorers had feared. It had all the characteristics of treachery and surprise which were to arouse a thirst for vengeance in settlers during the next two and a half centuries throughout the continent. It displayed a type of Indian savagery in the treatment of the dead which was to horrify generations of civilized men. So far as such atrocities are concerned, there is of course nothing to be said in extenuation of the Indian. It was stark, brutal savagery. This was the characteristic of Indian warfare that no self-respecting European could contemplate without feeling his blood boil in helpless rage. Could this factor alone have been eliminated, it seems conceivable that some tolerance of the Indian might have been managed, and his race have been enabled to settle down on some terms of decent friendship with the whites. But his maltreatment of the dead, of women and of the injured was more than the European stomach could digest. It led inevitably to the wiping out of the red man as an inhabitant of civilization. Here at Chatham in 1606 the process of annihilation that went on in New England through King Philip's and the French and Indian wars began. The logical sequel to this episode speedily followed.

Champlain and his party sailed down through Vineyard Sound as far as Woods Hole. They sighted Martha's Vineyard, and proceeded as far as the narrow entrance to Buzzards Bay. Unfavorable winds turned them back, as they had turned back

Waymouth off Nantucket, and they returned to Chatham, still burning with resentment at the natives.

"Seeing now the wind continuing contrary, and being unable to put to sea, we resolved meanwhile to get possession of some savages of this place, and taking them to our settlement, put them to grinding corn at the handmill, as punishment for the deadly assault which they had committed on five or six of our company. But it was very difficult to do this when we were armed, since if we went to them prepared to fight, they would turn and flee into the woods, where they were not to be caught. It was necessary, accordingly, to have resort to artifice, and this is what we planned; when they should come to seek friendship with us, to coax them by showing them beads and other gewgaws, and assure them repeatedly of our good faith; then to take the shallop well armed, and conduct on shore the most robust and strong men we had, each one having a chain of beads and a fathom of match on his arm; and there, while pretending to smoke with them (each one having an end of his match lighted as not to excite suspicion, it being customary to have fire at the end of a cord in order to light the tobacco) coax them with pleasing words so as to draw them into the shallop; and if they should be unwilling to enter, each one approaching should choose his man, and putting the beads about his neck, should at the same time put the rope on him to draw him by force. But if they should be too boisterous, and it should not be possible to succeed they should be stabbed, the rope being firmly held, and if by chance any of them should get away there should be men on hand to charge them with swords. Meanwhile the little cannon on our barque were to be kept ready to fire upon their companions in case they should come to assist them, under cover of which firearms the shallop should withdraw in security. The plan above mentioned was well carried out as it had been arranged."

Later in the account it becomes clear that the mild statement of this hideous plan's being "well carried out" is a euphemism for a thoroughly executed piece of butchery in which a number of Indians were coolly slaughtered, not without a few wounds being sustained by the French in the process. There is again no more moral extenuation of this dark chapter of capital punishment without trial than of the earlier Indian atrocity. It is simply the sequence of events that always follows upon warfare at the barbarian level, and few of us moderns, faced with the same situation, would have survived on any other level once such a train of events was set in motion. No one ever treated natives in more kindly fashion than had Champlain and his company up to this point in their travels. At Nauset, no such retribution was demanded of the Indian— the French had leaned over backwards in forgiveness of a murder. But these same men, faced with the savagery at Chatham, after due meditation returned to Chatham and secured their savage revenge. Only then were they content to return to Nova Scotia. Champlain's last word on the event is significant of his attitude; "We withdrew, but with the satisfaction that God had not left unpunished the misdeeds of these barbarians." The scalps of the executed Indians were given to a Passamaquoddy native who had accompanied them on the voyage.

III. Farewell to Champlain

When Champlain and Poutrincourt left Chatham, they put in for a day or two at Nauset, and then sailed directly to Isle Haute on the Maine coast. After an exceedingly rough passage, during which they avoided shipwreck only by a small margin, they arrived at Port Royal on November 14th and were received with a boisterous welcome by the colonists. There is nothing to indicate that they became aware of Martin Pring's visit to the Maine coast that same year. Champlain was never to see New England again. The three years of work he had done were utterly wasted so far as any resulting advantage to the French was concerned. No doubt the company obtained a great deal of information that was of general use to them in their later Canadian adventures. But Champlain's report of these voyages was the only fruit which posterity inherited from the New England venture. This fact delayed the opening up of New England for fifteen years. Could steady occupation of the country have been maintained on the basis of Champlain's findings, there is no doubt that history might have followed quite a different course in New England.

The abandonment of the French project came about in this way: after a rather pleasant and constructive winter at Port Royal, word came in the spring that the Sieur de Monts, who had been managing the colony's affairs in France, had lost the king's support for the venture. Briefly, this situation had arisen because of strong opposition on the part of rival traders to the royal monopoly which de Monts held in the fur trade of the whole region. Since this trade was the only source of income to the colony and the only means of financing its supply ships and the salaries of its men, the whole venture had to be abandoned when this monopoly was withdrawn. Here once again is the specter of economics stepping in to control the direction of history. These ventures had to pay their way, and the fur-trading voyages of Pont Gravé to the northward had been a necessary accompaniment always to the more interesting explorations of Champlain to the south that we have been considering. It was over this stumbling block that the Port Royal colony fell. Under conditions of open competition in the fur trade no such income was possible as would be sufficient to carry on the colony. For this reason the summer of 1607 found the French packing up their belongings and sorrowfully returning to France.

We all know that Champlain's work was by no means done. Within two years he had re-established himself at Quebec near Cartier's old site, and during the next thirty years his persistent and untiring activities carried the French empire southward into upper New York State and westward to Ottawa and throughout the eastern half of the Great Lakes region. He there laid the foundation of the Dominion of Canada. There is some irony in the fact that the New England which was his training ground never became part of his greatest achievement, despite the fact that his work here was of a technique and excellence years in advance of any contemporary English empire builder. New England was left to be worked over and chipped at by dozens of desultory traders for fifteen years before another well-conceived effort at colonial exploitation was attempted. Long before that time the French project had established itself over a broad front deep in the heart of the continent. In the light of subsequent history it seems amazing that the wilderness of Canada was chosen for development ahead of the comparatively fertile shores of New England. That this happened was, as we have seen, by a deliberate choice of the Port Royal colonists in the first instance, and secondly by the failure of a royal monopoly in the fur trade. In so far as the abandonment of New England was a deliberate choice, it was probably due to the populousness of the Massachusetts Indians together with their hostile response to the friendly overtures of the French explorers. The less numerous Hurons and Montagnais of the upper St. Lawrence country received Champlain warmly, and he secured a firm alliance with them by assisting them in their wars with the Iroquois. But the Indians of Massachusetts, at Gloucester and at Chatham, resisted successfully the incursions of these first friendly Europeans to make a real study of their colonial possibilities hereabouts. It is perhaps not too much oversimplification to sum this all up by saying that the New England Indians succeeded in protecting their territory from the French and then obligingly died before the arrival of the English Pilgrims. For these two years of Champlain's splendid work marked the beginning and the end of French colonial enterprise in Massachusetts.

Chapter Seven

A KENNEBEC VIRGINIA FAILS, 1607–1608

THE YEAR in which Champlain's New England project was abandoned was the same one in which England began its first great effort at colonization of New England. We have spoken of the voyages of Gosnold, Pring and Waymouth as though they were relatively weak and isolated reconnoiterings of traders upon the coast; considered singly and in the light of their technical inferiority to the French program, such they were. They appeared to have no such uniformity of leadership or plan as did the exploits of Champlain, de Monts, Poutrincourt, and Pont Gravé. Nevertheless, there were certain linkages among the personnel of the several English voyages which, as we have already hinted, might indicate that they were derived from a common group of English adventurers. We have already noted that Bartholomew Gosnold and Gabriel Archer were both later concerned in the settlement of Jamestown in Virginia. Robert Salterne participated in both Gosnold and Pring voyages. James Rosier, who had been with Gosnold in 1602, became the chronicler of the Waymouth voyage. Bartholomew Gilbert of the Gosnold voyage was the brother of Raleigh Gilbert, one of the leaders of the Sagadahoc colony we are about to describe. And finally we remember that Sir Ferdinando Gorges, who had observed the fruits of the Waymouth voyage in 1605, sent Pring out again in 1606 with one of Waymouth's captive Indians, and that while we have no journal of this voyage, Gorges said that it was the means "of putting on foot and giving life to all our plantations." One may note that Gorges was to be increasingly a motive force behind New England voyages.

It is more difficult to form a nice, integrated picture of the organization of the English colonial program than of that of the French. But the usual muddling-through process was producing its usual surprisingly effective result. The apparently futile pleadings of Raleigh and of Hakluyt in the previous generation had seemed to fall on deaf ears after the disasters to Humphrey Gilbert and to Roanoke. But they had not. With Raleigh in the Tower of London, a group of adventurers began to appear who themselves were willing to hazard the costs of voyages aimed at settlement. Merchants of Bristol, nobility like Arundel and Warwick and Southampton, the sons of Sir Humphrey Gilbert, and governors of seaports like Gorges, were definitely interested in increasing the English profits from the New World, prefer-ably, of course, in the form of gold and silver. It was a period of postwar unemployment in England, and poverty cried out for the undertaking of new ventures. Furthermore, England at this time, despite her maritime strength, had no colonial empire. She had gradually become aware of the fact that other nations were displacing her wares in foreign trade through the medium of new colonial products and, even more important, through their monopoly of the new colonial markets. The commerce of the world was becoming increasingly concerned with providing manufactured supplies to colonial outposts and receiving raw products in return. The pattern of the world was changing.

The pinch of circumstance proved an even better teacher than the foresighted pleas of Raleigh. By 1606 the scattered men interested in North American ventures represented in such tentative experiments as those of Gorges and Southampton, con-verged on London, with the demand that king and Parliament reassign Raleigh's dormant monopoly over American trade to this new group of adventurers now becoming interested in pur-suing the enterprise. The result of this was the formation under a common royal charter of two new companies, usually referred to as the London, or Virginia, Company, which was to settle in the area between North Carolina and New Jersey, and the Plymouth Company, to which was assigned the area from New Jersey to Maine. The London Company was made up of adventurers from London, and included among its council Richard Hakluyt. The Plymouth Company comprised men of Bristol, Exeter, and Plymouth, and among them were Sir Ferdinando Gorges and George Popham, nephew of the Lord Chief Justice of England. Raleigh Gilbert, son of Sir Humphrey, was another of the Plymouth Councilors. The Earl of Southampton was one of the petitioners for the charter.

Thus we find brought together and associated in the new American enterprise Richard Hakluyt, Raleigh's close friend, and Raleigh's nephew and namesake, young Gilbert, together with several of those who had promulgated the voyages of Gosnold, Pring and Waymouth to New England. This is of interest in that it shows the line of succession by which the merchant tradition was handed down. Names like Hakluyt, Gilbert and Raleigh are not commonly thought of as founders of New England; yet here they are affixed to New England's first public document, dated April 10, 1606, under which the Sagadahoc colony sailed. And we should recall that it was Hakluyt who had been instrumental in sending out Martin Pring in 1603, with the consent of Raleigh.

In an attempt to form some appraisal of the caliber of the men responsible for the Plymouth Company's activities, we cannot depend much on names, however. Aging Richard Hakluyt was probably from the beginning more interested in Virginia than in New England, and we can dismiss him immediately. Of young Raleigh Gilbert we shall have more to say later. The outstanding initiators of the New England venture between 1605 and 1620 were without question Sir Ferdinando Gorges and various members of the Popham family, which was at the outset represented by the Lord Chief Justice of England, Sir John Popham, and his nephew, George Popham. Of the chief justice we can get a hint as to his character by admitting at once that it was he who had presided at the trial of Sir Walter Raleigh, and that he had earned the hisses of the populace by coarsely denouncing Raleigh in open court, although to his credit he did probably invest a good deal of money in the Plymouth enterprises.

Thus we have introduced into the situation a circumstance which would be hard to explain in any other way than as a deliberate scheme to turn Raleigh's downfall into private commercial gain by those involved in discrediting him. How much Gorges was involved in this apparent scheme it seems impossible to determine, but there was certainly no attempt to keep the Popham name concealed in the shadows when the roster of incorporation of the Plymouth Company was made up, even though the chief justice himself was not included. Obviously here was one of Raleigh's outspoken enemies enjoying the position of inheriting his monopoly of North America. This seems true in spite of the curious fact that both Popham and Gorges seem to have been related to Raleigh by marriage.

There is not space here to go into an extended discussion of the politics and tangled motives of the Plymouth Company; indeed, the information available is not always sufficient to justify more than the above sort of snap judgment. In so far as we can reach conclusions, however, the picture is not like that of a Raleigh supporting out of his own funds a gallant ideal of patriotism. Roanoke, through repeated and prodigious failure, had inspired the heroic tenacity of one of the world's great men. The New England of the Plymouth Company shared little of this heroic quality. Arising out of the downfall of great Raleigh, it was the spiritual heir, principally, of that motive of plunder which had possessed the followers of Drake and Hawkins. Nevertheless, the fact that Raleigh's tragic epic has seized on the imaginations of successive generations should not blind us to the fact that some fragment of his prophetic insight was now mingled with the more sordid phases of the profit motive in men who were his enemies and his inferiors. Had Raleigh possessed the practical sagacity of these later men, the foundations of his

colony might have been more firmly laid. Likewise, had these
men owned the tenacious idealism of Raleigh, we might be now
celebrating a permanent settlement in Maine rather than one in
Massachusetts.

Gosnold and Pring had both returned to England with
profitable cargoes. The voyage of Waymouth had borne out
that earlier evidence of commodities to be had for the taking.
It was unquestionably this testimony of profit that stimulated
Popham and Gorges to promulgate the Plymouth Company.
Both Plymouth and London companies now immediately went
into action. In May of 1606, one month after the charter of the
two companies was granted, Chief Justice Popham sent out
Captain Haines "in a tall ship belonging to Bristol and the river
Severn, to settle a plantation in the river of Sagadahoc," on the
coast of Maine. In August of the same year Sir Ferdinando
Gorges sent a second ship, under command of Henry Challons,
with two of Waymouth's kidnaped savages as pilots, which was
intended to join the expedition of Haines. Both these ships were
captured by Spanish corsairs and therefore never reached New
England. In October, 1606, the chief justice sent out a third
vessel under Thomas Hanham, one of the incorporators of the
company, with Martin Pring as master, and this ship, as we
already have had occasion to mention, made that "most exact
discovery" of the Maine coast with the help of a third captured
native, Nahanada, but finding no trace of Challons and Haines,
returned to England without establishing a settlement. Nahanada
was allowed to remain in Maine. It was in consequence of the
failure of these three expeditions that Virginia was settled before
Maine, for Captain Newport's expedition under the aegis of the
London Company, sailed in December, 1606, and landed in
Jamestown on May 13, 1607. Only eighteen days later a fourth
party of Plymouth Company settlers sailed from Plymouth for
the Sagadahoc under command of George Popham and Raleigh
Gilbert, and it was this expedition which had the distinction of
making the first concerted effort to found a colony in New
England.

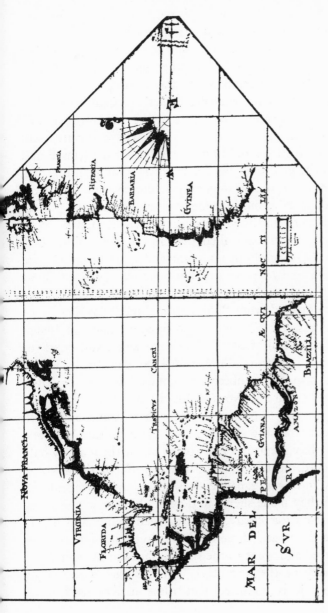

FIG. 6—THE VIRGINIA COMPANY CHART, 1606–1608. A unique representation, probably issued by the Virginia Company. The first map to show "Cape Kod" by name. "James Towne" is also shown. Only the work of Gosnold, Pring, and possibly Waymouth are indicated in New England. The map records very fully and exactly the very information which we may suppose Hudson to have possessed when he set sail on his memorable third voyage, on which he was to discover the great river which bears his name. The region of Hudson's explorations between Cape Cod and Chesapeake Bay is very sketchily and inaccurately delineated. (Reproduced from the original in the Phelps-Stokes collection in the New York Public Library.)

Our best, though fragmentary and inadequate, account of the Sagadahoc settlement is derived from a manuscript by one William Strachey, Gent, who was associated with the James-town Colony. An even more inadequate account exists, probably from the pen of James Davies of the ship *Mary and John.* Inasmuch as Davies's narrative for the main part duplicates Strachey's chronicle, and terminates earlier, we shall here utilize the latter. After describing the failure of the earlier voyages of the Plymouth Company Strachey says: "Howbeyt, the aforesaid late Lord Chief Justice would not, for all this hard hansell and Spanish mischief, give over his determination for planting of a colony within the afore said so goodly a country, upon the river of Sachadahoc; but against the next yeare prepared a greater number of planters, and better provisions, which in two shipps he sent thither; a fly-boat called the *Gift of God*, wherein a kinsman of his, George Popham, commanded; and a good ship, called the *Mary and John*, of London, wherein Raleigh Gilbert commanded; which with one hundred and twenty persons for planters broke ground from Plymouth in June, 1607."

On July 31st they "came to an anchor under an island, for all this coast is full of islands, but very sound and good for shipping to passe by them." There is little to identify this island, but judging from their subsequent courses, it was probably along the eastern shore of Nova Scotia. In any case, "They had not been at anchor two hours, when there came a Spanish shallop to them from the shoare, in her eight salvadg men and a little salvadg boy, he at the first rowed about them and would not come aboard, notwithstanding they proffered them bread, knives, beads and other small trifles; but having gazed awhile upon the ship they made shewe to departe; howbeyt when they were a little from the shoare, they returned againe and boldly came into the shipp, and three of them stayed all night aboard, the rest departed and went to the shoare, shewing by signes that they would returne the next daye." In the brief narrative by Captain Davies it is recorded that these natives used many French words.

"The first of August, the same salvadges returned with three women with them in another biskey shallop, bringing with them many beaver skyns to exchange for knyves and beades; the saganio of that place they told them Messamot, seated upon a river not farr off, which they called Emanuell. The salvadges departing, they hoisted out their bote; and the pilott, Captain R. Davies with twelve others rowed into the bay wherein their ship road, and landed on a galland island, where they found gooseberries, strawberries, raspices, hurts, and all the island full of hugh high trees of divers sorts; after they had delighted themselves there awhile, they returned abourd againe and observed the place to stand in 44 degrees one-third."

As if Gosnold's story of Indian yachting in European boats were not incredible enough, here is double the evidence! Where on earth did these Indians get their Spanish boats? Surely Strachey, Archer, and Brereton were in no naïve state of mind with regard to Indian canoes, and the matter is further confirmed by a note in the Jesuit Relations, that in 1611 on the Penobscot "we found a fleet of 80 Indian canoes, and one shallop." Henry Hudson likewise saw Indians in a shallop on the Maine coast in 1609. Here is the story; we must take it at whatever value we choose.

Five days of Maine coast cruising down past the Camden Hills and Matinicus Island brought the *Mary and John* on August 7th into the region explored two years before by George Waymouth. The ship's log is given in considerable detail in Strachey's chronicle, and yachtsmen would enjoy the sketched profiles of island horizons with which he adorns the story. On August 7th, on one of the many islands, they eventually came upon "a crosse set up, one of the same which Captain George Weyman, in his discovery, for all after occasions, left upon this island." This was the island "the which they afterwards named St. George his island." And here they were met by the *Gift of God*, which, separated from them during the Atlantic passage, steered straight for this rendezvous in as pretty an example of navigation as one could wish to see.

"About midnight, Captain Gilbert caused his shipp's boat to be mannd with fourteen persons and the Indian Skidwares (brought into England by Captain Wayman) and rowed to the westward from their shipp, to the river of Pamaquid [New Harbor], which they found to be four leagues distant from the shipp, where she road. The Indian brought them to the salvadges houses, where they found two hundred men, women, and childrene; and theire chief commander, or sagamo, amongst them, named Nahanada, who had been brought likewise into England by Captain Wayman, and returned thither by Captain Haman, setting forth for those parts and some part of Canada the year before; at their first comyng the Indians betooke them to their arms, their bowes and arrowes; but after Nahanada had talked with Skidwares and perceived that they were English men, he caused them to lay aside their bowes and arrowes, and he himself came unto them and ymbraced them with much chierfulness, and did they like wise him; and after two houres thus enterchangeably spent, they returned abourd againe.

"[August] 9, Sunday, the chief of both the shipps with the greatest part of all the company, landed on the island where the crosse stood, the which they called St. George's Island, and heard a sermon delivered to them by Mr. Seymour, their preacher and soe returned abourd againe."

On August 10th Captains Popham and Gilbert with a company of fifty went again to Pemaquid, and again the Indians appeared fully armed and refused to allow all of the fifty to land. After a conference, the Indians withdrew into the woods, and with them went Skidwares, who was not "desirous to returne with them any more abourd. Our people, loth to proffer any vyolence unto him by drawing him by force, suffered him to stay behind, promising to returne to them the next day following, but he did not." This loss of Skidwares, their only interpreter, must have seemed a severe blow to the colony.

The two ships now set sail for Sagadahoc, but were delayed by a three-day storm in which one of their shallops, or tenders, was badly damaged. At length, on August 15th, they reached

Seguin Island and the next day got both ships safely at anchor off the mouth of the Sagadahoc, now of course known as the Kennebec. We recall that Champlain had spent a week on this river in 1605. We may assume that Hanham and Pring had also been here in 1606, since the site for which Popham and Gilbert were now searching was apparently well known to them, though not visited, so far as we can determine, by Waymouth in 1605.

(On the 17th) "Captain Popham; in his pynnace, with thirty persons, and Captain Gilbert in his long boat, with eighteen persons more went early in the morning from their shipp into the river Sachedehoc, to view the river, and to search where they might find a fitt place for their plantation. They sayled up into the river neere forty leagues, and found it to be a very gallant river very deepe, and seldome lesse water than three fathome, when they found sest; whereupon they proceeded no farther, but in their returne homewards they observed many goodly islands therein, and many braunches of other small rivers falling into yt.

(August) "18 They all went ashore, and there made choise of a place for their plantacion, at the mouth or entry of the ryver on the west side (for the river bendeth yt self towards the nor-east and by east), being almost an island, of a good bigness, so called of a sagamo or chief commander [Sebenoa] under the graund bassaba. As they went ashoare, three canoes full of Indians came to them, but would not come neere, but rowed away up the river." The site they chose for their plantation was the modern Sabino Head, sheltered by the hook of Popham Beach from the ocean at the Kennebec's mouth. Here in an uneasy anchorage, beset by swirling currents and frequent fogs, they moored their ships. Only a few acres of sloping hillside broke the expanse of spruce-covered ledges on islands and points about them.

(August) "19 They all went ashoare where they made choise of their plantation, and where they had a sermon delivered unto them by their preacher; and after the sermon, the president's commission was read with the lawes to be observed and kept." These laws gave the usual liberal English provision to the president and council of assistants, namely, that they were empowered to make laws needful and proper for the government of the colony, providing that they be consonant with the laws of England. "George Popham, gent, was nominated president: Captain Raleigh Gilbert, James Davies, Richard Seymour, preacher, Captain Richard Davies, Captain Harlow, the same who brought away the salvadges at this tyme shewed in London, from the river of Canada, were all sworne assistants; and soe they returned back againe."

(August) "20 All went to shoare againe and there began to entrench and make a fort, and to buyld a storehouse, soe contynewing the 21st, 22nd, 23rd, 24th, 25th, 26th, 27th." In Captain Davies's version, he says that on the 23rd Captain Popham went in his shallop to the ryver of Pashipskoke [Sheepscot]. "Thear they had parle with the Salvages again who delyvered unto them that they had been at wars with Sasanoa and had slain his sonne in fyght. Skidwares and Dehanada weer in this fyght."

On the 28th Raleigh Gilbert set out on a brief exploring trip across Casco Bay to the westward, investigating Cape Elizabeth and Richmond Island. There was nothing particularly noteworthy found during the three days he was gone, and he apparently did not get as far as the Indian village so well described by Champlain at the mouth of the Saco. The work of building went on at Sagadahoc during his absence, and for four days after his return the entire settlement was wholly occupied with building and furnishing the fort and storehouse. The Davies chronicle says that on September 1st "thear cam a canooa unto us in the which was 2 great kettles of brass."

On September 5th, nine canoes filled with whole families of Indians appeared at the fort, to the number of forty, and among them Nahanada and Skidwares. Greetings were friendly on both sides, and the natives proposed to guide Raleigh Gilbert to the Penobscot to visit the "bassaba." Two days later young Gilbert left with a party of twenty-two and merchandise for barter, but being held up by easterly gales he did not meet his rendezvous with the Indians, at Pemaquid, for three days, and by that time the natives had departed. Gilbert sailed for three days to the eastward among the islands and was unable to find the Penobscot. He again returned empty-handed from his cruise, with nothing but his labor for his pains. We remember that Waymouth had sidestepped the Penobscot trading trip out of suspicion of the savages. All the larger by contrast looms Champlain's bold cruise to the land of Bessabez, with his little party of twelve men going twenty-five leagues up the broad Penobscot in 1604. We may see here how serious a loss to the Sagadahoc colonists was their failure to maintain the confident friendship of Skidwares. Guides and interpreters were of the essence of success in these exploring enterprises; their friendliness was the hinge on which the door to accomplishment opened. For the next week the entire company was occupied in building. But on September 23rd Raleigh Gilbert again set out on an exploring expedition, this time "for the head of the river of Sachadahoc. They sayled all this day, and the 24th the like, untill six of the clock in the afternoone, when they landed on the river's side, where they found a champion land and very fertile, where they remayned all that night.

"In the morning they departed from thence and sayled up the river and came to a flatt low island where ys a great cataract or downfall of water which runneth by both sides of this island very shold and swift [Swan Island]. In this island they found great stores of grapes, both redd and white; good hopps, as also chiballs and garlike; they haled their boat with a strong rope through this downfall perforce, and went neere a league further up, and here they lay all night; and in the first of the night there called certaine salvages on the further side of the river unto them in broken English; they answered them againe and parled long with them, when towards morning they departed." These events are believed to have occurred near Vassalboro.

(September) "26. In the morning there came a canoo unto them, and in her a Sagamo called his name Sebenoa, and told us how he was Lord of the river Sachadehoc. They entertayned him friendly, and tooke him unto their boat and presented him with some triffling things, which he accepted; howbeyt, he desired some one of our men to be put into his canoo as a pawne for his safety, where upon Captain Gilbert sent in a man of his, when presently the canoa rowed away from them with all the speed they could make up the river. They followed with the shallop, having great care that the Sagamo should not leape overbourd. The canoa quickly rowed from them and landed, and the men made to their houses, being neere a league on the land from the river's side, and carried our man with them. The shallop making good waye, at length came to another downfall, which was so shallowe, and soe swift, that by noe meanes they could passe any further, for which, Captain Gilbert, with nine others, landed and tooke their fare, the salvadge Sagamo, with them, and went in search after those other salvages, whose howses, the Sagamo told Captain Gilbert, were not far off; and after a good tedious march, they came indeed at length unto those salvages' howses, wheere found neere fifty able men very strong and tall, such as their like before they had not seene, all newly painted and armed with their bowes and arrowes, Howbeyt, after that the Sagamo had talked with them, they delivered back again the man, and used all the rest very friendly, as did ours the like by them, who shewed them their commodities of beads, knives, and some copper, of which they seemed very fond; and by way of trade, made shew that they would come downe to the boat and there bring such things as they had to exchange them for ours. Soe Captain Gilbert departed from them, and within half an houre after he had gotten to his boat, there came three canoes down unto them, and in them some sixteen salvages, and brought with them some tobacco and certaine small skynes, which were of no value; which Captain Gilbert perceaving, and that they had nothing ells wherewith to trade, he caused all his men to come abourd, and as he would have putt from the shore; the salvages perceiving so much subtilely devised how they might put out the fier in the

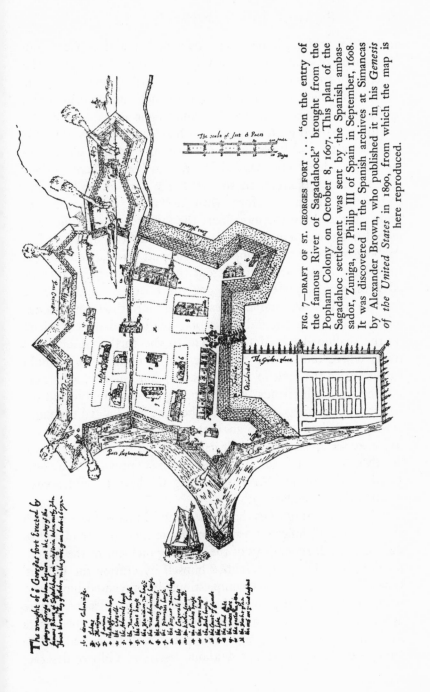

FIG. 7—DRAFT OF ST. GEORGES FORT . . . "on the entry of the famous River of Sagadahock" brought from the Popham Colony on October 8, 1607. This plan of the Sagadahoc settlement was sent by the Spanish ambassador, Zuniga, to Philip III of Spain in September, 1608. It was discovered in the Spanish archives at Simancas by Alexander Brown, who published it in his *Genesis of the United States* in 1890, from which the map is here reproduced.

shallop, by which meanes they sawe they should be free from the danger of our men's pieces [guns], and to performe the same, one of the salvadges came into the shallop and taking the fier brand which one of our company held in his hand there by to light the matches, as if he would light a pipe of tobacco, as sone as he had gotten yt into his hand he presently threw it into the water and leapt out of the shallop. Captain Gilbert seeing that suddenly commanded his men to betake them to their musketts and the targettiers too, from the head of the boat, and bad one of the men before, with his targett on his arme, to stepp on the shore for more fier; the salvages resisted him and would not suffer him to take any, and some others holding fast the boat roap that the shallop could not putt off. Captain Gilbert caused the musquettiers to present their peaces, the which the salvages, seeing, presently lett goe the boat-roap and betooke them to their bowes and arrowes, and ran into the bushes, nocking their arrowes, but did not shoot, neither did ours at them. So the shallop departed from them to the further side of the river, where one of the canoas, came unto them, and would have excused the fault of the others. Captain Gilbert made shew as if he were still friends, and entertayned them kindlye and soe left them, returning to the place where he had lodged the night before, and there came to an anchor for that night." The next day they set up a cross at their campside and spent the next two days exploring the rapids of the Sasanoa, previously investigated by Champlain, before returning to the fort, which they reached on September 29th.

It is interesting to us that these inland Indians knew enough about the Englishmen's firearms to dowse their firebrand and so disarm them. It reminds us of the amusing incident of the henchman of Gosnold's who defended himself by cutting the Indians' bowstrings. The maneuver unquestionably prevented bloodshed in this instance, and proved the Indians' quick-wittedness quite as much as it demonstrated the fact that Gilbert's men were momentarily off their guard. The party may be considered to have been lucky to escape without loss, and Gilbert deserves credit for his courage in proceeding to the Indian village to reclaim his hostage. All too many such instances culminated in ambush.

So ended Gilbert's third sortie into the surrounding country, still with no tangible gains either in profitable furs or other commodities or in appreciable improvement in the relationship between settlers and Indians. The same sort of trial encounters were at this time going on around Jamestown in Virginia, as we can read in Captain John Smith's chronicles of the southern colony. In Virginia more progress was made in securing corn from the natives in exchange for trifles, but the situation so far as permanent friendship with the natives was concerned was little if any better, for skirmishes involving the death of a few colonists were common, and only a succession of relief expeditions from England kept that colony alive. It was soon to become evident that the most determined sort of personnel, energetic leadership in the settlement, and rapid increase in white population were to be the essential factors for success in these colonial ventures. Neither colony knew this yet. Certainly these expeditions of Raleigh Gilbert were not calculated to teach the Indian wholesome respect for Englishmen.

(On October 3rd) "there came a canoa unto some of the people of the fort as they were fishing on the sand, in which was Skidwares, who badd them tell their president that Nahanada, with the Bashabaes brother and others were on the further side of the river, and the next daie would come and visit him.

(October) "4. There came two canoas to the fort, in which were Nahanada and his wife, and Skidwares and the Bashabaes brother, and one other called Amenquin, a Sagamo; all whome the president feasted and entertayned with all kindness, both that day and the next, which being Sundaye, the president carried them with him to the place of publike prayers, which they were at both morning and evening, attending yt with great reverence and silence.

(October) "6. The Salvadges departed all except Amenquin the Sagamo, who would needes staye amongst our people a longer tyme. Upon the departure of the others, the president gave unto everyone of them copper beads, or knives, which contented them not a little, as also delivered a present unto the Bashabae's brother and another for his wife, giving them to understand that he would come unto his court in the river of Penobscot, and see him very shortly, bringing many such like of his country commodities with him."

At this point in Strachey's chronicle the daily narrative suddenly breaks off without explanation, and the chapter is terminated with the following three paragraphs which all too inadequately summarize the succeeding affairs of the colony:

"You maie please to understand how, whilst this business was thus followed here, soone after their arrivall, that had dispatch't away Capt. Robert Davies, in the *Mary and John*, to advertise of their safe arrival and forwardnes of their plantacion within this river of Sachadehoc, with letters to the Lord Chief Justice, ymportuninge a supply for the most necessary wants to the subsisting of a colony, to be sent unto them betymes the next yeare.

"After Capt. Davies' departure they fully finished the fort, trencht and fortified yt with twelve pieces of ordinance, and built fifty howses therein, besides a church and a storehouse; and the carpenters framed a pretty Pynnace of about some thirty tonne, which they called the *Virginia;* the chief ship wright being one Digby of London.

"Many discoveries had likewise been made both to the mayne and unto the neighbour rivers, and the frontier nations fully discovered by the diligence of Captain Gilbert, had not the wynter proved soe extreme unseasonable and frosty; for yt being in the yeare 1607, when the extraordinary frost was felt in most parts of Europe, yt was here likewise as vehement, by which noe boat could stir upon any busines. Howbeyt, as tyme and occasion gave leave, there was nothing omitted which could add unto the benefit or knowledge of the planters, for which when Capt. Davies arrived there in the year following (set out from Topsam, the port towne of Exciter, with a shipp laden full of victualls, armes, instruments, and tooles, etc.) albeyt, he found Mr. George Popham, the president, and some other dead yet he found all things in good forwardness, and many kinds of furrs obteyned from the Indians by way of trade, good store of sarsparilla gathered, and the new pinnace all finished. By the reason that Capt. Gilbert received letters that his brother was newly dead, and a faire portion of land fallen unto his share, which required his repaier home, and noe mynes discovered nor hope there of, being the mayne intended benefit expected to uphold the charge of this plantacion, and the feare that all the other wynters would prove like the first, the company by no means would stay any longer in the country, especyally Capt. Gilbert being to leave them, and Mr. Popham as aforesaid, dead; wherefore they all ymbarqued in this new arrived shipp, and in the new pynnace, the *Virginia,* and sett saile for England. And this was the end of that northerne colony upon the river Sachadehoc.

"Finis."

On the face of Strachey's chronicle, I suppose it is fair to assume that whoever provided Strachey with the narrative (for it seems very doubtful that he ever went to the Sagadahoc) probably sailed home with one of the ships in the autumn and that this accounts for the sharp breaking off of his narrative of the colony. Unfortunately there is no other primary source available to complete the story, and there have been many surmises among historians as to the actual character of events that led to the abandonment of the enterprise. The Jesuit Father Biard was informed by the Indians in 1611 that they killed eleven of the settlers in retribution for cruelties and injustices perpetrated by the English. The evidence in Strachey's concluding paragraphs is plain enough as to essentials. Gorges says that their storehouse and most of their provisions burned during the winter, and obviouly there was a breakdown in the leadership of the project through the death of seventy-year-old George Popham and the withdrawal of Gilbert. In a letter to Lord Cecil, Gorges described President Popham, as "an honest

man, but old and of an unwieldy body, and timorously fearful
to offend or contest with others that will or do oppose him;
but otherwise a discreet, careful man." Gilbert seems to have
conspired with some English friends to secure complete control
of the colony through an attempt to revive the old patent of
his father, Sir Humphrey Gilbert of Newfoundland fame; but
this attempt was thwarted by Gorges. We can thus readily
understand Gorges's private estimate of Gilbert as "desirous of
supremacy and rule, a loose life, prompt to sensuality, little zeal
in religion, humorous, head strong, and of small judgment and
experience, otherwise valiant enough."

No mention is made of the fate of Popham's flyboat
Gift of God, and despite Strachey's assertion that "they all
ymbarqued" in the other two vessels, some zealously patriotic
Maine writers have ventured the opinion that some of the
Popham settlers remained in Maine, perhaps at Pemaquid, and
carried on a fragmentary persistence of the colony as a trading
base for the known subsequent voyages of vessels sent out in
the following years by Gorges and the Popham family to ply
the fur trade and the fishing industry along this coast. No adequate basis for this theory exists, and the numerous narratives
of voyagers in the region during the subsequent ten years fail
to mention such a possibility. It seems incredible that so voluminous a writer and so steadfast a promoter of colonization as Sir
Ferdinando Gorges should not have left in his writings some
mention of so glorious a claim to continuous settlement as the
Pemaquid removal theory would substantiate if it had actually
happened. James Phinney Baxter, reasoning from Gorges's own
correspondence, believes that the *Mary and John* set sail to
England in September of 1607, and that in December, after the
Virginia was completed, the *Gift of God* was also sent home,
probably with all but forty-five of the colonists. In March
Gorges sent two supply ships out to the colony, one of them
being the *Mary and John* again. These ships brought the news
of the death of Chief Justice Popham, and of course arrived to
find that George Popham was also dead. A third supply ship

sent out in July of 1608, brought the news of Sir John Gilbert's death, and, necessitating the return of Raleigh Gilbert, dealt the final blow to the colony's leadership. We may conclude that by one schedule or another the colony of Sagadahoc was definitely abandoned during the summer of 1608, to the intense sorrow and regret of Gorges, as he amply indicates.

It is true, however, that the Pemaquid and Monhegan area was visited every summer from 1608 on by an increasingly large fleet of fishing and trading vessels from the west ports of England. The Sagadahoc failure called attention to the immense potentialities of that area as a fishing center. The Virginia Colony soon began sending vessels north to Maine for fish and, as we shall soon see, vessels of Sir Francis Popham and of Gorges himself reappeared there every year. Sir Samuel Argall in 1613, Captain John Smith in 1614, Hobson, Hawkins, Hunt, Dermer, and many others appeared at Monhegan over the next dozen years to maintain the contact with Maine that Waymouth and the Sagadahoc planters had established. It should never be forgotten that when the Pilgrims in 1622 were suffering desperately from famine, Edward Winslow went in search of food to the fishing fleet at Damariscove, near Pemaquid, "about which place," Winslow wrote, "there fished about thirty sail of ships." Among these fishermen Winslow found "a willingness to supply our wants which were done so far as able; and would not take any bills for the same, but did what they could freely, wishing their store had been such as they might in greater measure have expressed their love and supplied our necessities, for which they sorrowed."

The northern colony at Sagadahoc is recorded in history as a failure. From the standpoint of its continuity as a settlement, and especially as contrasted with Jamestown, Plymouth, and Boston, it was a failure. It was so considered at the time. Its abandonment broke down the integrity of the Plymouth Company's organization and delayed a continuance of the major program of settlement in New England for twenty years. Its planters did not possess that half-mad loyalty to an idea which twice turned back homeward-bound shallops under Champlain, and its leaders, with the exception of Gorges, certainly were not capable of the selfless devotion of Raleigh, still desperately contemplating colonial projects from his prison cell. Henry O. Thayer sums up the situation as follows: "Liberal expenditures and foresight had prepared the way; abundant supplies were subsequently forwarded, vigilant care of devoted patrons followed the colony; but an inward disease, more than outward ills, not indeed wanting, weakened it, so that a slight stroke in the end broke the resolution of the company."

But granting all this, there is still more to be said to the credit of this failure, and some revision of our estimate of the importance of the Sagadahoc venture is needed. Considered as a preparatory program, the series of voyages beginning with Gosnold's and culminating in the abandoned Sagadahoc colony represent a colonial movement comparable in scope and intensity with Champlain's three years in New England. In each case the major settlement was abandoned, but in each case also a permanent trading post, that of Poutrincourt at Port Royal and that of Gorges and the later settlers at Monhegan and Pemaquid, eventually resulted. Thus in both instances the program resulted in an eventual commercial foothold which maintained the several claims of France and England in the new territories. Had it not been for these preliminary explorations of the coast and the establishment of profitable trading stations, it seems inconceivable that the Pilgrims and Puritans would have been able to settle and remain in Massachusetts. We may credit the faltering Plymouth Company with the glory of having placed England's claim to New England on a somewhat firmer basis than that of France. Thus all was not lost with the departure of Raleigh Gilbert from the plantation at Sagadahoc.

Chapter Eight

THREE PORTENTOUS VISITORS, 1609–1611

THE ECHOES of the Sagadahoc disaster were cumulative. It seemed as though everything connected with the Plymouth Company's fortunes went wrong. As if it were not enough to have lost two expeditions to Spanish pirates, to be deprived of half the prime movers in the project through death, and thereby to have lost a colony, a more subtle blow now fell. The council of the southern colony at Jamestown, hearing of the failure of the Sagadahoc enterprise, now approached the corporation of the Plymouth group, soliciting support for their own venture. They set forth the advantages of their more southern climate, and of course the fact that Virginia was still a going concern, however torn by dissension, famine and massacres, was a powerful argument to win them converts. The result was necessarily a further weakening of the Plymouth Company. When in the spring of 1609 the London Company gathered its ships in the harbor of Plymouth, under the very eyes of Ferdinando Gorges, who was Plymouth's military governor, the little *Virginia*, built at Sagadahoc, went along with them to Jamestown. The Earl of Southampton, who had sent Gosnold and Waymouth to New England, now transferred his major attentions to Jamestown, and later became treasurer of the Virginia Company. Captain James Davies, he of the *Mary and John*, joined the Jamestown colonists, along with Robert Davies, another of the Sagadahoc men. There were doubtless others of whom we are ignorant. Bartholomew Gosnold and Gabriel Archer were already in Virginia. Thus into the Virginia enterprise was poured much of whatever colonial enthusiasm there was left in the New England group. This was fortunate for Virginia, and in the long run redounded to the advantage of New England, since Jamestown's power was on several later occasions useful to New England. But from the viewpoint of Gorges and his New England charter it was, no doubt, a bitter setback. This was the reason why Gorges was not able to finance a further colonial venture. As we have seen, he and other merchant adventurers continued to send numerous trading and fishing vessels to Monhegan, and in this way maintained contact during the subsequent years, but New England remained still a coast line, and in no sense a plantation, for yet another dozen years.

From Jamestown, indeed, came the impulse for the next two New England voyages of which we have any record. To assign the first of these to Virginia is slightly amusing, but that there is a devious connection will become apparent in what follows.

1. Henry Hudson, 1609

Henry Hudson was an Englishman whose grandfather had been active in the formation of the English Muscovy Company, that amazing brain child of the old age of Sebastian Cabot, which had opened English trading routes to Russia, by way of Archangel, and thence even across Russia to Persia. In the years 1607 and 1608, when Sagadahoc was pursuing its tragic course, young Hudson was making, for the Muscovy Company, two voyages in search of a northern or a northeastern passage across the Arctic to Cathay. In 1607 he was turned back by the ice pack at the northern point of Spitsbergen, and in 1608 he sailed to Nova Zembla in a vain attempt to round the frigid northern coasts of Russia. In 1609 the great merchants of Amsterdam under the auspices of the Dutch East India Company engaged him for a second attempt at Nova Zembla. We can do no better in describing the first portion of this voyage than to quote the contemporary account of it by the Dutch writer Emanuel Van Meteren, published in 1610:

"This Henry Hutson left the Texel on the 6th of April, 1609, doubled the Cape of Norway the 5th of May, and directed his course along the northern coasts towards Nova Zembla; but he there found the sea as full of ice as he had found it in the preceding years, so that they lost the hope of effecting anything during the season. This circumstance, and the cold, which some of his men, who had been in the East Indies, could not bear, caused quarrels among the crew, they being partly English, partly Dutch, upon which Captain Hutson laid before them two propositions. The first of these was to go to the coast of America, to the latitude of 40°, moved thereto mostly by letters and maps *which a certain Captain Smith had sent him from Virginia*, and by which he indicated to him a sea leading into the western ocean, by the north of the southern English colony. Had this information been true (experience goes as yet to the contrary), it would have been of great advantage, as indicating a short way to India. The other proposition was to direct their search through Davis' Strait. This meeting with general approval, they sailed thitherward on the 14th of May with a good wind at the Faroe island, they sailed on, till on the 18th of July they reached the coast of Nova Francia under 44°, where they were obliged to run in, in order to get a new foremast, having lost theirs. They found one, and set it up. They found this a good place for cod-fishing as also for traffic in good skins and furs, which were to be got there at a very low price. But the crew behaved badly towards the people of the country, taking their property by force, out of which there arose quarrels among themselves. The English, fearing that between the two they would be outnumbered and worsted, were therefore afraid to pursue the matter further. So they left that place on the 26th of July, and kept out to sea till the 3rd of August, when they came near the coast in 43° of latitude."

Van Meteren thus outlines for us the extraordinary circumstances by which that fabled character, Captain John Smith, of whom we will soon have much to relate in our New England story, turned a Dutch voyage of the East India Company to Nova Zembla into an exploration of New England and the Hudson River. Smith had indeed written a letter to Hudson from Jamestown, outlining his speculations concerning a possible westward passage through North America. He may have been referring to Delaware Bay or to the Hudson River. In any case it is perfectly clear that it was Smith, from Virginia, who brought Hudson to these shores. Inasmuch as it was this voyage which turned the Dutch interest toward the possibilities of trade about the New York area, we may without too great a stretch of imagination credit Smith with some responsibility for the founding of New Amsterdam. Apparently two Englishmen brought the Dutch to North America.

For the New England portion of Hudson's voyage we can turn to what amounts to the ship's log, written by one "Robert Juet, of Limehouse," who was an officer of the *Half Moon*. This was published in *Purchas his Pilgrimes*, in 1625. We can extract from among the soundings and weather observations certain passages that are of interest to our New England viewpoint.

Approaching the Maine coast in the latitude of 43° 25′ on July 13, 1609, Juet writes that "at sixe of the clocke wee had sight of the land and saw two sayles on head off us." On July 16th "in the morning it cleared up, and we had sight of five islands lying north, and north and by west of us, two leagues. Then wee made ready to set sayle, but the myst came so thicke that we durst not enter in among them." Here he says: "I caught fifteene cods, some of the greatest that I have seene." "The seventeenth, was all mystie, so that we could not get into the harbour. At ten of the clocke two boats came off to us, with sixe of the savages of the countrey seeming glad of our coming. We gave them trifles, and they eate and dranke with us; and told us that there were gold, silver and copper mynes hard by us [*sic!*]; and that the French-men doe trade with them; which is very likely, for one of them spake some words of French.

"The eighteenth, faire weather, wee went into a very good harbour, and rode hard by the shoare in foure fathoms water. The river runneth up a great way, but there is but two fathoms hard by us. We went on shoare and cut us a fore mast; then at noone we came aboard againe, and found the height of the place to be in 44 degrees, 1 minute, and the sunne to fall at a south south-west sunne. We mended our sayles, and fell to make our fore-mast. The harbour lyeth south and north, a mile in where we rode." This was probably somewhere in the southern portion of Penobscot Bay.

On the 19th the crew found a supply of fresh water and fished for cod and lobsters, both of which were very plentiful. "The people coming aboord, shewed us great friendship, but we could not trust them." "On the twentieth wee espied two French shallops full of the country people come into the harbour, but they offered us no wrong, seeing we stood upon our guard. They brought many beaver skinnes and other fine furres, which they would have changed for redde gownes. For the French trade with them for red cassocks, knives, hatchets, copper kettles, trivets, beades, and other trifles." This gives us some notion of how active the unchronicled French trade had become along this coast, for if Juet found all these articles among a small group of Indians in the one harbor, certainly the total volume of such commerce must have been enormous on the coast generally. Again we are astounded at the Indians' use of "French shallops." Champlain's Nova Scotian trading settlement at Port Royal had remained abandoned now for two years, and was not to be reoccupied by Poutrincourt's son Biencourt until 1610. Yet here is plain proof that French traders maintained their commercial foothold in northern Maine even as Gorges and Francis Popham were attempting to do only fifty miles farther south. It was inevitable that the two nations soon would come to blows over their trading rivalry, and we shall see in our next chapter how that century and a half of struggle was to begin.

From July 21st to 24th Hudson's men busied themselves about stepping the new mast and rerigging it, between intervals of fishing. "We kept good watch for fear of being betrayed by the people," says Juet, "and perceived where they layed their shallops. The five and twentieth, very faire weather and hot. In the morning we manned our scute [small boat] with foure muskets and sixe men, and tooke one of their shallops and brought it aboord. Then we manned our boat and scute with twelve men and muskets, and two stone pieces or murderers, and drove the savages from their houses and tooke the spoyle of them, as they would have done of us. Then we set sayle." We can imagine what desire for revenge such gratuitous treachery aroused in the minds of these natives. Was it any wonder that the French were later able to employ these Indians as willing and fierce allies against English-speaking settlers?

Hudson now sailed southward with varying winds for a week, having some difficulty with shoals and tide rips on July 31st, perhaps on Georges Bank. On August 3rd "we had sight of the land, and steered in with it, thinking to go to the north-ward of it. So we sent our shallop with five men to sound in by the shore: and they found it deepe five fathoms within bow-shot of the shoare: and they went on land, and found goodly grapes and rose trees, and brought them aboord with them." This was probably off the extinct Points Gilbert and Care which Gosnold had found protruding from the easterly Cape Cod shore. On August 4th "we stood to the north-west two watches, and one south in for the land, and came to an anchor at the northern end of the headland, and heard the voyce of men call. Then we sent our boat on shoare, thinking they had beene some Christians left on the land; but we found them to bee savages, which seemed very glad of our comming. So we brought one aboord with us, and gave him meate, and he did eate and drinke with us. Our master gave him three or foure glasse buttons, and sent him on land with our shallop againe.

And at our boats comming from the shoare he leapt and danced, and held up his hands, and pointed us to a river on the other side [Pamet?]: for we had made signes that we came to fish there. The body of this headland lyeth in 41 degrees 45 minutes. We set sayle againe after dinner, thinking to have got to the westward of this headland, but could not: so we beare up to the southward of it, and made a south-east way; and the souther point did beare west at eight of the clocke at night. . . . The people have green tobacco and pipes, the boles whereof are made of earth and the pipes of red copper. The land is very sweet."

Hudson now kept offshore from the southern point of the headland, "for wee feared a great riffe that lyeth off the land, and steered away south and by east. . . . Upon this riffe we had observation, and found it lyeth in 40°, ten minutes. And this is that headland which Captaine Bartholomew Gosnold discovered in the yeare 1602, and called Cape Cod, because of the store of cod-fish that hee found there-about."

The *Half Moon* had the usual difficulties in circumventing Nantucket Shoals, "for there the tyde of ebbe laid us on, and the streame did hurle so, that it laid us so neere the breach of a shoald that wee were forced to anchor." And, as this frequently happened in such voyages, the experience on these shoals was so unpleasant that Hudson put to sea for nearly three weeks and did not again sight land until in the latitude of Delaware he began to retrace his steps northward along the coast in search of that fictitious westward passage about which John Smith had speculated in his letter. He did not court the wrath of the English by sailing in to the Virginia settlement, despite his friendship for Smith, who was at that time governor at Jamestown, but proceeded northward to explore Delaware Bay and the Hudson River, thus determining finally that there was no passage, by way of either route, westward into the Pacific. Verrazano and Gomez had much earlier come to the same conclusion, and it is almost certain that both French and unofficial Dutch traders had explored the Hudson prior to 1600. It is amazing to recall that Champlain had been assisting his Canadian allies in their battle with the Iroquois near Ticonderoga only two months before Hudson's arrival at Albany. Vermont was thus discovered from the north. So, English New England was almost completely surrounded by foreign competitors eleven years prior to its settlement. Yet Hudson probably knew little or nothing about the previous activities on this shore except of course the discoveries of Gosnold, which Juet mentions. It is not a part of our New England story to recount Hudson's exploration of the river that bears his name. A later portion of Juet's narrative gives the circumstances of the *Half Moon's* progress up the Hudson to the head of navigation near Albany, of skirmishes with the natives, and of the excellent fur trade. In all, the ship spent a month on the river, setting sail for England on October 5th. At Dartmouth the ship was detained by the English authorities, so that information about the voyage became immediately accessible to the English.

Henry Hudson was the beginning and the end of an era. He was the last of our New England explorers to be chiefly motivated by the search for a short route to the Orient. As such he was the last of the great navigators in New England's history. We all know how he died in the following year, set adrift in arctic Hudson's Bay through the despicable plottings of his mutinous crew, one of the leaders of whom, we regret to recall, was the same Robert Juet who wrote our New England narrative. Juet himself died on that homeward voyage. Apart from his many contributions to the science of geography, Hudson's great achievement was in drawing the attention of the Dutch to the possibilities of profitable trade and settlement about New York.

Thus he set in motion yet another rivalry to the English hold on New England. The succeeding years were to see the English ventures from Maine to Connecticut pinched between French Canada and Acadia and Dutch New Netherland. Parts of Maine and Connecticut were for a considerable period to be occupied by these competing nations, and for a time the area of New England was to be practically considered as extending only between the Penobscot and Connecticut rivers.

Before leaving the great navigators, let us consider briefly the notions of North American geography that had gradually evolved since 1492. Columbus never touched the North American continent, and perhaps died believing that his islands were off the coast of Asia. The Cabots' discovery was, on the contrary, immediately termed the New Found Land, though John Cabot thought he was north of the China coast. Ponce de León discovered Florida in 1512. The 1524 voyage of Verrazano was apparently the first to join Florida to Nova Scotia in a continuous sweep of coast line. That this was of enormous significance was probably realized by those who sent out Gomez in the following year, and he of course confirmed Verrazano's findings. This continent was thus proved to be a New World, rather than a part of Asia. The Spaniards had by 1525 become familiar with the Gulf of Mexico through the explorations of Cortes and De Soto, but what lay behind the northern coasts as yet could only be guessed at. Consequently any speculative conclusion about this northern area by a map maker whose work became widely disseminated inevitably must have enormous influence upon the geographic ideas of succeeding generations until such time as the hinterland of the United States and Canada should be actually explored. Such a map was that of Verrazano's brother, Hieronimo, produced in 1529. This map represented Florida as joined to the more northern regions by a narrow isthmus, to the west of which lay a great expanse of water, the "Sea of Verrazano." For the greater part of the sixteenth century this legendary Sea of Verrazano was faithfully reproduced by successive cartographers in varying forms. Sir Francis Drake's circumnavigation voyage in 1578 might be thought to have been sufficient evidence to destroy this notion, since he lingered on the California coast for a considerable period, but it did not, for no one as yet had any idea of the three thousand miles separating California from Virginia or New England. Even the explorations of Cartier and Champlain, pressing deeper westward into the heart of the continent, did not wholly rid geographers of the idea that somewhere between New France and Florida there was an isthmus, like that at Panama, across which, with the aid of a bay or river, one might sail through to the great South Sea, and so to China. Thus we may be fairly sure that Captain John Smith and Henry Hudson, in 1609, were still dreaming of the Sea of Verrazano. Indeed, Smith seems to have sailed up Chesapeake Bay not wholly in search of corn for the Virginia planters, but quite as much in high hopes that around the next bend might be revealed that glorious vision

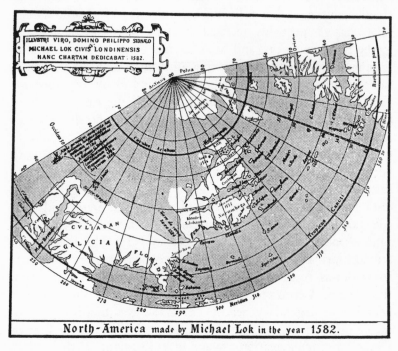

FIG. 8—MAP OF NORTH AMERICA MADE BY THE ENGLISH MERCHANT MICHAEL LOK
IN 1582.

Lok is known to have had in his possession a copy of Hieronimo Verrazano's map on which the "Sea of Verrazano" was first portrayed. Lok's map may be cited as an illustration of the persistence of the theory of a possible westerly passage through North America which motivated Henry Hudson in his voyage of 1609. (Reproduced from J. G. Kohl's *History of the Discovery of Maine*, Portland, 1869.)

of all navigators, a passage through the North American obstacle. We should picture Cartier on the St. Lawrence, Allefonsce in Massachusetts Bay, and Champlain on the Bay of Fundy and the Penobscot, as all drawn on by the same gorgeous possibility. Certainly Hudson was inflamed with it, and it must have amounted to a ruling passion with him, for he already, like Columbus, had fought the reluctance of a mutinous crew at Nova Zembla, and he was to die in the arctic a martyr to the same insistent urge. In his brief career he tried all the practical possibilities then or since considered likely, eliminated all except the Northwest Passage, and died in search of that only route left unexplored, having gone farther in the northwest than Frobisher in 1578 or Davis in 1585. Only in the nineteenth century was this Northwest Passage idea finally conquered. Into four brief years, 1607-1610, Henry Hudson packed all that we know of this amazing life's achievement. That his crew attacked the Indians of Maine is of small consequence in the light of his meaning in history. That he honored New England shores with his casual visit, and cut a mast from the forests of Maine, adds interest and glory to the story of our coast. By setting the stage for the founding of New Netherland he further complicated the New England picture.

II. Samuel Argall, 1610

Meanwhile the fortunes of the Jamestown colony had gone from bad to worse. The original company of a hundred men who had set out in 1607, of whom fifty-two were classed as "gentlemen," the remainder as mechanics and tradesmen, dwindled within four months to half that number through starvation, fever and the attacks of Indians. There were few among the "planters" who had the least notion of agriculture, and almost none who were willing or able to do the hard labor of setting up a colony. Had it not been for the energetic leadership of Captain John Smith, the colony would surely have perished. Smith was new at colonization himself, but he had

had a resourceful military career during which he had been left for dead on a battlefield in Hungary, sold into slavery in Turkey, and had made his way on foot through the wilds of Russia. As John Fiske says: "He was full of shifts and expedients, and in the early colony at Jamestown was the only man capable of taking the lead. He sailed up and down the coast, explored the great rivers, coaxed or bullied the Indians, and got supplies of food from them." So he kept the colony going for two years.

In the spring of 1609, as we have seen, a relief expedition was sent out by the Virginia Company in command of Sir Thomas Gates and Sir George Somers, setting sail from Plymouth under the jealous eyes of Ferdinando Gorges. The nine ships containing five hundred men must have made a brave showing as they departed from Plymouth. Alas, the flagship *Sea Venture*, with all the commanders aboard, was wrecked at Bermuda, and the rest of the leaderless fleet arrived at Jamestown "only to make confusion more hideous." Poor Smith maintained some semblance of authority only with the greatest difficulty and the new colonists, planted in villages farther up the river, proved wholly incompetent to support themselves in the new environment. Smith was injured in the autumn of 1609, lost the confidence of the settlers during his illness, and returned to England at about the time that Henry Hudson sailed home from New York. In June, 1610, only sixty of the five hundred men were left alive. At this point Gates and Somers, having built themselves two pinnaces in Bermuda, arrived at the colony and found things in such desperate straits that they determined to abandon the effort and return to England. The Jamestown colonists had actually embarked in their four pinnaces, one of which was Sagadahoc's *Virginia*, when the new governor of Virginia, Lord Delaware, arrived at Hampton Roads and intercepted them, bringing three ships and abundant supplies. Shades of St. Croix and Port Royal! Under Delaware's strong hand, and that of Sir Thomas Dale who followed him, Virginia began to thrive. Again the force of leadership was being demonstrated.

Participating in both 1609 and 1610 in voyages to Jamestown, carrying out assignments under the Virginia Company, was Sir Samuel Argall, a bold skipper who was one day to be a rather unscrupulous deputy governor of Virginia. On June 19, 1610, eleven days after the arrival of Lord Delaware at Jamestown, Argall and Sir George Somers set sail in two pinnaces to go to Bermuda in the effort to get a cargo of hogs which Somers had found running wild in abundance during his residence there after the wreck of the *Sea Venture*. After beating about in contrary winds for twenty-eight days, and apparently being unable to find Bermuda, a difficult piece of navigation in those days, the two captains determined on July 16th to head for Cape Cod. Reading between the lines one may suppose that codfish might be an acceptable substitute for the hogs which they were unable to locate.

Reaching New England latitudes, and fishing banks which we may suppose were the Georges, the two vessels agreed on July 26th to sail to the River of Sagadahoc. Shortly thereafter the pinnaces became separated in thick fog, and Argall, from whose own account of the voyages we quote, makes no further mention of Somers's craft. The first land sighted was Seal Rock, off the Penobscot, on which Argall landed July 30th and "killed three seales with my hanger. This island is not halfe a mile about, nothing but a Rocke, which seemed to be very rich marble stone . . . About ten of the clocke I came aboord again, with some wood that I had found upon the Iland, for there had beene some folkes that had made fiers there. Then I stood over to another Iland [Matinicus] that did bear north off me about three leagues; this small rockie Iland lyeth in forty foure degrees. About seven of the clocke that night I came to an anchor among Ilands in eight fathoms water; and upon one of these Ilands I fitted my selfe with wood and water, and Balast."

Argall now stayed among the islands of Penobscot Bay for

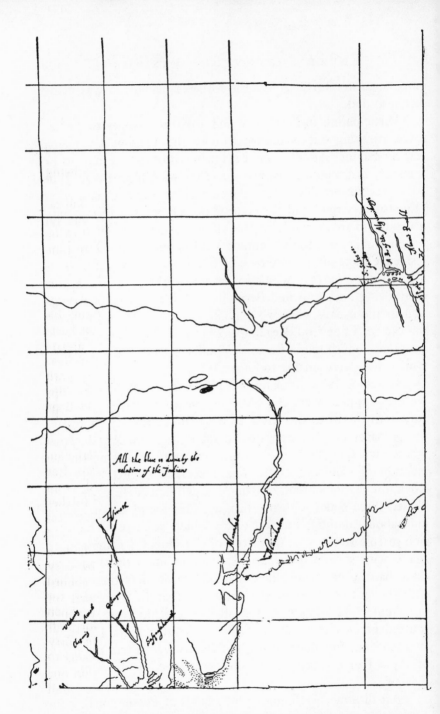

All the blue is done by the relations of the Indians

FIG. 9—NEW ENGLAND PORTION OF A MAP OF NORTH AMERICA MADE IN VIRGINIA BY AN UNKNOWN ROYAL CARTOGRAPHER ABOUT 1610. It gives abundant evidences of the work of Gosnold, Pring, Champlain, Waymouth, the Sagadahoc colony, and Henry Hudson. The map was unearthed in the Spanish archives

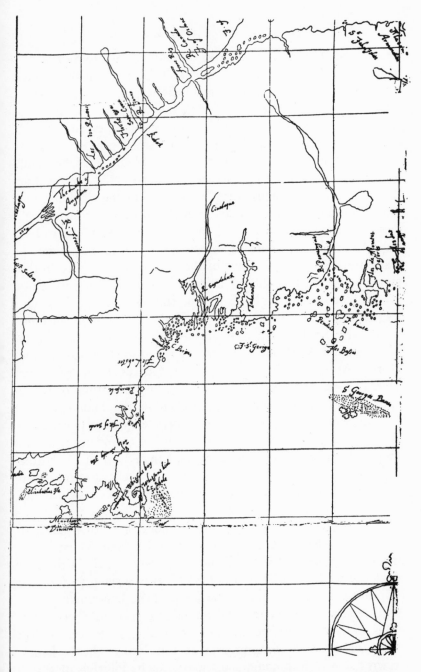

by Alexander Brown, in whose *Genesis of the United States* it was published in 1890, and from which it is here reproduced. Presumably the map was stolen by the Spanish ambassador at London and sent to the King of Spain. No English copy is known.

eleven days, fishing. He returned on August 12th to Seal Rock to attempt to get some more seals, "for I did find that they were very nourishing meate, and a great reliefe to my men, and that they could be very well saved with salt to keepe a long time. But when I came thither I could not by any meanes catch any." Finding that the fishing began to fail, Argall now abandoned any intention he may have had to proceed to Sagadahoc and now set out for Cape Cod, "to see whether I could get any fish there or not." On August 19th "about two of the clocke in the afternoone I did see an Hedland, which did beare off me South-west, about foure leagues; so I steered with it, taking it to bee Cape Cod: and by foure of the clocke I was fallen among so many shoales, that it was five of the clocke the next day in the morning before I could get cleere of them. It is a very dangerous place to fall with all; for the shoales lie at the least ten leagues off from the Land; and my Barke did draw seven foot. This Land lyeth South-west and North-east, and the shoales lie off from it South and South by west, and so along toward the North. At the North-west by west Guards I observed the North-starre, and found the ship to be in the latitude of fortie one degrees, fiftie minutes, being then in the middle of the Sholdes; and I did finde thirteene degrees westerly variation then likewise. Thus finding the place not to be for my turne, as soon as I was cleare of these dangers, I thought it fit to returne to James Towne in Virginia, to the Lord Delaware, my Lord Governor, and there to attend his command: so I shaped my course for that place."

There seems at first sight to be nothing in this narrative of any considerable importance to New England. What is immediately significant about it, however, is that here is the first evidence we have of New England fisheries serving to feed the Virginia Colony. From this time forward the Jamestown people sent vessels to the New England fishing grounds every year. This of course steadied the hold that English fishermen had upon this coast. More than that, it eventually brought the Jamestown colonists into communication with the Pilgrims of Plymouth, and it was a Virginia vessel returning from Monhegan which informed William Bradford in 1622 of the possibilities of securing supplies from the Monhegan fishermen. We have already mentioned Edward Winslow's voyage to Damariscove in that year.

The special significance of this fragmentary narrative lies, further, in the fact that it constituted Sir Samuel Argall's introduction to these shores. For it was Argall who was commissioned, in 1613, to break up the French settlements in Maine and Nova Scotia. Argall likewise was to give the Dutch their first warning that they were trespassing, at New Amsterdam, on English ground. Thus we may consider that this minor voyage was indeed a portentous one, for here was introduced into New England the man who was to act in the capacity of the first colonial navy. The hapless Plymouth Company was to depend on this soldier from Virginia to defend its title to New England, even as it was to depend on Virginia's Captain John Smith as a cartographer and publicity man.

III. Edward Harlow 1611

The Hudson and Argall voyages serve to fill in the gap between the failure of Sagadahoc and the further explorations of our coast by Plymouth Company men. These years of 1609 and 1610 no doubt brought a lull in the activity on the New England front. England's best efforts were being devoted to keeping Jamestown alive, and the shattered remnants of the Plymouth Company were in no position financially to embark on new ventures to a coast that many now considered too cold in winter to be habitable for Englishmen. Dissipation and intrigue at the court of the weak King James were becoming obstacles to colonial ventures of any kind. Sir Ferdinando Gorges was beset with troubles even in finding sufficient funds to pay the soldiers of his garrison in English Plymouth, and the succeeding years were to demonstrate even more forcefully that if he was ever to succeed in exploiting New England it must be out of funds advanced from his own purse. He still had his grant in New England, to be sure, but neither he nor Francis, John Popham's only son, nor any of the other dwindling group of incorporators could summon the interest or the investment of adventurers eager to re-enter the New England project. Thus the few New England ventures that were undertaken by the English between 1608 and 1613 were private voyages in the same class with those of Gosnold and Pring in 1602 and 1603. Gorges seems to have been unable even to finance a single ship on his own account until in 1614 he sent out Richard Vines to settle in the country and become his agent there. In the meantime we know of only two other English ventures, and of these we have only the most fragmentary mention. John Smith tells us that "Sir Francis Popham sent divers times one Captaine Williams to Monahigan onely to trade and make core-fish, but for any Plantations there was no more speeches." In what years these visits of the Popham men were made we have no definite information, save that from the context we may judge that they preceded Smith's own voyage of 1614.

The Earl of Southampton, whose primary objective we know had now become Jamestown, did keep up a desultory interest in New England. Since he had been the original promoter of Gosnold's voyage, it would be surprising indeed if he had dropped entirely his New England motive. As military governor of the Isle of Wight he was in a position similar to that of Gorges at Plymouth, and we know from Gorges's writings that the two remained in occasional touch over problems both of defense and of the colonial ambition which they shared in common. The fear of Spanish raids, as well as of English pirates, was constant in the southern ports of England throughout the reign of James. We learn that about 1611 Southampton sent one Edward Harlow, probably the same that had been master of ordnance at Sagadahoc, to do some exploration at Cape Cod. John Smith gives us what little we know of this voyage in the following passage: "The right Honourable Henry Earle of South-hampton and those of the Isle of Wight, imploied Cap-

taine Edward Harlow to discover an Isle supposed about Cape
Cod, but they found their plots [maps] had much abused them,
for falling with Monahigen, they found onely Cape Cod no
Ile but the maine, there they detained three Salvages aboord
them, called Pechmo, Monopet, and Pekenimne, but Pechmo
leapt over board, and got away; and not long after with his con-
sorts cut their Boat from their sterne, got her on shore, and so
filled her with sand, and guarded her with Bowes and Arrowes
the English lost her. Not farre from thence they had three men
sorely wounded with Arrowes." Here is the first known light
to be thrown on the methods by which Indians obtained their
European boats.

"Anchoring at the Ile of Nohono, the Salvages in their
Canowes assaulted the Ship till the English Guns made them
retire; yet here they tooke Sakaweston that, after he had lived
many yeeres in England, went a Souldier to the warres of Bohemia.

"At Capawe [Martha's Vineyard] they tooke Coneconam
and Epenow, but the people at Agawom [Ipswich?] used them
kindly. So with five Salvages they returned for England."

This voyage of Harlow's illustrates for us again the chain
of hostilities of which we have seen recurrent evidence in the
voyages of Waymouth, Champlain and Hudson. It also continues our series of kidnaped Indians. It gives curious additional
testimony to the fact that Indians could be quite as successful in
stealing European boats as were the Dutch and English under
Pring and Hudson in stealing them back from the natives. The
superstitious awe with which the Indians had greeted Verrazano in 1524, and perhaps even Gosnold in 1602, had disappeared, to be replaced by an increasingly open rivalry in treachery between the two races. In five short years this trend had
developed at Cape Cod, from the first New England bloodshed
under Champlain, to the competitive, eager banditry of this
voyage of Harlow's. In 1602 and 1603 the English had been content with nothing worse than the stealing of Indian canoes, at
Cuttyhunk and Plymouth. Waymouth in 1605 had shanghaied

the five chiefs of Pemaquid, two of whom had been returned to Maine. In 1606 occurred Champlain's little massacre at Chatham. The Jesuit Relations tell that there were skirmishes, with bloodshed, about Sagadahoc in 1608. Hudson in Maine, in 1609, "drove the savages from their houses and tooke the spoyle of them."

And here at Cape Cod in 1611 Harlow added five to the roster of kidnaped aborigines before being forced to take to his heels. This is not a pretty record for the apologists of European civilization, though mild when compared to the deeds of bloody Spain. It perhaps accounts for Harlow's fruitless search for "an Ile supposed about Cape Cod." In Monhegan the English had a haven free of Indian hostility, uninhabited by natives, and possessed of a harbor of refuge. Nowhere else along the coast was there another one known. Could the Earl of Southampton have located, at Nantucket perhaps, a similar stronghold, the coasts of Massachusetts might have been more extensively exploited, and perhaps settled upon earlier. But Nantucket was populated by natives, and as Champlain had already learned, the Massachusetts Indians were able and willing to defend their shores. The English could not find even a trading post in these southern latitudes, but fell back again upon Monhegan, which was to remain "the usual place" for yet another decade.

Harlow's voyage is notable for one other matter. In Epenow he had captured an Indian who was to become more famous than Nahanada and Skidwares, and almost as important as the Squanto and Samoset of the Pilgrims. We shall hear of him further in connection with the voyages of Captains Hobson and Dermer in 1614 and 1619. In the meantime he was taken to London, where he was exhibited in public "for a wonder," and eventually fell into the possession of our old friend Ferdinando Gorges. Gorges lodged him with Assacomet, one of Waymouth's Pemaquid natives. As soon as the two had contrived to resolve their language difficulties, which consisted of differences, Gorges says, similar to those between dialects in the south and the north of England, Gorges began to learn considerable information about the Massachusetts coast. This led to further explorations of Massachusetts by his men, and may be considered to have laid the foundations of the 1614 expedition of Captain John Smith, who produced the best-known English map of early New England. Harlow's voyage, therefore, may be interpreted as of comparable significance to those of Hudson and Argall, despite our fragmentary account of it. On these several counts, it strikes us as noteworthy.

So despite the hapless fortunes of the Plymouth Company, things were not standing still as regards New England. The Dutch were soon to explore its southern shores as a consequence of the portentous discoveries of the last of the navigators, Henry Hudson. Argall brought Jamestown into habitual communication with its fishing. Harlow returned to the degenerating Plymouth Company with an ominous report of Massachusetts, and brought with him Epenow who served as an unwilling pilot to those shores. We must now digress from English interests to take up a more pressing problem for New England—the second serious attempt of France to establish herself on the coast of Maine.

Chapter Nine

PIERRE BIARD,
JESUIT EXPLORER OF MAINE, 1611

A NEW MOTIVE for the exploration and colonization of New England now began to appear on the European
horizon. We have seen how painfully and slowly the commercial impulse, through scattered organization and the discouragement of repeated failures, had accumulated momentum
sufficient to maintain a constantly changing but nevertheless
steady traffic on these shores. Elsewhere in the New World, in
Virginia, the Caribbean and South America, the foothold was
much stronger. In some of those areas, notably in Mexico and
Brazil, a religious impulse had fortified the commercial one.
French Protestants had found momentarily a haven in exile in
Brazil, and the Spanish conquerors throughout their realms were
followed by priests who interested themselves in carrying the
gospel to the conquered Indians. To the Protestants, the New
World offered freedom from persecution; to the Roman Catholics, an opportunity for the extension of Christianity to be-
nighted heathen. The rivalry of these two phases of the religious motive had thus far left New England untouched except
for Rosier's fleeting reconnaissance during the Waymouth
voyage, but the warfare between them was soon to influence the
directions of colonial ventures hereabouts to a degree that was
to become even more significant than the commercial impulse.
The roots of this unchristian warfare are to be found in the religious history of France and of England in this period, and it

is not within the function of this book to review them. It is sufficient for our purposes to note that Roman Catholicism was increasing its influence in both countries, that the effect of this in France was to produce a wave of enthusiasm for Jesuit missions and in England to harass further the Puritan sects. These tendencies, already afoot, were to motivate settlements by both Jesuits and Puritans in New England and were to reach the height of their rivalry in the later French and Indian Wars, which were in their New England phases almost as much religious wars as international ones.

The Puritans were scarcely a factor in New England prior to 1620. All of the English voyages that we have reviewed were manned so far as we know principally by good Church of England men. The crosses erected by Waymouth and his "Pentecost Harbor," were in essence no more heretical than the paternosters that Champlain presented to the Indians of Boston. There is some evidence, as we have indicated, that Rosier, who chronicled the Waymouth voyage, was himself a Roman Catholic following instructions from Rome to investigate the opportunities in Maine for a refuge for English Papists. But if this was his intention, there was no evidence in the Sagadahoc story to suppose that it bore fruits. Richard Seymour, the colony's preacher, was apparently a good Anglican, along with the other officers of that northern plantation. Surely the New England Indians were subjected to no more heretical doctrine than that of the Anglican faith, unless through unchronicled contacts with Huguenot fishermen from the west of France.

But the French Roman Catholic interests now initiated a bid for control of northern New England, starting from a base at Port Royal, the abandoned Acadian colony of de Monts and Champlain. We remember that Port Royal was evacuated in 1607. Through a series of political exigencies in France, Champlain and de Monts had removed their fur-trading activities to Quebec. Since then Port Royal had lain fallow, untended by any save the friendly Micmac Indians. Its title had passed to the Sieur de Poutrincourt, whose affection for the place had maintained his interest in it. Henri IV had confirmed this grant, making his ownership of it secure. Through three long years in France Poutrincourt waded through lawsuits and the settling of his affairs in an attempt to renew the colonial undertaking. It was in this interval that the Jesuits began to gain strong influence at the French court. When in the beginning of 1611 Poutrincourt was finally ready to set sail with a new group of colonists, he found himself saddled with royal instructions to take a missionary along with him. The motive of saving of souls was to be combined with his commercial enterprise. The Jesuit Pierre Biard, professor of theology at Lyons, was the man designated to accompany the expedition.

Poutrincourt was a good Roman Catholic, as had been Champlain and de Monts before him, but he foresaw difficulties in the intrusion of the powerful Society of Jesus upon his private commercial venture. He therefore arranged matters in such a way that a priest of his own choosing sailed with him from Dieppe in February, 1611, leaving the indignant Father Biard waiting futilely at Bordeaux for a ship that never came. So began a source of friction that echoed in the subsequent years of the colony.

Poutrincourt saw to it that baptisms were carried out wholesale among the Micmacs from the moment of his arrival at Port Royal. He was clever enough to appreciate that his political fences needed rebuilding as much as the buildings and furnishings of his long-abandoned settlement. In July, his eighteen-year-old son Biencourt carried back to France a glowing report of Christian awakening among the heathen Indians of Nova Scotia.

Meanwhile Henri IV had been assassinated. In his place reigned infamous Marie de Medici, as regent for her imbecile son. "Coarse scion of a bad stock, false wife and faithless queen, paramour of an intriguing foreigner, tool of the Jesuits and of Spain," Parkman calls her. Needless to say, Biencourt found matters in a mess. Madame de Guercheville, indefatigable supporter of the Jesuits and lady of honor to the queen, had bought out a controlling interest in Port Royal and in the Quebec venture as well, and all Canada was now to be a Jesuit mission. Biencourt's ship was outfitted by Jesuit money and sailed back to Port Royal bearing Father Biard and another Jesuit, Enemond Massé, to begin activities in Acadia. One can imagine the consternation of Poutrincourt and the triumph of Biard, face to face on the landing stage of the little settlement. Poutrincourt soon sailed back to France in an attempt to readjust his shattered fortunes, leaving to his capable young son the thankless task of co-ordinating the spiritual and temporal functions of the colony.

Our narrative of the New England voyage that follows is derived wholly from Father Biard's letter, written from Port Royal to his superiors, dated January 31, 1612. From other evidence it is known that quarrels were frequent between the two elements in the Port Royal group, but these must be left to the imagination in the sauve narrative at our disposal. Biard gives apparently full credit to the high character and diplomacy of young Biencourt, and we must assume that there was in the character of both men admirable restraint and high courage, if only from the fact that the voyage was able to accomplish so much under the above circumstances. The leaders of all the French enterprises in New England command respect for their powers of leadership.

"I have been on two journeys with M. de Biencourt," writes Biard, "one of perhaps a dozen days, the other of a month and a half, and we skirted all the coast from Port Royal to Kinibequi, west-southwest." The longer of these seems to have occurred in the months of October and November, 1611, and we may therefore place it as in the year following Argall's reconnaissance of Penobscot Bay, and probably in the same season with Harlow's discreditable kidnapings from Monhegan to Nantucket. Pont Gravé's son was at the same time trading in the Bay of Fundy, and Biard makes it clear that there were English fishermen at Monhegan. Biard tells of yet more in the continuation of his letter: "We entered the large rivers, Saint John,

Saint Croix, Pentegoet [Penobscot], and the aforesaid Kinnibequi; we visited the French, who wintered here this year in
two places, on the river St. John, and on the St. Croix; the
men from St. Malo on the St. John, Captain Plastrier on the St.
Croix." Thus we have here casual evidence of six distinct groups
of vessels on the short coast from Port Royal to Monhegan in
this 1611 season, *three of them spending the winter!* This is
surely striking testimony to the degree of development of semi-
permanent French trading posts just outside New England
shores. We have no knowledge that any Englishman had wintered on these coasts up to this period, with the single exception
of the Sagadahoc colony. But Frenchmen had wintered on the
Bay of Fundy through the seasons of 1604 to 1607 inclusive,
and again here in this season of 1611–1612.

"Returning from that river St. John," goes on Father Biard,
"our way was directed toward the Armouchiquoys." The Jesuit
thus refers to the Indians about the Kennebec rather than to
Champlain's "Almouchiquois" of the Saco area. "For this two
chief reasons actuated M. de Biencourt; the first to receive news
of the English and to know whether he could get the better of
them; the second to barter for grain with the Armouchiquoys, to
help us pass the winter without starving, in case we received no
relief from France.

"To understand the first reason, you must know that a
little before, Captain Platrier of Honfleur, before mentioned,
wishing to go to Kinibequi, was taken prisoner by two English
ships, which were at an island called Emmetenic [Monhegan],
eight leagues from the aforesaid Kinibequi. His release was obtained by means of some presents (so called for appearance sake)
and the promise which he made to submit to the commands
given him, not to trade on that entire coast. For these English
pretend to be masters of it, and to this intent produce letters of
their king, which we however believe to be forgeries."

This passage is of interest to us as indication that "these
English" here referred to must have carried copies of the Plymouth Company patent of 1606. If so, then these were not

ordinary fishermen or unlicensed traders, for such could hardly have been supposed to "produce letters of their king." All this suggests that these were Popham or Gorges men at Monhegan. Or was this an unrecorded escapade of the Southampton-sponsored Edward Harlow voyage? In any event, it was the opening gun of a century and a half of conflict on the coasts of Maine.

Biard continues: "Now M. de Biencourt, having heard all this from the very lips of Captain Platrier, earnestly pointed out to these people how it was incumbent on him, officer of the crown and lieutenant of his father, and also on every good Frenchman, to resist this usurpation of the English so obstructive to the rights and possessions of his Majesty. 'For,' said he, 'it is well known to all (not to go further back) that the great Henry, whom may God pardon, according to the rights acquired by his predecessors and himself, gave to M. des Monts, in the year 1604, all this region from the fortieth degree north latitude to the forty-sixth. Since this grant the aforesaid Seigneur des Monts, through himself and through M. de Poutrincourt my much honored father, his lieutenant, and through others, has often taken actual possession of the whole region, and that, too, three or four years before the English settled, or before one had ever heard anything of their claim.' This and many other things the said Sieur Biencourt recounted, encouraging his people." Scarcely could Biard or Biencourt imagine that the vexed question would need a hundred and fifty years, and three wars, to settle. Certainly at the moment, much was to be said in favor of the French view, on the basis of possession.

"As for myself," writes the priest, "I had two other reasons for undertaking this journey; the one to act as spiritual advisor to the said Sieur de Biencourt and his people; the other, to become acquainted with and see the disposition of those natives to receive the Gospel. Such then were the reasons for our expedition." We may assume from the circumstances that followed that Biard had also in mind the finding of a site for a new Jesuit mission.

"We arrived at Kinnibequi, eighty leagues from Port

Royal, the 28th of October, day of St. Simon and St. Jude, of the same year 1611. Our people immediately landed, eager to see the fort of the English; for we had heard in various ways that there was no one there. Now, as in a new thing all is fine, each one strove to praise and extol this undertaking of the English, and to relate the advantages of the place; every one said what he most valued in it. But in a few days we changed our opinion very much; for we saw that it was easy to make a counterfort which would have shut them up and deprived them of the sea and river; also that although they had been left alone, yet would they not have enjoyed the advantages of the river, since it has several other fine mouths some distance from there. Moreover, what is worse, we do not believe that for six leagues round about there is a single acre of arable land, the soil being wholly stony or rocky." The French criticism is of course justified. Anyone who has visited rugged Sabino Head and observed its bleak ledges above the sandy meadow, hemmed in by rocky islands and swift currents of the Kennebec's mouth, feels a quick sympathy for this comment of Biard's about the Sagadahoc site. The French criticism is of course that of enemies and subject to the bias thus incurred. Nevertheless, it is well justified when considered as an example of differences in approach to the colonial problem. The French looked first to military defense, and second to a food supply from the soil, the outlook of soldiers and feudal farmers. But to the English of Sagadahoc, the commodities of trade came first, exchangeable for supplies in ships from home, the merchants' attitude. Before either nation should make its foothold sure, it must learn the viewpoint of the homebuilder, self-sufficient in family units deriving livelihood from their own toil. This was the lesson now painfully being learned at Jamestown, where literally hundreds were dying for lack of that knowledge. Certainly Sagadahoc as a *site* was no worse than the St. Croix of de Monts and Champlain. Not sites, but men and their philosophies make colonies.

Biard and Biencourt now sailed up the Kennebec. "We had gone already about three leagues, and the tide ebbing **we had** anchored in the middle of the river, when suddenly we saw six canoes of the Armouchiquoys coming toward us. There were twenty-four people in them, all warriors . . . the night coming, they lodged on the other bank of the river, if not beyond the range, at least beyond the sighting of our cannon. All that night there was nothing but haranguing, singing, dancing; for such is the life of all those people when they crowd together. But since we presumed that probably their songs and dances were invocations to the Devil, in order to resist the domination of this accursed tyrant, I had our people sing some hymns of the Church, as the Salve, the Ave Maris Stella and others. But when once they had begun to sing, spiritual songs failing, they seized on the others which they knew. These in turn being exhausted, as it lies in the French nature to imitate everything, they began to mimic the song and dance of the Armouchiquoys who were on the bank, counterfeiting them so well in every respect that the Armouchiquoys kept still in order to hear them, and then our people becoming silent, they commenced again in turn. Truly it was prime fun; for you would have said that they were two choruses, which agreed very well, and scarcely could you have distinguished the genuine Armouchiquoys from the spurious." This reminds us faintly of Martin Pring's guitar episode at Plymouth in 1603. Surely the explorer's life was not entirely grim!

"Morning came, we continued our way up the river. They accompanying us, said to us if we wished some piousquemin (that is their wheat), we could easily turn to the right, and not go up river with great labor and danger; that by turning to the right, through the arm of the river which was shown to us we could in a few hours reach the great sachem Meteourmite, who would supply us with everything; that they would act as guides to us, for they too were going to make him a visit. . . . A part of them went before us, a part behind us, a part of them also with us in the vessel. Nevertheless M. de Biencourt was always on his guard and often had the longboat go before with the plummet. We had gone not further than half a league, when, coming into a great lake, the leadsmen cries out: 'Two fathoms of water, one fathom, only one fathom everywhere.' Immediately: 'Strike sail, strike sail, let go the anchor.' 'Where are our Armouchiquoys? where are they? The traitors! how well God has helped us! They had led us to the snares. Go about, go about!' We return on our track.

"Meanwhile Meteourmite, having been informed of our approach, was hastening to meet us, and although he saw us turn back he certainly followed after us. M. de Biencourt profited much by being more discreet than many of his command who were then urging him to kill all comers. For they were in a great rage and in as equally great fear; but rage made the greater noise.

"M. de Biencourt restrained himself, and in no other way receiving Meteourmite unfriendly, learned from him that there was a way by which we could get through; that, so that we might not miss it, he would send to our vessel some of his own people; that furthermore we should go to his wigwam and he would try to satisfy us. We believed him but soon thought we should repent it, for we passed such dangerous rapids and narrows that we thought we should hardly ever escape alive. In fact, in two places, some of our people cried out piteously that we were all lost. But, praise be to God, they cried out too soon." Champlain had had his difficulties also with these Hell Gate rapids, in 1605.

"Once there M. de Biencourt put on his arms to visit Meteourmite in that dress. He found him in his grand decorations of savage majesty, alone in a hut well thatched, both top and bottom, and some forty powerful men about the hut, as a bodyguard, each one having his shield, his bow and his arrows on the ground before him. Those people are no ninnies, not at all, and you can believe me.

"For my part I received that day the larger share of the embraces; for as I was without arms the most distinguished, forsaking the soldiers they seized on me with a thousand protestations of friendship. They led me into the largest of all the huts, which held at least eighty people. The seats filled, I threw myself on my knees and having made the sign of the cross recited my Pater, Ave, Credo, and some prayers; then, at a pause, my hosts, as though they understood me well, applauded in their way crying out 'Ho! ho! ho!' I gave them some crosses and images making them understand what I could. They eagerly kissed them, made the sign of the cross and, each by himself, endeavored to bring me their something. Thus passed that visit and another which I afterward made."

Here was an element in the approach to the Indian which the English traders lacked. The mystery of the ritual, recited by the unarmed priest in his black robes, must have made a powerful impression on the ingenuous Indian. Here was the seed of that blind loyalty with which the tribes were to follow French priests into scores of battles with the infidel Puritans through years of French and Indian warfare. This was the beginning of that long tragedy of annihilation through which New England Indians must pass. For here, in the person of the first of a long line of warrior priests, was the root of that loyalty to the French which spelled their doom. Throughout the length and breadth of the north country other Biards were to minister to other tribes in terms of the mysteries that the savage instinct loved, and thereby to hold them in a bond of fealty that no Puritan reasoning could ever shake. Here indeed was a new impulse, on these northern shores. These Indians were to become an obstacle to English settlement that would denude the towns of Maine of their English planters for a century, that would drive them back upon the Saco and the Piscataqua time after time. In Pierre Biard the French introduced their most powerful weapon against the English, as time would prove.

"Now Meteourmite had answered M. de Biencourt that, as for wheat, they did not have much; but that they had some skins if he wished to trade. The day of the barter having come I went away with a boy to a neighboring island to there offer up the consecrated host of our reconciliation. Our ship's people in order not to be surprised, under pretense of trading, had armed and barricaded themselves, leaving space for the savages in the middle of the deck; but to no purpose for the latter rushed on in such a crowd and with such eagerness that they immediately filled the whole vessel, all mixed up with our men. We began to cry: 'Go back, go back.' But of what avail? They also cried out on their side.

"It was then our people thought they were truly captured and already it was all clamor and uproar. M. de Biencourt has often said that many times he had his arm raised and his mouth open to shout, while giving the first blow: 'Kill, kill'; but that this consideration alone restrained him, I know not how, that I was away, and consequently if there was a fight, I was lost. God made use of this good intuition of his, not only as regards my safety but also as regards that of the whole expedition. For, as all now see clearly if this mad act had been committed, not one would have escaped and the French would have been forever in bad repute along the entire coast.

"God willed that Meteourmite and some other leaders should perceive the danger and thus withdraw their men. Evening having come and all gone away, Meteourmite sent some of his people to apologize for the insolence of the morning, affirming that the whole disturbance had come not from him, but from the Armouchiquoys; that they had also stolen from us an ax and a gamelle [a large wooden bowl], which utensil he returned to us; that this theft had displeased him so much that, immediately on discovering it, he had dismissed the Armouchiquoys; that for himself he was well intentioned and knew well that we neither killed nor beat the savages of that region, but rather received them at our table, often made the tabagi with them, smoked with them, and brought them many good things from France, for which they loved us. These people are, I believe, the greatest speechifiers in the whole world: they do nothing without much talk."

This incident places young Biencourt on the same high plane of leadership and good judgment that we noted in de Monts and Champlain at Mallebarre. Out of a difficult crisis he emerged with friendship and good will. Not like Gosnold and

Pring and Waymouth and Harlow, running away with the proceeds of crime, nor like Raleigh Gilbert, glad enough to get away with a whole skin, but coming to a friendly reconciliation without bloodshed. Here once again the French made friends with the enemy.

"But since I have mentioned the English in this place," continues Biard, "perhaps some one may wish to know about their experience, which we learned there. It is then as follows: In the year 1608 [Biard is of course in error as to this date], the English commenced to settle on one of the mouths of this river, the Kenibequi, as we said before. They had then a very honorable leader [Popham], and one who demeaned himself excellently toward the natives. They say, however that the Armouchiquoys feared such neighbors, and therefore caused the death of the aforesaid captain. These people have a way, in use with them, of killing by magic. Now in the second year, 1609 [should be 1608], the English changed their tactics under another leader [Raleigh Gilbert]. They shamelessly drove away the savages; they beat them, overburdened them, and tore them with dogs beyond all measure; consequently the poor abused people irritated at the present and divining worse things for the future, made a resolve, as the saying is, to kill the wolf's cub before he has stronger teeth and claws. Their opportunity came one day when three longboats had gone fishing. Our conspirators followed on their track, and drawing near with a fine pretense of friendship (for they thus lavish the more caresses when they plan the more treachery), they enter the boats and, at a given signal each one chooses his man and kills him with slashes of the knife. Thus eleven Englishmen were dispatched. The others, overawed, abandoned their undertaking that same year and have not followed it up since, being satisfied to come in the summer to fish at that island, Emetenic [Monhegan], which we have said was about eight leagues from the fort they had begun.

"For this reason, the abuse offered to the person of Captain Platrier by the said English having taken place on this island, Emetenic, M. Biencourt determined to reconnoiter it, and to leave there some mark of revindication. This he did, erecting on the harbor a very handsome cross bearing the arms of France. Some of his people advised him to burn the boats which he found there; but since he is mild and humane he would not do so, seeing that they were boats not of soldiers, but of fishermen."

This is an additional hint that Plastrier had encountered at Monhegan an English voyage of more or less unofficial character, for the French here distinguished between fishermen and soldiers. The erection of the cross was a curious gesture of futility under the circumstances—no doubt the English fishermen cut it down the moment the Frenchmen departed. It is also to be noted that neither French nor English apparently considered unlicensed fishing a violation of trading monopolies.

Let us return a moment to Biard's comments on the fate of the Sagadahoc colony. Of course his version of it is subject to the criticism that it is the story twice revised by enemies of the English, first by the Indians and then by Biard. It has the ring, however, of accuracy as to the death of Popham and as to the contrasting characters of Popham and Raleigh Gilbert. It is further accurate in representing the abandonment of the colony and the subsequent visits of fishing voyages to Monhegan each summer. Thus in its outline of the events it agrees very well with what little we know from other sources of the activities of the Popham and Gorges interests in the disintegrating stages of the Sagadahoc venture. What, then, must we say of the alleged cruelties to the Indians and the tale of eleven Englishmen being massacred by the Armouchiquoys? I think the best that can be said is that, judged by Raleigh Gilbert's behavior on his Kennebec River cruise in the fall of 1607, coupled with Gorges's estimate of Gilbert, the Biard story is not improbable. Nor does it seem unlikely that the death of eleven good men by Indian butchery may have been quite as strong an argument for abandonment of the venture as the settling of Gilbert's brother's English estate. The plain inference seems to be that Raleigh Gilbert lacked the splendid qualities of either his father or his noble uncle and namesake. If Biard or the Indians were determined to destroy the reputation of all the English settlers, why would they otherwise have taken the trouble to designate Popham as "honorable leader" and contrast his excellent demeanor toward the natives with the change of tactics under Gilbert? All this confirms one's original notion that Sagadahoc was a failure of leadership far more than of any other factor. Jamestown succeeded because of Captain John Smith; Sagadahoc failed for lack of his double.

"From there," goes on Biard after the Monhegan episode, "inasmuch as the season urged us on, being already November sixth, we set sail to return to Port Royal, landing at Pentegoet [Penobscot] as we had promised the savages.

"Pentegoet is a very fine river and can be likened to the French Garonne. It empties into the French Gulf [Bay of Fundy] and has several islands and rocks at the mouth; so that if you do not go up the river some ways you think it is a great bend or bay of the sea, there where you begin clearly to recognize the bend and course of a river. Its mouth is about three leagues broad, at forty-four and a half degrees from the equator. You cannot divine what is the Norumbega of the ancients if it is not this; for otherwise both the others and myself inquiring after this word and place have never been able to learn anything." This of course agrees with Champlain's comment on the same subject, and brings up memories of Thevet.

"We then, having gone upstream three leagues or more, encountered another fine river called Chiboctous [Naramisic?] which comes from the north-east to empty into this great Pentegoet. At the meeting of the two rivers there was the finest gathering of savages that I have yet seen. There were eighty canoes and a long-boat, eighteen huts and about three hundred souls." This was the Kadesquit toward which the Jesuit colony of 1613 was heading when it was diverted at Mount Desert Island. "The most prominent chief was called Betsabés, a prudent and conservative man; and in truth one often finds in these savages natural and political merits, which put to blush whoever is not shameless when, in comparison, he looks at a good share of the Frenchmen who come to these parts." This is certainly a singular tribute to the Indian by one who, more than any previous explorer, took an interest in the Indian for his soul's sake. Biard elsewhere indicates that he had no such high regard for the Nova Scotia natives. In Betsabés we recognize Champlain's friend Bessabez.

"After they recognized us they showed great joy at night, according to their custom, by dances, songs, and speeches. And we were also very glad to be in a friendly country; for among the Etchemins, such as are those here, and the Souriquois, such as are those of Port Royal, we are not on our guard any more than we are among our own domestics and, God be thanked, we have not yet fared ill by it.

"The next day I visited the savages and proceeded in my usual way, as I have related concerning Kinibequi. But this in addition here, since they having told me there were some sick ones there. I went to see them and in my character as priest, as is laid down in the ritual, read over them the gospel and prayers, giving a cross to each one to hang on his neck.

"Among others I found one stretched out near the fire, as is their custom, the eyes and face much distorted, sweating great drops from his head alone, being hardly able to speak, in a great access of fever. They told me he had been ill for four months and that from his appearance then he would not live long. Now I know not what his sickness was, whether it was periodic or not I do not know; but what is certain the second day after that I saw him in our vessel, hale and hearty, wearing his cross on his neck, and he showed his gratitude to me with a very good countenance, taking me by the hand. I had no way of speaking to him, since they were then bartering, and for this reason the deck was filled with people and all the interpreters busy. In sooth I was very glad that the goodness of God was beginning to make these poor and abandoned nations feel that there is nothing but good and prosperity in the sign of the holy and redeeming cross.

"In short, not to repeat often the same thing, both here and every where else that we have been able to talk with these poor Gentiles we have tried to impress on them some elementary conceptions of the greatness and truth of Christianity, as much as the means allowed. And to give a general summary, this is the fruit of our journey. We have begun to know and to be known; we have taken possession of these regions in the name of the Church of God, placing there the royal throne of our Saviour and Monarch, Jesus Christ, his holy altar; the savages have seen us pray, extol, enjoin by our sermons, the images and cross, the manner of living and like things; they have received the first apprehension and seeds of our holy faith, which will shoot forth and germinate abundantly some day, if it please God, when they receive a longer and better cultivation."

So ended what was commercially a dubiously successful voyage. Biencourt probably obtained a moderate cargo of beaver skins, but not sufficient to induce him or his father ever to return to Maine so far as we know. Apparently very little corn was obtained. The men returned to Port Royal to a miserable exist-ence of bickering and discontent, broken only in January, 1612, by the arrival of a small supply ship from Poutrincourt bring-ing yet another Jesuit, the lay brother Gilbert du Thet, sent out by Madame de Guercheville to take over the business affairs of the mission. Indeed as a trading venture Port Royal was already dead, for the Jesuits in France were quietly but surely ruining Poutrincourt, and the quarreling in the colony was but a prelude to the complete victory of the black-robed priests.

It is therefore as Pierre Biard's voyage that we should measure the exploration of Maine just concluded. Francis Park-man, in the classic *Pioneers of France in the New World*, takes the part of Poutrincourt in this episode, and there indeed is much in the story to draw one's sympathies that way. But in their historical perspective these events were a part of the Jesuit program in North America, of a piece with the missions that opened the Great Lakes and the Mississippi to the French. The New England phase of the movement was destined to explode grotesquely in the curious anticlimax to be discussed in our next chapter. But the villainous character of Biard which Parkman draws seems not entirely justified in the light of what the Jesuits were trying to do. These priests were shrewd, and worldly-wise, and cared little for a commercial victim of their policy like Poutrincourt. If their plans for New England had succeeded, they would have set the stage for a savage Christian empire as vast on the Atlantic seaboard as it proved to be in the north country. None of the English ever developed a talent for Indian alliance comparable to what we have seen exemplified in this Maine voyage by Pierre Biard.

What Biencourt's admirable discretion and trade in French trinkets could never achieve, the awesome mysteries and images of the priest had already accomplished among the Indians of Maine. With miracles of healing, and a Christian counterpart of their own speechifying and ritual chanting, the lone Jesuit had already begun to make of the Indians of Maine a fanatic horde that would need be annihilated as a prerequisite to any English settlement. As an omen of French conquest by the cross, this voyage represents a signal event in New England history. Pierre Biard's closing prophecy, had it been fulfilled, might have altered New England fully as much as though Champlain had founded a Quebec in Boston Harbor.

"They have received," to repeat his words, "the first apprehension and seeds of our holy faith, which will shoot forth and germinate abundantly some day, if it please God, when they receive a longer and better cultivation." Even the voluminous hopes and predictions of Sir Ferdinando Gorges could contain no more powerful portent of possible events in New England than that single sentence by the astute priest at the end of his first sally into Maine. But his extravagant boast was not to bear its fruit.

Chapter Ten

SAMUEL ARGALL AND
VIRGINIA'S CONQUEST OF MAINE, 1613

FRANCIS PARKMAN well outlines the situation at Port Royal in 1612:

"The dark months wore slowly on. A band of half famished men gathered about the huge fires of their barn-like hall, moody, sullen, and quarrelsome. Discord was here in the black robe of the Jesuit and the brown capote of the rival trader. The position of the wretched little colony may well provoke reflection. Here lay the shaggy continent from Florida to the Pole, outstretched in savage slumber along the sea, the stern domain of Nature, or to adopt the ready solution of the Jesuit, a realm of the powers of night, blasted beneath the sceptre of hell. On the banks of James River was a nest of woe-begone Englishmen, a handful of Dutch fur-traders at the mouth of the Hudson, and a few shivering Frenchmen among the snowdrifts of Acadia; while deep within the wild monotony of desolation, on the icy verge of the great northern river, the band of Champlain upheld the Fleur-de-lis on the rock of Quebec. These men were the advance guard, the forlorn hope of civilization, messengers of promise to a desert continent. Yet, unconscious of their high function, not content with inevitable woes, they were rent by petty jealousies and miserable feuds; while each of these detached fragments of rival nationalities, scarcely able to maintain its own wretched existence on a few square miles, begrudged to the others the smallest share in a domain which all the nations of Europe could hardly have sufficed to fill." So passed a year of bickering at Port Royal.

The Jesuit leadership in France, under the willing offices of Madame de Guercheville, now secured from the young king, Louis XIII, a new grant of the whole of North America, from Florida to the St. Lawrence. Bent on utilizing Poutrincourt's Acadian colony for the Jesuit purpose, they succeeded in seizing his ship in satisfaction of his indebtedness, throwing him into prison, and reoutfitting the vessel to bear a new group of colonists. Thus the veteran ship *Jonas*, which had originally carried supplies to Port Royal for Champlain and de Monts, was now drafted into the service of still a third French colonial venture. With Charles Fleury as master, she set sail from Honfleur on March 12, 1613, with 48 settlers, artisans and laborers under command of the Sieur de La Saussaye, and with him another Jesuit, Father Quentin, and the lay brother and business representative Gilbert du Thet, who had already made one trip to Port Royal. Horses and goats were included in the cargo. Touching at Lahave on May 16th, they soon arrived at Port Royal, where they found Biencourt and his followers busily searching the woods for food. Taking Fathers Biard and Massé on board, waiting only a few days for favorable winds, they set sail for Kadesquit on the Penobscot, which apparently Biard had chosen in 1611 as the site for a new mission. "But God willed otherwise," wrote Biard, "for when we had reached the southeastern coast of the Island of Manan, the weather changed, and the sea was covered with a fog so dense that we could not distinguish day from night. We were greatly alarmed, for this place is full of breakers and rocks, upon which, in the darkness, we feared our vessel might drift. As the wind did not permit us to put out to sea, we remained in this position two days and two nights, tacking sometimes one way, sometimes another, as God inspired us. Our tribulations led us to pray to God to deliver us from danger, and send us to some place where we might contribute to His Glory. He heard us, in His mercy, for on the same evening we began to discover the stars, and in the morning the fog had cleared away. We then discovered that we were near the coast of Mount Desert, an island which the savages call Pemetic. The pilot steered towards the eastern shore, and landed us in a large and beautiful harbor. We returned thanks to God, elevating the Cross, and singing praises with the holy Sacrifice of the Mass. We named the place and harbor Saint Sauveur." The ship was anchored not far from Schooner Head.

Sailors and colonists now fell into an angry discussion as to whether the term of the sailors' stay in the country should be reckoned from the landing at Lahave or from their arrival at Mount Desert. This expedition was at no point an example of the usual enlightened leadership of the French. While this argument was proceeding, Biard met some Indians with whom he had become acquainted two years before, and they urged him to settle here at Pemetic, which was "quite as good a place as Kadesquit." The Jesuits were unwilling to change their plans, until the astute natives, claiming that their sagamore, Asticou, was sick, urged the priests to go to him and baptize him into the faith, lest he burn in hell. No priest could ignore such a summons. Biard, his interpreter, and La Motte, mate of the *Jonas*, traveled in Indian canoes to the native village on the eastern shore of Somes Sound, where they found no sick sagamore, but did come on a splendid place for their settlement on Fernald's Point, opposite the Indian village. "This place," says Biard, "is a beautiful hillside sloping gently from the seashore, and supplied with water by a spring on either side. There are from 25 to 30 acres covered with grass, which in some places reaches the height of a man. It fronts the south and east. The soil is rich and fertile. The harbor is smooth as a pond being shut in by the large island of Mount Desert, besides being sheltered by certain smaller islands which break the force of the winds and waves, and fortify the entrance. It is large enough to hold any fleet, and ships can discharge within a cable's length from the shore. It is in latitude 44 and one half degrees north, a position more northerly than that of Bordeaux."

The ship was now brought in to the chosen site. "When we had landed in this place," continues the priest, "and planted the Cross, we began to work, and with the work began our disputes, the omen and origin of our misfortunes." Even the colonists themselves seem to have felt the cloud of misfortune that surrounded this expedition in every phase of its progress. "The cause of these disputes was that our captain, La Saussaye, wished to attend to agriculture, and our other leaders besought him not to occupy the workmen in that manner, and so delay the erection of dwellings and fortifications. He would not comply with this request, and from these disputes arose others, which lasted until the English obliged us to make peace in the manner I am about to relate."

How long the work and the disputes lasted we have no exact way of knowing. Biard elsewhere says that in mid-June they planted, at St. Sauveur, grain, peas, and all kinds of garden herbs. In view of the May 16th arrival at Lahave, they could not at the time of this sowing have been at Mount Desert longer than a week or two, and this is further borne out by the fact that, as we have seen above, La Saussaye "would not comply" with the request of his opponents, but immediately set about his gardening. In any case, we know that it was in May that our old friend Samuel Argall, he who had reconnoitered these shores in 1610, left Jamestown in the ship *Treasurer* of 130 tons, carrying fourteen guns and sixty men. He wrote to a friend that he was bound for islands off the coast of Maine to fish for cod, but the Virginia records prove the contrary. He bore, instead, a commission from Sir Thomas Dale, governor of Virginia, to expel the French from any settlement they might have made within the limits of King James's patents, which extended from the 34th to the 45th parallels of north latitude. This area included the whole of the coast of Maine and the southern half of Nova Scotia, in which Port Royal was situated. His ship was outfitted as a ship of war, and the justification for this lay in the terms of the London and Plymouth companies' charters, which expressly permitted either company or colony to "encounter, expulse, repel, and resist, as well by Sea as by Land, by all ways and Means whatsoever, all and every such Person and Persons, as without the especial License shall inhabit within the said Precincts and Limits of the said several Colonies and Plantations." The first instance of the enforcement of this provision of the charter had been in the case of Captain Plastrier, described by Biard in our preceding chapter. In that instance both Biard and Biencourt had apparently doubted the existence of any such charter. Any doubts the Jesuits still entertained were now to be destroyed.

For Argall, fogbound in Penobscot Bay, we may suppose sometime in the latter part of June, was approached by canoes whose occupants indicated to him by bows and flourishes that they had been talking with Frenchmen. Learning through signs that the "Normans," as all these Indians called the French, were in the neighborhood, Argall was piloted by one of the natives to the half-built settlement. Under full sail, the *Treasurer* soon was racing into the Western Way before a strong southwester, "the drums and trumpets making a furious noise." Argall's men prepared for battle. The poor deluded Indian pilot wrung his hands in shame and despair. There on the shore were four white tents on the grassy slope. The colony was utterly surprised.

"But as for us," writes Biard, "seeing this ship a long way off approaching under full sail, we never thought to question whether it was a friend or enemy, Frenchman or alien. Because of this our pilot set out in a shallop to meet them, even while the English were arming themselves. La Saussaye remained ashore, keeping most of his men there with him, while Lieutenant la Motte, Ensign Rousève, Sergeant Joubert, and all the more resolute men went aboard our ship. Thus things were arranged properly for a reception to gentlefolk.

"The English ship came in as swift as an arrow, with a favorable wind, the sails red, the English flag flying, and three trumpets and two drums making a furious din. Our pilot, who had gone to investigate, did not return to his ship because (as he said), the English had the advantage of the wind, and there-

fore he went off around an island so that he would not fall
into their hands. Our ship was thus deprived of half of its
sailors, and had for its defense only ten others in all, and of
these there were none who were versed in fighting aboard ship,
except Captain Flory, who indeed lacked neither judgment nor
courage. But he had no time to get ready, nor men to help him;
hence he could not even get up the anchor to get under way,
futile as this would have been in view of the fact that the sails
were furled. For since it was summer, and the ship was lying
in port without apprehension of peril, the sails had been hung
as awnings from the poop to the bit, so as to shade the deck,
and they could not be bent so quickly. This mischance had a
fortunate outcome, however, for our men stayed thus very well
concealed during the fight, so that the English could aim at no
one in particular with their muskets, unless he was already dead
or wounded.

"On the approach of the English, pursuant to the custom
of calling out one's identity, our men shouted their mariner's
greeting: 'O-o-o!' But the Englishmen did not reply in kind;
rather, with quite a different voice: great volleys of musketry
and a broadside of cannon. She had fourteen pieces of artillery
and sixty mariner-musketeers, who opened fire broadside, raking
the poop and the meadow, wherever our men were, in ranks and
volleys as orderly as infantrymen use on land.

"The first English broadside was terrific: the whole ship
spat flame and smoke. On our side there was only a cool response and our artillery was wholly silent. Captain Flory
shouted bravely enough: 'Fire the cannon! Fire!' but the can-
noneer was not there. Gilbert du Thet, however, who had never
been a fop or coward, when he heard this shout, and seeing no
one carry out the order, seized the match and made our gun
speak as loudly as the enemy's. The only trouble was that he
did not take aim; had he done so, he might have produced something more formidable than noise.

"After this first furious volley, the English came about and
ran up alongside with an anchor, preparing to fasten on to our

bit. Captain Flory began to pull in his anchor line in order to stop the enemy and make him veer off to the side, for he was afraid that his ship was going to be pushed on a shoal. Seeing our ship in recovery and being manoeuvered, the enemy again began attacking with musket-fire as before. In this second attack Gilbert du Thet received a musket-wound in the body and fell, stretched out on his back on the deck. Captain Flory was also wounded in the foot, and three others elsewhere, who began to signal and shout that they surrendered. It was obviously no equal fight. At this point the English got into their ship's boat in order to board. Our men inadvisedly tried to get into theirs in order to get ashore, for they were afraid of facing the victors. The English were very soon aboard our vessel, since they had not far to come, and they began firing at them in the attempt to bring them back. Frightened, two of our men threw themselves into the water, trying to get ashore, but they drowned, either because of wounds previously received, or from being shot while swimming. These were two promising young fellows, one from Dieppe, named Le Moyne, and the other, Nepveu, from the city of Beauvais: their bodies did not appear until nine days later. We found means of recovering them and giving them religious burial. Such was the story of the capture of our ship.

"The triumphant Englishman now went ashore, where our tents were, and the buildings we had just begun to construct. There he searched far and wide for our Captain [La Saussaye], saying that he wanted to see our credentials: that this country belonged to the English, and that it was for that reason that they had hurled themselves on us upon finding us there; nevertheless that if we made it clear that we were there under authority of our King, they would respect that fact, not wishing in any way to go counter to the warm alliance between our two Kings. The misfortune was that no one could find La Saussaye, and because of this the shrewd and subtle English leader took possession of his chests, skilfully picked the locks, and after finding and seizing our commissions and royal letters, put back all the other belongings in their places just as he had found them, and neatly closed the lids. The next day, when La Saussaye had returned, the English Captain, who knew his job well, received him kindly, and made preliminary inquiries of him with courteous ceremony. Then coming to the point, he asked of him his credentials in order that there should be no doubt that they were actually dealing with the instructions and authority of our great King. La Saussaye replied that his letters patent were in his chests. They brought him the chests, and before he had opened them with his keys, suggested that he examine them well to see if anyone had meddled with them. La Saussaye saw that everything was in good order, but alas, he did not find his papers there! Thereupon the English leader changed his manner and tone, becoming very severe as his role demanded. 'How is it, then,' he said, 'that you trespass here? You give us to understand that you have a commission from your King, and can't produce any evidence of it. You are treacherous pirates and free-booters worthy of death.' And from that time on he gave shares of the plunder to his soldiers, spending a whole afternoon in doing so. We on shore looked on while they made away with all our supplies, for the English left us on shore while they stayed aboard ship, appropriating our vessels to their own uses. We had two of them, that is our ship and a small bark built over here which was equipped for nine men. We were reduced to a pitiful state, but this was not the whole story. The next day they came ashore and robbed yet more of whatever we had, not all at once, but by raiding parties, and each time they landed, there was always some pillaging of our clothes and other belongings. Once they laid violent hands on two of our men and subjected them to atrocious treatment, which so frightened some of the others that they fled into the woods like poor roving animals, half-naked and without food, not knowing what would become of them.

"Now as to the Jesuits, I have said that Gilbert du Thet was downed by a volley during the battle. The English who came aboard the vessel placed him in the hands of their surgeon, both him and all the others who were wounded. This surgeon was a Catholic, and known to be such, and there was no one more kind—he did us a great many favors. But Father Biard, finding that Gilbert du Thet had been wounded, asked of the English Captain that the wounded be brought ashore, which was granted, and thus Gilbert had the means of obtaining confession, and blessing and praising God. He then died among his brothers, with the greatest resignation and devout spirit, twenty-four hours after he was wounded. He had his wish, for on leaving Honfleur, in the presence of the whole gathering he had lifted his hands and eyes toward heaven, praying to God that he should never return to France, but that he should die working for the conquest of souls and the salvation of the savages."

La Saussaye, Father Massé and thirteen others were allowed by the English to take the bark, probably a pinnace, amply provisioned, accompanied by the pilot, Bailleul, and they sailed across to Nova Scotia, where they were rescued by two French trading vessels, who returned them safely to St. Malo. Parkman rather harshly states that these men were set adrift, but it seems clear that they elected this course of action. Even Biard admits that they were given the alternative of spending a year in Virginia working out their freedom, after which they would be shipped back to France. The remainder of the prisoners were treated well, Biard again agrees, for the Jesuits were accepted at Argall's own table. Indeed Biard wrote the following estimate of Argall: "from what we have experienced since, he was a fine Captain, very wise and shrewd, but nevertheless a gentleman full of courage; his men also were not all inhumane, nor cruel against any of us." The whole company was taken to Virginia, aboard the *Jonas* and *Treasurer*. There Governor Dale at first threatened severe punishment, until Argall rather reluctantly produced the stolen credentials of the colony, whereupon the governor was content to hold them as prisoners. They were returned to England in 1614.

The governor was now aware of the existence of St. Croix and Port Royal. He promptly commissioned Argall to return to the Bay of Fundy and destroy those French footholds also. Accordingly the *Treasurer* and *Jonas* set sail in the late summer again. Biard and Quentin accompanied this expedition, probably as guides, though the English seem to have regarded Biard as a traitor to the French, which may have meant an enemy of Biencourt. Stopping at St. Sauveur the English pulled down the Jesuit cross and leveled the half-completed buildings. In this connection Biard writes of the seeds which had been planted shortly after their arrival at Mount Desert in mid-June: "three months later, that is in mid-September, we returned to see our husbandry; the wheat did not appear at all (of course it had been sown out of season), the barley was in spike, but not ripe," and so on. This helps us in estimating the brief duration of the colony, for surely two of those three months must have been occupied in the voyage to Virginia and return, and at least nine days seem to have been spent at the colony after the battle. It seems reasonable to suppose, therefore, that the St. Sauveur settlement was in existence for a matter of only about two or three weeks. La Saussaye's love of agriculture was indeed a costly error.

Proceeding to St. Croix, Argall's men destroyed the island buildings of de Monts and Champlain, which we remember had been used in 1611 by Captain Plastrier as winter quarters. Finally the buildings at Port Royal were burned, the crops uprooted, and the stock carried away. Biencourt and his men managed to keep themselves alive through a winter of misery, until rescued by a relief ship sent by Poutrincourt, who now abandoned the venture. Biencourt later returned and partially rebuilt the settlement. In Nova Scotia the impulse of trade was more deeply rooted than the religious one, and outlived it despite all obstacles.

The *Jonas*, its pinnace, and the *Treasurer*, having completed their errand of destruction, set sail for Virginia, but became separated in a storm. The pinnace with six Englishmen foundered. The *Jonas*, in command of Argall's lieutenant, Turnell, and with Fathers Biard and Quentin aboard, was forced to bear away to the Azores, and eventually made port at Pembroke in Wales, whence the two priests returned to France. Argall reached Virginia in safety, and in the following year returned the remaining French prisoners to England. After protest by the French Government, the *Jonas* was returned to France, but no further redress was ever made by the English. In lives lost during the whole adventure, the English paid a heavier price than the French, six against three, but possibly the St. Sauveur plunder can be credited as saving a few lives in Jamestown to square the issue.

From several points of view this whole episode of the Mount Desert colony and its annihilation deserves thoughtful review. In Parkman's intensely interesting and almost rollicking narrative of the affair the chief personalities are crystal clear and the dramatic qualities therefore brilliant and engaging. His is the classical literary presentation of the events, and nothing can dull the glory of his version. Biard is the arch villain of the piece and Argall only slightly less so, while poor Biencourt and Poutrincourt call up one's heartiest sympathies as the originators and rightful heirs of the project who are mercilessly imposed on. All this is patent, and inherent in the dramatic character of the story as narrative. But as history, one has to call these opinions in question.

In so far as Biard's personal characteristics are concerned, there is much to sustain Parkman's view. He was apparently willing to sell his patriotism to the English in payment for his life. He was heartily detested by both the French of Port Royal and the English of Jamestown, and came near to being murdered by Biencourt's men when Argall brought him back to Port Royal. Yet one has the strange impression that as a representative of the Jesuit ministry to the Indians he did an able piece of work. Let us grant that he was a conspirator against the traders, that he served as the ready tool of the English when his life was threatened—still he seems to have left us an impression of ability as a missionary and as an explorer. His voyage with Biencourt in 1611 seems to have been successful.

This is faint praise for the man's character, but perhaps allows him something of credit for his achievement.

For Poutrincourt and Biencourt we can have only feelings of admiration. Men of courage and of persistence, to be sure motivated by the desire for profit chiefly, they clung to a vision and failed. Had they been able to play a game of cooperation with the Jesuit power it is conceivable that they might have accomplished more, even as Champlain was doing at Quebec. Poutrincourt got off on the wrong foot with the Jesuits at the outset. Yet according to his own lights he was a worthy successor to Champlain and de Monts, though faced with intolerable and insurmountable opposition. One marvels at the hardihood with which he and his son clung to their objective.

Sir Samuel Argall, it seems to me, is in a different category from that in which Parkman places him. The historian prejudices the reader to view him almost as a pirate, and strains truth to picture him as the sort who would deliberately set men adrift in an open boat, omitting the fact that they were amply provisioned and chose that course. Is it not fairer to judge Argall as one of the last of the Elizabethan sea dogs? He was a soldier carrying out a commission. Perhaps one is prejudiced against him by his bold theft of La Saussaye's credentials. What was the man to do otherwise? The patent of King James and that of Louis were in clear conflict. The nations were not at war. International law in such matters was confused. What should the soldier do in such circumstances but to seize on the one piece of evidence by which his conduct could be questioned? Your frank pirate would never have subsequently admitted to Governor Dale that he had stolen the Frenchman's commission. He would have destroyed it and that would have been the end of the matter! But Argall, however grudgingly, admits his crime, saves his noble prisoner from the gallows. The best proof of Argall's character is in the fact that the records of the Jamestown colony mention that he was given a certificate under the seal of the colony, declaring that he had in no way exceeded the commission given him.

It is profitable to go beyond this vindication of his character and pursue somewhat further the historical significance of Argall's act. We have already indicated that, had the Jesuit plans succeeded, the subsequent history of New England would have followed a quite different course, more in consonance with the prophecy of Pierre Biard in January of 1612. Biard might then have been looked upon as some sort of a national hero. Instead, we look upon Argall as a brash but nevertheless effective savior of New England. The poor floundering Plymouth Company was wholly unable to defend its charter. It is curious in this connection to notice Lescarbot's remark that up to 1613 there was never a vessel lost in the French enterprise. This strikes us the more forcibly when we remember that the Plymouth Company's first two expeditions to Maine in 1606 were captured by pirates. Ferdinando Gorges had no more than a single small trading vessel now at his disposal. Had Jamestown not come to the rescue, it seems quite likely that New England might easily have become New France. Nowhere in England at this time were there resources available for the colonization of New England comparable to those possessed by the French Jesuits. In this situation only military force could conceivably have turned the tide. The English were exceptionally fortunate in having a sea rover of the caliber of Argall in North American waters at this juncture, for if St. Sauveur had had time to make itself impregnable, with the addition of supplies from such supporting voyages as the Jesuits could easily command, it is almost inevitable that the French would have made it impossible for a Pilgrim colony to establish itself in Massachusetts. Thus the remnant of the tradition of Drake and his sea dogs in the person of Sir Samuel Argall should be regarded as a brilliant and decisive force in the history of the English colonization of North America. To Virginia and her admiral New England owes her very existence.

This was the end of serious French colonization of New England. Up to the moment of Argall's arrival at Mount Desert, the French had decidedly the better of the argument. The progressive series of expeditions beginning with Champlain's splendid efforts, resumed by Poutrincourt and his capable young son and culminating in the disaster at St. Sauveur, should be regarded as a far more consistent and sustained colonial endeavor than the badly co-ordinated ventures of the English from Gosnold to Sagadahoc. The English had not yet proved their capacity to live and support themselves amid the rigors of the wilderness, but the French had repeatedly demonstrated their ability to do so, in however wretched circumstances. It appears as a curious anticlimax that this qualification, which would appear to us as the essential one, did not become the determining factor in the Anglo-French rivalry. Instead, what settled the matter was a curious throwback to the sea-dog tactics with which the French a hundred years earlier had been so successful against the Spaniards, and which the English under Drake and Hawkins had vastly improved upon. As so often happened in the history of the British Empire, sea power became decisive. By the same means that France lost Florida to the Spaniards, she now lost New England to the English. Here, by the same naval superiority that extended the mercantile activities of her adventurers throughout the known world, England now established her dormant claim to the coast of Maine. What neither the profit nor the colonization motive of Gorges had been as yet able to accomplish, power on the seas proved competent to defend. This was a turning point. Never again did the Jesuits attempt a settlement on these shores. And the desultory activities of French traders who subsequently appeared in Penobscot Bay must have been carried on furtively, in constant fear of raids by a British ship of war. Oh, for a Verrazano or a Cartier! Madame de Guercheville must have ground her teeth. Of what use now was her grant from Florida to the St. Lawrence? King James had set his seal upon New England!

Chapter Eleven

ADRIAEN BLOCK EXPLORES
SOUTHERN NEW ENGLAND, 1614

THE ERASURE of St. Sauveur and Port Royal from the map of northern Virginia did not quite finish Argall's work. For in the course of his return voyage from Nova Scotia in November, 1613, he seems to have observed some unexpected evidences of activity in New York Bay. Turning the *Treasurer's* prow in through the Narrows, he came upon a Dutch ship, the *Fortune*, anchored off a little colony of crude huts on Manhattan Island, and a group of men busily at work on the frame of a small "yacht." Here he found Adriaen Block and Hendrick Christiaensen, Dutch fur-trading captains, and from them he learned their story, that they had been on the point of returning to Holland with full cargoes of Hudson River furs when their second ship, the *Tiger*, commanded by Block, had suddenly caught fire and been completely destroyed. Winter was imminent, and under the circumstances they had put up some shelters against the weather, until such time as they could build themselves a little 16-ton vessel for the journey home.

Had Argall been the freebooter that some have pictured him, we may suppose that he might have seized this vessel with its valuable cargo, and turned these Dutchmen loose to forage in the woods. Instead of following such a course, something in the man made him content to reprimand the traders for trespassing on King James's territories. Fiske says he made them haul down their Dutch flag and substitute the English, and then sailed off to Jamestown. In so doing he probably made New Netherland possible. Had he been indeed a ruthless pirate, there never would have been any occasion for this chapter.

For the little yacht *Onrust* (Restless) with Adriaen Block at the helm, was destined the following summer to produce for us our first good map of southern New England. 1613 was the second successive year that Block and Christiaensen had made voyages to Manhattan, following in the track of great Henry Hudson, now three years a corpse in arctic wastes. And it was the circumstance of the burning of the *Tiger* that provided the occasion for a more leisurely examination of the surrounding shores. The Dutch worked all winter on the *Onrust*, only 44½ feet long, and in the spring of 1614 she made her trial voyage, pushing sturdily through the whirlpools of the East River, which Block so well named Hell Gate, and on into the broad reaches of Long Island Sound. We have no original narrative of this voyage, but there exists in the work of the distinguished Dutch writer Johannes de Laet, a director of the Dutch West India Company and friend of the Plymouth Pilgrims, an excellent summary of the voyage, written between 1621 and 1624. This, in conjunction with the Figurative Map of Adriaen Block, which was presented to the States-General of Holland in October, 1614, provides the substance of the chronicle that follows:

"Hellegat, as named by our people, is another river, according to the description of Captain Adriaen Block, that flows from the great bay [Long Island Sound] into the great river [Hudson], and the current according to his statement comes a distance of about thirty-seven leagues east of the great river. The two currents of the great river and the Hellegat meet one another near Noten Island [Governors]. In coming from the great river to the bay, the reaches extend east by north, and east-northeast and east-southeast, formed entirely by islands. The natives here bring on board the ships oysters, squirrels and wild ducks."

Passing eastward, Block came in the vicinity of Norwalk,

Connecticut, to "a number of islands, so that Captain Adriaen Block gave the name of Archipelagus to the group. The great bay is there about four leagues wide. There is a small stream on the main that does not extend more than half a league in from the shore, when it becomes perfectly dry. The natives here are called Siwanois, and dwell along the coast for eight leagues, to the neighborhood of Hellegat."

Block apparently missed the mouth of the Housatonic, but farther along at the present New Haven he saw the Quinipiac River, which he "called the River of Royenberch," which "stretches east-northeast, and is about a Bow-shot wide, with a depth of three and a half fathoms at high water. It rises and falls about six feet. . . . The natives who dwell here are called Quinipeys. They take many beavers, but it is necessary for them to get into the habit of trade, otherwise they are too indolent to hunt the beaver."

The *Onrust* next sailed fully sixty miles up the Connecticut River past the present site of Hartford and probably to the point where the Enfield rapids made further progress impossible. This inland voyage is described in the following terms: "Next, on the same south coast, succeeds a river named by our countrymen Fresh River, which is shallow at its mouth, and lies between two courses, north by east and west by north; but according to conjecture, its general direction is from the north northwest. In some places it is very shallow, so that at about fifteen leagues up the river there is not much more than five feet of water. There are few inhabitants near the mouth of the river, but at the distance of fifteen leagues above they become more numerous; their nation is called Sequins. From this place [Middletown] the river stretches ten leagues, mostly in a northerly direction, but is very crooked; the reaches extend from northeast to southwest by south, and it is impossible to sail through them all with a head wind. The depth of water varies from eight to twelve feet, is sometimes four and five fathoms, but mostly eight and nine feet. The natives there plant maize, and in the year 1614 they had a village resembling a fort for

protection against the attacks of their enemies." This was at
South Windsor, just above Hartford. Apparently Block landed
here and had a meal with the Indians, for he says: "They are
called Nawaas, and their sagamore was then named Morahieck.
They term the bread made of maize, in their language, *leganick*.
This place is situated in latitude 41° 48′. The river is not navigable with yachts for more than two leagues farther, as it is
very shallow and has a rocky bottom. Within the land dwells
another nation of savages, who are called Horikans; they descend
the river in canoes made of bark. This river has always a down-
ward current so that no assistance is derived from it in going
up, but a favorable wind is necessary."

Proceeding eastward from the mouth of the Connecticut,
Block noticed the Niantic River at East Lyme, and called it
the Frisian River. Here "some trade is carried on with the natives, who are called Morhicans." At New London he sailed
into the Thames, "which our countrymen call the river of
Siccanamos after the name of the Sagimos or Sacmos; here is a
good roadstead behind a sand-point about half a league from the
western shore in two and a half fathoms water. The river comes
for the most part from north-by-east, and is in some places
very shallow, having but nine feet of water, and there is but
little current, and in other places six feet. But there are holes
with full five fathoms water, but navigation for ships extends
only five or six leagues. Salmon are found there. The people
who dwell on this river . . . are called Pequatoos [Pequots]
and are the enemies of the Wapanoos [Wampanoags]. A small
island lies to the southwest by south from this river, as the
coast runs." Here was indeed the first yacht to visit New London, and probably the only one that ever fished for salmon
there.

Block now pushed on to the eastern end of Long Island
Sound, or "Great Bay, which is situated between the main land
and some broken land or several islands." He was the first
to appreciate the insular character of Long Island. His name
for its easterly end, Fisher's Hook, was originally applied to

Montauk Point, but the name has subsequently been transferred to Fisher's Island. "In their Great Bay," writes de Laet, "are many islands both large and small, that have no particular names, so far as is known to us, except that on a chart of this quarter made some years since, several small islands at the entrance to this great bay, near Fisher's Hook, of which we shall speak presently, are named Gesellen [The Companions]. And another, called Long Island, lies over across the bay, to avoid which, when rounding Fisher's Hook, and running for the small Frisian River, one must steer to the Northwest." Thus Block seems to have given Long Island also its name. The harbor of Stonington appears in the following: "On the main land within the bay lies a curved promontory, behind which there is a small stream or inlet, which is called by our people East River since it extends toward the east."

The *Onrust* now emerged from Long Island Sound and visited "an island to which our countrymen have given the name of Block's Island, from Captain Adriaen Block. This island and Texel [the present Martha's Vineyard] are situated east by north and west by south from one another, and the distance is such that you can see both from the quarter deck when you are half way between." Block Island, as we know, had been discovered by Verrazano just ninety years previously. A curious error on the part of the geographers had in the meantime altered the name of "Louisa," which he gave it, to "Claudia," another member of the family of François I, and as "Claudia" the island had become known. Now, however, Block's name became securely attached to the island, and there is as a result no remnant, even, of a Verrazano name along our coast.

"To the north of these islands and within the main land, is situated first the river or bay of Nassau, which extends from the above-named Block's Island northeast by east and southwest by west." Like Verrazano, Block now sailed in among the islands of Narragansett Bay. "This bay or river of Nassau is very large and wide; and according to the description of Captain Block is full two leagues in width; it has in the midst of it a number of islands, which one may pass on either side. It extends inward east-north east about eight leagues, but in the rear it is not more than two petard shots wide, and has generally seven, eight, nine, five and four fathoms of water, except in a shallow at the uppermost part of the bay, at a petard shot's distance from an island in that direction, where there is but nine feet of water. Beyond this shallow we have again three and a half fathoms of water, the land in this vicinity appears very fine, and the inhabitants seem sturdy and fairly tall. They are somewhat shy, however, since they are not accustomed to trade with strangers, otherwise there are beaver and fox skins, etc., to be had, as in other places in that quarter.

"From the westerly passage into this bay of Nassau to the most southeastern entrance of Anchor Bay [Sakonnet River], the distance is seven leagues according to the reckoning of our skippers, and the course is east by south and west by north. Our countrymen have given two names to this bay, as it has an island in the center and discharges into the sea by two mouths, the most easterly of which they call Anchor Bay, and the most westerly Sloop Bay. The southeast shore of this bay runs northeast by north and north-northeast. In the lower part of the bay dwell the Wapenocks [Wampanoags], a nation of savages like the rest. Captain Adriaen Block calls the people who inhabit the west side of this bay Nahicans [Nahigansetts or Narragansetts], and their sagamore Nathattou, another chief was named Cachaquant. Towards the northwest side there is a sandy point [still called Sand Point], with a small island bearing north by west, and bending so as to form a handsome bay with a sandy bottom [Greenwich Bay]. On the end of this sandy point there is but two fathoms of water, and farther on three and three and a half fathoms, with a sharp bottom, where lies a small rocky island. From Sloop Bay, or the most westerly passage of this inlet, it is eight leagues to the Great Bay."

It is interesting to compare Block's account of Narragansett Bay with the earlier one of Verrazano. It is at once obvious that the viewpoints of the two men were quite different: Block was primarily concerned with the problems of navigation, and gives us what is actually an outline for a Coast Pilot Handbook of the region, whereas Verrazano was more immediately interested in the inhabitants and their way of life. We do learn accurately for the first time from Block, however, the names of the tribes and their approximate distribution, and indeed, considering his observations of such tribal names along the entire Connecticut and Rhode Island shore, we can add surprisingly little from subsequent colonial sources to the information he assembled in this one brief voyage. He also gives us the impression that there was little European contact with these Indians after the first three decades of the sixteenth century, and this is in accordance with what we know up to the time of Gosnold. It would be of interest to know whether the extensive villages about the Potawomut River and Sand Point, whose stone relics fill many a Rhode Island archaeologist's collection today, were flourishing at the time of Block's visit to Greenwich Bay, but he gives no sign.

It seems that it might be profitable to make comparisons between Block's description of the next area he visited, namely, Martha's Vineyard and the Elizabeth Isles, with those of Gosnold twelve years earlier. Unfortunately, from this point on our text is rather scanty, and such a comparison is quite impracticable; indeed, de Laet seems to have borrowed somewhat from voyages of other Dutch captains like Cornelis Jacobszen May and Hendrick Christiaensen, as well as from Block, in order to throw light on this region. Happily, Block's own map of 1614 is helpful here in determining the extent of his own knowledge. Reference to it reveals at once that the scantiness of the text is well borne out by the inaccuracy of the map. Martha's Vineyard and Nantucket are joined together as one island, and are placed south and west of a reduplicated and much widened Buzzards Bay, which is called "De Zuyder Zee." We are not surprised, therefore, to find some confusion in de Laet's account of these islands. He says: "Three leagues to the west of Cape Mallebarre [Champlain's old haunt on Cape Cod] lies an island about two leagues from the shore, and one league in extent or thereabout; but at a distance one might suppose that it was part of the main land; it was called by some, as I conjecture, Petockenock." This was undoubtedly Nantucket, one of whose subsidiary islands is still known as Tuckernuck. "In respect to the bearing of the coast in this quarter, I do not find it laid down in any statements of our countrymen that have come to my hands. But a number of islands lie off this coast, as, for instance, one that is commonly called by our Dutch captains, Texel; and by others, Cape Ack. It is a large island and appears white and clifflike, according to the description of Captain Cornelis Jacobszen May." This was of course Martha's Vineyard, which Captain John Smith several times refers to as Capawack. The Dutch reference to Gay Head is clear in association with their approach to Martha's Vineyard from the west. "About a league and a half from the southwest extremity of this island Texel, lies another small island, which was named by our countrymen Hendrick Christiaensen's Island [Noman's Land], and by others Marten vinger's Island. In this vicinity are likewise several small islands, called Elizabeth's Islands, which are upon the starboard side in coming from the river or bay of Nassau; and in order to run on the outside of Hendrick Christiaensen's Island, it is necessary to steer a south-east course."

These sailing directions are essentially correct as far as they go. It is not particularly surprising that a navigator leaving Narragansett Bay and sailing eastward might feel that he was entering an impenetrable maelstrom among the complex currents between the Elizabeth Islands, which form a difficult barrier even in our own day. Consequently we may visualize Block as sailing out to sea to get out of trouble, passing the end of Martha's Vineyard and observing Noman's Land offshore. He then apparently kept outside Nantucket, approaching only close enough to appreciate that it was not part of the mainland. De Laet seems to have confused the "Marten vinger" name with Noman's Land, as many another later writer did, and apparently de Laet provided the Gosnold place names in the narrative. There is no indication on Block's map that he was familiar with Gosnold's work. His map did for the first time supply us with the name "Rood Eylant," though the area to which Block applied it seems to have been somewhere on the southerly shores of Cape Cod. Abundant evidences of Champlain's explorations appear to the northward on this map, and some "shoals Of Cape Mallebarre" are indicated to the south of Nantucket.

"Our Netherland ship-masters do not quite agree about the shoals in this quarter," writes de Laet about these, "although according to some accounts there are sand banks or a reef extending out to sea in a southerly direction for the distance of thirty leagues. Not that it is very shallow for so great a distance, but only that the bottom can be reached with the lead; and there is the least depth of water eight or nine leagues off from the shore and out of sight of land [Nantucket Shoals]. The soundings are very unequal, so that one will sometimes have thirty fathoms, at one cast, and at the next only seven or eight. But on the other hand it is said by others, that no such shoals or reefs lie so far out to sea to the south of this cape, but only to the eastward of the bay or port of Malebarre. We shall leave this matter to be settled among the skippers by the more complete discoveries hereafter."

We may take this as an excellent summary of the difficulties which beset Block and other navigators in their attempts to approach Cape Cod and Nantucket from the southward. We remember how George Waymouth and even the great Henry Hudson gave up and put to sea after encountering the Round Shoals and Pollock Rip. Verrazano seems to have given them a wide berth. Thus far only the Norsemen, Gosnold, Champlain, and perhaps Edward Harlow had penetrated the waters of Nantucket Sound. These islands, which in 1602 had looked so hopeful as a site for settlement, were to lie untouched until an approach from plantations on the mainland could make them more easily accessible. In the light of these difficulties, Block contributed a good deal of information in this area that was useful. Actually, his map, so amazingly accurate along the shores to the southward, here distorted the reality, but tended to correct Edward Harlow's misleading statement in 1611 that he found "onely Cape Cod, no Ile but the maine," though we may also recall Harlow's report, in all fairness, that their "plots [maps] had much abused them." Block's map certainly must have been the first to connect up the Gosnold discoveries with the coasts to the southward, and it is significant that de Laet correctly interpreted this relationship. Juet's narrative indicated that Hudson was familiar only with Gosnold's work. Block's map suggested that he was familiar only with Champlain's. Not until this work of de Laet, written no earlier than 1621, do we find brought together for the first time the fruits of the geographic labors of all three nations on New England's shores.

For the remainder of Adriaen Block's New England voyage we have only fragmentary material. That he coasted Cape Cod, which he called Cape Bevechier, we can be sure. That he entered Massachusetts Bay and coasted its northern shore in the latitude of Salem, which the Dutch called Pye Bay, is almost equally certain from de Laet's account. Block's map would suggest that he was familiar with the inner shore of Cape Cod Bay in that he placed Dutch names on such harbors as Plymouth, which he called Cranes Bay.

De Laet's only contribution to this problem is the following, at the beginning of his chapter on the coast of New Netherland: "To understand somewhat better the situation of the coast and the shape of these countries, we shall begin somewhat farther to the north than their limits actually extend, namely at Pye Bay [Salem] as it is called by some of our navigators, in latitude 42° 30'. The distance from thence to the longitude of the Lizard [England], according to the observations and reckoning of Captain Adriaen Block, is 690 leagues or thereabout. Around the cape of this bay the ground is muddy sand; a numerous people inhabit there, who are extremely well looking, but timid and shy of Christians, so that it requires some address to approach them. From this place to a point called by the aforementioned Captain Block Cape Bevechier (from its

FIG. 10—THE FIGURATIVE MAP OF ADRIAEN BLOCK, 1614. This map was presented to the States General of the Netherlands in October, 1614, in connection with an application for trading monopolies in the area depicted. It portrays the results of Adriaen Block's exploration, together with knowledge of the work of Champlain. It is the earliest map on which Manhattan appears as an island, and the first on which the tribe of "Manhates" is located. Also, the name of "Niev Nederlandt" appears here for the first time. (Reproduced from the copy in the Phelps-Stokes collection in the New York Public Library.)

great resemblance to Bevechier, the land being cliffe-like, and not very elevated), across Wyck Bay (another bay so called by our people, extending to the southeast) [Massachusetts Bay], the distance is twelve leagues, and the course to the northwest by west and southeast by east. The coast trends from this cape, in the first place northwest and southeast for five leagues, and then north by east and south by west for six leagues, to another sandy point. From the latter to Cape Malebarre, the distance is nine leagues, and the direction of the coast northeast by north and southwest by south. This cape was also called by our countrymen Flat Hook; the surf breaks very much upon the point at its extremity, although there is three fathoms water at low tide, so that there are treacherous currents, rendering the navigation dangerous to those who are not acquainted with them." Flat Hook, on Block's map, is identified with the site of the modern Chatham. In the above description of the easterly shore of Cape Cod, de Laet seems to add another description of the easterly projections of Cape Cod, first discovered by Gosnold, which the ocean has subsequently devoured.

Block's map gives the name "Wyngard's Hook" to Cape Ann, "Broken Hook" to Kittery Point, and "Schoonhaven" to Portsmouth Harbor, outside which the cluster of the Isles of Shoals appears. "Graf Hendrick's Bay is applied to some harbor south of Cape Ann, and "Cos Haven" to another in the vicinity of Boston. Both these harbors are filled with islands. Massachusetts Bay is here called "De Noord Zee" and Cape Cod Bay appears as "Staten Bay." Cape Cod on the map is called not "Cape Bevechier," but "Staten Hook." As above noted, Plymouth is "Cranes Bay."

The question here arises whether the Dutch may have applied their fanciful names to areas which they had not in fact explored, in the hope that they might thus lay claim to regions beyond the extent of their voyages. No perfectly reliable answer can be given to this problem, but de Laet's naïve statement at the beginning of his chapter that he is describing territory "somewhat farther north" than the New Netherland limits "actually extend," is a hint that the Dutch did not lay serious claim to these territories. It will become apparent in our next chapter that there was a small fleet of French and English vessels fishing and trading in the neighborhood of Monhegan and even along the Massachusetts coast in the spring of 1614, and it seems likely that the appearance of a Dutch vessel in that area for any length of time would not have avoided mention in the voluminous chronicle of Captain John Smith, who was there that summer, and records the presence of French and other English ships. De Laet says that it was Block who calculated the distance from Pye Bay to the Lizard, and the Figurative Map certainly suggests by its accuracy that Block did explore Massachusetts Bay rather thoroughly. As one follows the map northward, the first place name that is not Dutch is Champlain's Chouacoet, in Saco Bay. It seems to me quite likely that Block extended his voyage about as far as the Isles of Shoals before turning back down the coast to rejoin Christiaensen. Block seems to have returned to Cape Cod, and there encountered Christiaensen in the *Fortune*, which had likewise been exploring northward from Manhattan. Block turned the *Onrust* over to Cornelis Jacobszen May, a mate of the *Fortune*, and Block and Christiaensen proceeded to return to Holland in the *Fortune*. The *Onrust* was used in later explorations in Delaware Bay.

We may imagine that during the voyage home Block and Christiaensen got their heads together over Block's notes, and produced a master map of their combined experiences. Inasmuch as we have no knowledge of Christiaensen's voyage from Manhattan to Cape Cod, we can give no estimate of his contributions to the Figurative Map, except to note that it was deemed fitting to give his name to Noman's Land. In any case the map was finished and presented as a part of Block's report to the newly organized Amsterdam Trading Company, and by the company to the States-General in an application for a trading monopoly in the new "unoccupied" region lying between Virginia and Canada. This monopoly was granted for a period of three years, and the name "New Netherland" applied to a region extending from Philadelphia to Eastport, Maine. Subsequently the claim was shortened to include only the coast from the Delaware River to Pye Bay.

Adriaen Block ranks highest as the discoverer of Long Island and Connecticut. The caliber of his geographical work in the *Onrust* along that coast and up the rivers was comparable with that of Champlain in Maine and Massachusetts. While we have no narrative from his pen, we can appreciate from the painstaking detail of his observation that he was both capable and bold. The voyage up the Connecticut River must take rank with Champlain's work on the Penobscot as an enterprise of audacity and calm judgment. Aside from the dangers of navigation inherent in that inland voyage, which were considerable, one must credit the man with confidence in his ability to circumvent the perils of Indian hostility, and yet return with as good a knowledge of the natives as he seems to have obtained. We are the losers in having none of the human details of his voyage. There is nowhere any suggestion of the difficulties encountered, and de Laet's dispassionate narrative is really so restrained as in some ways to conceal the magnitude of the achievement.

In Rhode Island and Massachusetts, Block's efforts were a repetition of work that had gone before. It was probably less detailed as the distance separating him from Manhattan increased. But if indeed Adriaen Block entered "Cranes Bay," then he was the third European navigator to look upon the site of a Plymouth yet to be. Curiously enough two other captains, Englishmen, were severally visiting that harbor during the same season, and how it was that Captain John Smith or Thomas Hunt failed to sight the *Onrust* in Massachusetts Bay that summer of 1614 is one of those curious matters of history that are stranger than fiction. Nor is it less a coincidence that Smith and Block were at the same time preparing maps of Massachusetts Bay, and that, while Block was presenting his New Netherland to the States-General of Holland, John Smith was in consultation with Prince Charles of England over his chart of New England. Thus while Samuel Argall had thrust the French from one end of New England, he had failed to eliminate the Dutch from equal competition with the English at the other end. Adriaen Block had set in motion another problem for Northern Virginia which fifty years would not suffice to solve.

Chapter Twelve

CAPTAIN JOHN SMITH,
NEW ENGLAND'S RALEIGH, 1614

1. Smith's Colonial Policy for New England

WITH CAPTAIN JOHN SMITH, the preparatory period of New England's history entered a completely new phase. Rarely has there been a more striking example of the power of one forceful personality to reverse the trends of an unpromising situation than in the instance of Smith's impact on the New England of 1614. Since 1498 there had been thirty recorded voyages to these shores by five nations. Of these the Spanish and Portuguese had early withdrawn of their own volition, leaving the territory to be worked over by the French and English, with the Dutch only recently making their appearance as challengers. The English had made twice as many voyages to this area as the French, and had succeeded, at least for the moment, in ejecting the French. Yet matters were as much in the doldrums among English promoters of overseas enterprise as among the French. Indeed, we have become convinced that the French pioneers in Maine and Nova Scotia had had, until the naval defeat of 1613, rather the better of the argument. The one promising wave of enthusiasm that had propelled the Popham group to Maine in 1607 had proved to be of disappointingly short duration, and was not followed by any resumption of colonial initiative on the part of Englishmen. Champlain's abandonment of the area, on the contrary, had led to a second wave of Jesuit enterprise that had required resort to military violence to quell. But military coups do not build colonies, and as yet no organized move to counter the French colonial effort had appeared even distantly on any English horizon.

Curiously enough, such a constructive impulse was now developing in the mind of one man whose forcefulness was to prove equal to the occasion where organizations were wanting. In the face of an England which had decided that New England's climate was unfavorable for habitation; in defiance of the bankruptcy of the Plymouth Company; and despite the discouragement of its only persistent sponsor, Ferdinando Gorges, Captain John Smith was to bring about the colonization of New England. He was his own explorer, geographer, historian and promoter in this enterprise, and the only element he did not himself provide was the band of colonists, though he came close to accomplishing this also. He set the scene unaided; circumstance provided the planters.

There grew up in America during the nineteenth century a strangely distorted legend about Captain John Smith which was unfortunately abetted by some of our most eminent historians. In the popular mind still, Smith's name is inextricably tangled with the dubious and sentimental myth of Pocahontas. Smith's obviously political exaggeration of this myth for his own purposes was made the starting point of a painstaking analysis of all his Virginia writings by assiduous historians, who would never think of applying such tests of textual accuracy to a modern political speech. Yet Smith always wrote as a candidate for office. The result was to draw around all his work a mantle of suspicion and distrust that is quite undeserved. Such illustrious historians as Charles Deane and Henry Adams busied themselves about this character-wrecking pursuit. While there is much to sustain their objections to Smith's handling of the Pocahontas story, they succeeded, in the process, in destroying the validity of Smith's whole work in the mind of the general public. We should attempt to judge John Smith not by his self-aggrandizing statements, but rather by what he accomplished.

I do not propose to enter further into this controversy. It needs mention in this place, however, because of the much-neglected fact that Smith was fully as important to the history of New England as he ever was to Virginia. Neither the Pocahontas story nor the more involved controversies over the merits of the early presidents of Jamestown Colony have any conceivable bearing on Smith's New England activities except as they have succeeded in submerging the value of those activities. Most biographies of Smith practically ignore his New England work. In attempting here to throw light on this phase of his career, we have a new opportunity to evaluate the man without recourse to the doubts that surround his Jamestown experiences. We can start fresh. Let us try to divorce ourselves from our historical preconceptions about Smith and look at him anew, and with the same eyes with which we have esteemed other explorers on this shore.

Smith's work in the New England field occupied the most mature period of his life. He gave seventeen years of unremitting and poorly rewarded effort to the promotion of colonization in New England; yet I know of no more than three New England monuments to his memory: those at Cohasset, Massachusetts, the Isles of Shoals, and on Monhegan Island. He came to the New England coast the first of any of its explorers to have had previous experience in the practical problems of colonization. His first years in Virginia, regardless of how one may look upon his leadership there, had been a schooling that had sharpened his eye to the requirements of a new country to be a proper site for planters. We shall see whether his work bears the mark of good judgment and caution with which such schooling should have endowed him.

Writing in 1615 his *Description of New England*, he began:

"In the month of April, 1614, with two ships from London, of a few Marchants, I chanced to arrive in New-England, a parte of Ameryca, at the Ile of Monahigan, in 43½ of Northerly latitude; our plot was there to take Whales and make tryalls of a Myne of Gold and Copper. If those failed Fish and Furres was then our refuge, to make our selves savers howsoever. We found this Whale-fishing a costly conclusion: we saw many, and spent much time in chasing them; but could not kill any: they beeing a kinde of Jubartes [Blackfish] and not the Whale that yeeldes Finnes and Oyle as wee expected. For our Golde, it was rather the Masters device to get a voyage that projected it, then any knowledge hee had at all of any such matter. Fish and Furres was now our guard: and by our late arrival, and long lingering about the Whales, the prime of both those seasons were past ere wee perceived it; we thinking that their seasons, served at all times: but wee found it otherwise; for, by the midst of June, the fishing failed. Yet in July and August some was taken, but not sufficient to defray so great a charge as our stay required. Of dry fish we made about 40,000 of Cor-fish about 7,000."

Smith thus began his chronicle by suggesting that his voyage had been a financial failure. So far was he in his opening paragraph from glossing over his deficiencies that he actually presented the reader with a rather ludicrous picture of what might, with some justice, be termed a wild-goose chase. He brought his emphasis pointedly and quickly to focus on the somewhat disappointing fact that profit was chiefly to be expected in this new country from fish and furs, and even the fish gave out unless one fished in the right season. If this man was truly the mountebank we have been led to believe, then perhaps he had not yet warmed to his subject.

"Whilest the sailors fished," he continued, "Myself with eight or nine others of them [that] might best bee spared: Ranging the coast in a small boat, wee got for trifles neer 1100 Bever skinnes, 100 Martins, and neer as many Otters: and the most of them within the distance of twenty leagues.

"We ranged the Coast both East and West much furder; but Eastwards our commodities were not esteemed, they were so neare the French who affords them better: and right against us in the Main was a ship of Sir Francis Pophammes, that had there such acquaintance, having many years used onely that porte, that the most parte there was had by him. And 40 leagues westwards were two French ships, that had there a great voyage by trade; during the time we tryed those conclusions, not knowing the Coast, nor Salvages habitation." All these observations ring true against the background of the previous voyages. It is interesting to learn that French trading vessels were still active despite Argall's conquest and that the prices of furs were rising among the Maine Indians as contrasted with the inhabitants of the coasts to the westward.

"With these Furres, the Traine [oil], and Cor-fish, I returned for England in the bark: where within six months after our departure from the Downes, we safe arrived back. The best of this fish was solde for five pound the hundreth, the rest by ill usage betwixt three pound and fifty shillings.

"The other Ship staied to fit herselfe for Spaine with the dry fish; which was sould, by the Sailers reporte that returned, at forty ryalls [20 shillings] the quintall, each hundred weighing two quintalls and a halfe."

This summary of the commercial aspects of the voyage completed, Smith launched out into a discussion of what he knew of the historical and geographical background of the New World, and gave as his excuse for this "because I have beene so oft asked such strange questions" about the new countries. In the course of this discussion he acknowledged his debt to the writings of De Soto, Sir Walter Raleigh, Bartholomew Gosnold and "Captaine Waymouth of Pemmaquid." But he complained: "I have had six or seven severall plots [charts] of those Northern parts, so unlike each to other, and most so differing from any true proportion of resemblance of the Country, as they did mee no more good then so much waste paper, though they cost me more. It may be it was not my chance to see the best; but least [lest] others may be deceived as I was, or throgh dangerous ignorance hazard themselves as I did, I have drawn a Map from Point to Point, Ile to Ile, and Harbour to Harbour, with the Soundings, Sands, Rocks and Land-marks as I passed close aboard the Shore in a little Boat; although there

FIG. II.

FIRST ISSUE OF CAPTAIN JOHN SMITH'S MAP OF NEW ENGLAND, 1614

—the foundation of New England cartography. After his return from Virginia in 1609, Smith devoted himself to the exploration of New England. He sailed thither with two vessels in 1614, and on his return presented Prince Charles a map of the coast from Penobscot to Cape Cod. He made three later but unsuccessful attempts to revisit New England—two in 1615, and one in 1617. The following map represents the place-names as altered by Prince Charles after the *Description of New England* (London, 1616) was written.

Continued on page 242

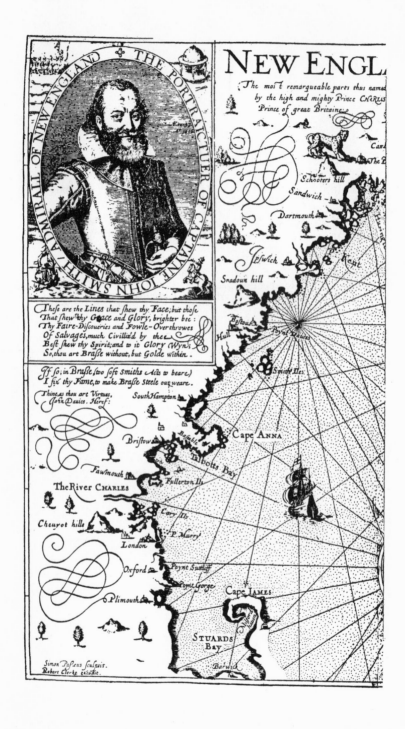

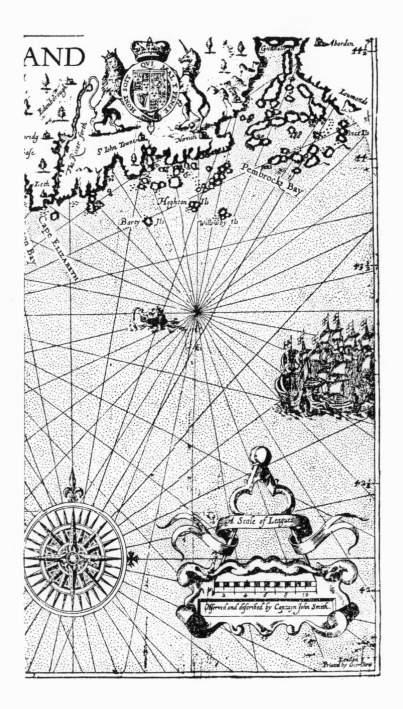

AND

QVI

HONI SOIT QVI MALY PENSE

Edinburgh

bridg
chase

Leth

St Iohn Towne

The River fonts

Cape ElizABeth

on Bay

Gudhullt an

Aborden

Lowmondes

Dutch Ils

Norich

Pembrock Bay

Heghton Ils

Barty Ils

Willowby Ils

44½

44

43½

43

42½

42

A Scale of Leagues

2   4   8   10

Obserued and described by Captayn Iohn Smith.

London
Printed by Geo Low

FIRST ISSUE OF CAPTAIN JOHN SMITH'S MAP OF NEW ENGLAND, 1614–*Continued*

Smith provides the list of changed names as follows:

The Old Names	The New
Cape Cod	Cape James
Chawum	Barwick
Accomack	Plimouth
Sagaquas	Oxford
Massachusetts Mount	Chevit Hill
Massachusetts River	Charles River
Totant	Fawmouth
Naemkeck	Bastable
Cape Trabigzanda	Cape Ann
Aggawom .	Southampton
Passataquack	Hull
Accominticus	Boston
Mount Sassanowes	Snowdon Hill
Sowocatuck	Ipswitch
Bahana	Dartmouth
Aucocisco's Mount	Shooters Hill
Aucocisco	The Base
Aumoughcawgen	Cambridge
Kinebeck	Enenborough
Sagadahock	Leeth
Pemmaquid	S. Johns Towne
Monahigan	Barties Iles
Sagocket	Norwich
Matinnack	Willowby's Iles
Metinnicus	Hoghtons Iles
Mecadacut	Dumbarton
Pennobscot	Aborden
Nusket	Lowmonds

(Map reproduced from the copy in the Phelps-Stokes collection in the New York Public Library. List of names from *Works of Captain John Smith*, ed. Edward Arber, Birmingham, 1884.)

be many things to be observed which the haste of other affairs did cause me omit. For being sent more to get present commodities then knowledge by discoveries for any future good, I had not power to search as I would; yet it will serve to direct any that should goe that waies, to safe Harbours and the Salvages habitations. What marchandize and commodities for their labours they may finde, this following discourse shall plainly demonstrate."

With this modest appraisal he introduced a map which for accuracy of detail and clarity of presentation far surpassed that which it took Champlain two seasons to produce in essentially the same area. Yet Champlain's sole task was to act as geographer, whereas Smith, like Adriaen Block, was primarily concerned in pursuing the fur trade. Smith betrays no indication of any familarity with Champlain's map. This is one of many instances that can be cited of Smith's characteristically indefatigable energy. As we have already suggested, Smith could derive more benefit from an unpromising situation than most men could from the most favorable circumstances. There will be further occasion for remarking on what extraordinary significance Smith managed to draw from the events of this one voyage. Had he done nothing more than produce this map he would have made of his voyage a signal achievement. It is the more unfortunate that Prince Charles saw fit to deface this map by replacing all Smith's accurately placed Indian place names with English names to suit his own fancy. Happily Smith's list of twenty-four of the original Indian equivalents has been preserved.

By way of introduction to further details about New England, our explorer next set down a patient little essay attempting to explain to his insular British reader how big America actually was, and why progress in colonization had proceeded so slowly. "It is not a worke for every one," he wrote, "to manage such an affaire as makes a discoverie and plants a Colony. It requires all the best parts of Art, Judgement, Courage, Honesty, and Constancy, Diligence and Industrie to doe but neere well. Some are proper for one thing then another; and therein are to be imployed: nothing breedes more confusion then mis-placing and misimploying men in their undertakings. Columbus, Cortez, Pitzara, Soto, Magellanes, and the rest served more than a prentiship to learne how to begin their most memorable at-tempts in the West Indies: which to the wonder of all ages successfully they effected, when many hundreds of others farre above them in the worlds opinion, beeing instructed but by relation, came to shame and confusion in acts of small moment, who doubtless in other matters, were both wise, discreet, gen-erous and couragious. I say not this to detract anything from their incomparable merits, but to answer those questionlesse questions that keep us from imitating the worthiness of their brave spirits."

There is a paragraph that we shall do well to pause and con-sider. This man starts talking about colonies before he even describes for us his own discoveries! For after dispensing with his commercial report in four brief paragraphs, and his splendid map in one, he here proceeds to put his finger on the weakest link in the whole English colonial problem. This is the first time that any New England chronicler has so much as men-tioned the technical problems of settlement. Even Champlain neglected to do so, and we may look long and vainly through the annals of all the previous English expeditions to this coast for any mature consideration of how the personnel of a planta-tion should be adapted to the local problems. But in Smith we are confronted with a man of experience in such undertakings, and his insight into the problem was keen enough to come to grips with the real issue. It is on men, not circumstance, that success hinges. Not only by scholarship but by *apprenticeship* must men be trained for colonial enterprise, and the men must be chosen to fit their employments! I venture to say that there were not a dozen men in England at this period who under-stood that fact as fully as Smith here expressed it. Certainly Gorges and Francis Popham, in their isolation, needed that knowledge if ever they were to succeed in their ambitions.

The Jamestown colony had learned it only by the bitterest of experience, among planters unfitted for planting.

Proceeding to his descriptive details, Smith began: "That part we call New England is betwixt the degrees of 41 and 45; but that parte this discourse speaketh of, stretcheth but from Pennobscot to Cape Cod, some 75 leagues by a right line distant each from other: within which bounds I have seene at least 40 severall habitations upon the Sea Coast, and sounded about 25 excellent good Harbours: in many whereof there is anchorage for 500 sayle of ships of any burden; in some of them for 5000. And more then 200 Iles overgrowne with good timber, of divers sorts of wood, which doe make so many harbours as requireth a longer time then I had, to be well discovered.

"The principall habitation Northward we were at, was Pennobscot. Southward along the Coast and up the rivers we found . . ." and there follows a list of twenty-eight Indian villages and eleven Indian tribes. From among the place names given we can clearly recognize the following familiar names: Pennobscot, Mecadacut (Megunticook), Pemmaquid, Nusconcus (Muscongus), Kenebeck, Sagadahock, Aucocisco (Casco), Accominticus (Agamenticus), Passataquack (Piscataqua), Aggawom, Naemkeck (Naumkeag), Massachuset, Pocapawmet (Ponkapoag), Quonahassit (Cohasset), Accomack (Plymouth), Pawmet (Pamet), and the Isle Nawset. Without any research into Indian dialect whatever, here are seventeen verifiable names out of Smith's twenty-eight, which are notable for their accuracy despite the difficulties in setting down a new language in English letters, and these are without exception given in the text in the proper order from north to south that they appear along the New England shore. An examination of the Smithsonian *Handbook of American Indians* reveals that three more of Smith's twenty-seven—Segocket, Aumoughcawgen, and Chawum (Sowams, or Pokanoket)—were confirmed by evidence from deeds or later sources. No more than six of all these seem to have been recorded by previous writers. How many of the remaining eight names would succumb to more knowledge of

Algonkian dialect than is available to me is conjectural, but it is interesting that all of the eight are, according to their order in the series, in the area swept by the great plague of 1616, and may therefore have disappeared before the Pilgrim migration appeared to preserve their names. Smith's map indicates that Sagoquas may have been Scituate, and Totant, Salem, Massachusetts. This constitutes obviously an amazing score of accuracy in the recording of place names in an alien tongue during so short a visit, and surpasses in detail the similar achievements of either Champlain or Adriaen Block. Smith even gives a correct summary of the tribal confederations under the Massachusets and Pokanokets. All this is further evidence of the intensity of Smith's powers of specific and honest observation. He has here provided in the evidence of his own work the best possible answer to those who consider him an arch liar and falsificator.

He next turned his attention to the general character of the various parts of the coast: "From Pennobscot to Sagadahock this coast is all Mountainous and Iles of huge Rocks, but overgrowen with all sorts of excellent good woodes for building houses, boats, barks, or shippes; with an incredible abundance of most sorts of fish, much fowle, and sundry sorts of good fruites for man's use.

"Betwixt Sagadahock and Sawocatuck [Champlain's Chouacoet, Saco Bay] there is but two or three sandy Bayes, but betwixt that and Cape Cod very many: especially the coast of the Massachusets is so indifferently mixed with high clayie or sandy cliffes in one place, and then tracts of large long ledges of divers sorts, and quarries of stone in other places strangely divided with tinctured veines of divers colours." In these latter we recognize the conspicuous dikes that decorate the granite ledges of Cohasset and Scituate. Smith was plainly delighted with the Massachusetts Bay shores, for he went on to say about this region: "And surely by reason of those sandy cliffes and cliffes of rocks, both which we saw so planted with Gardens and Corne fields, and so well inhabited with a goodly, strong and well proportioned people, besides the greatnesse of the

Timber growing on them, the greatnesse of the fish, and the moderate temper of the Ayre (for of twentie five, not any was sicke but two that were many yeares diseased before they went, not withstanding our bad lodging and accidental diet): who can but approve this a most excellent place, both for health and fertility? And of all the foure parts of the world that I have yet seene not inhabited, could I have but meanes to transport a Colonie, I would rather live here then any where: and if it did not maintaine it selfe, were wee but once indifferently well fitted, let us starve."

This opinion of Massachusetts, in such striking contrast with that of Champlain, was probably one of the chief influences on the promulgators of the Massachusetts Bay Colony. The Pilgrims did not appear to have made a premeditated choice of Massachusetts, but their chance settlement on that shore served only to confirm Smith's outspoken opinion. Smith's book, in slightly differing form, passed through three editions in England before 1628, and must have succeeded almost singlehanded in overturning the prevalent conception of New England as an un-inhabitable, subarctic land, a notion which the Sagadahoc failure had provoked. No one but Smith held a favorable opinion of Massachusetts at this time, for Gorges and Francis Popham had continued sending their ships to the Monhegan area, which was and still is a somewhat forbidding region from the standpoint of the planter. Thus no Englishman, save possibly Gosnold, had written as attractive a picture of any portion of Massachu-setts as did Smith here of the site destined to nurture the first permanent colonies. The combination of Smith's enthusiastic approval of this region with his untiring propaganda for its settlement were therefore apparently the only available source of favorable published information to English adventurers. Could we know the substance of the discussions that went on in the inner sanctums of the Plymouth Company and of the prospective Puritan emigrators to Massachusetts Bay during this period, I have no doubt we would find that Smith's book was the chief handbook on which decisions were based. His careful assurance that the region was healthful derives its importance from the fact that Jamestown had almost been annihilated by disease bred in its swampy surroundings, a fact of which the English were only too acutely aware. Nearly a thousand colonists had died in Jamestown at this time. And the fact that he drew a definite contrast between the desirability of Maine and Massachusetts largely nullified any possible disagreement between his estimates and those of the previous expeditions. In short, for all these reasons and others which might be cited, it seems only fair to credit Smith with the choice of Massachusetts as the site for northern English colonization. If this be true, then Captain John Smith was indeed an originator and chief sponsor of the Massachusetts colonies.

The narrative now turned to a consideration of the possibilities of profit from fishing. Smith reviewed the wealth the Dutch had obtained from this lowly occupation, and argued that England would do well to turn its energies away from highly speculative and often disastrous ventures in privateering and enter, rather, the certain profit which the Dutch had steadily maintained through their fisheries. "Never could the Spaniard with all his Mynes of golde and silver pay his debts, his friends and army, halfe so truly, as the Hollanders stil have done by this contemptible trade of fish." He described how the Portuguese and the Biscay men, with expensive imported equipment, "make 40 or 50 saile yearely to Cape-blank, and Newfound Land doth yearely fraught neare 800 sayle of Ships" with fish. If these fishermen could profit in the short season afforded by the Newfoundland fishing, "why should wee doubt—but to doe much better than they, where there is victual to feed us, wood of all sorts to build boats, Ships, or Barks; the fish at our doores; pitch, tarre, masts yards, and most of other necessaries onely for making." He appeals particularly to the unemployed and debt-ridden masses of England: "Here are no hard Landlords to racke us with high rents, or extorted fines to consume us; no tedious pleas in law to consume us with their many years disputations for Justice. . . . Here every man may be master and

owner of his owne labour and land. . . . If hee have nothing
but his hands, hee may set up his trade; and by industrie quickly
grow rich; spending but halfe that time wel, which in England
we abuse in idleness."

This, I suppose, is one of the earliest examples of the "land
of opportunity" argument. Smith here shows himself a shrewd
social propagandist, and nowhere is there a more effectively
applied summary of the colonial thesis which Hakluyt and
Raleigh had been pounding away at for thirty years than in this
brief plea by Smith. Soldier of fortune that he was, the energetic
captain was probably more in touch with the temper of the
English populace than the shipmasters, with whose narratives we
have been dealing hitherto. Thus again we meet a brand of insight in Smith that peculiarly qualified him for the task of selling
the colonial idea to the English. He could appeal to an element
in the British population that the nobility and intellectuals failed
to reach. It would be interesting to know how many indentured
servants and poor debtors who came to New England after
1628 had read Smith's book and been fired by his "*every* man
may be master and owner of his owne labour and land." That
was indeed a clarion call to the masses of England.

Smith discussed the climate of New England, pointing out
that it is in the latitude of Portugal, southern France and Italy.
He could find that these latter have no advantage over New
England "but this, They are beautified by the long labour and
diligence of industrious people and Art. This is as God made
it, when he created the worlde. Therefore I conclude if the
heart and intralls of those Regions were sought: if their land
were cultured, planted and manured by men of industrie, judgement and experience, what hope is there but it might equalize
any of those famous Kingdoms?" He found the ground fertile:
"Yet I made a Garden upon the top of a Rockie Ile in 43½,
4 leagues from the Main, [Monhegan], in May that grew so well
as it served us for sallets in June and July. All sorts of cattell
may here be bred and fed in the Iles, or Peninsulaes, securely
for nothing. In the Interim, till they encrease, if need be (ob-

serving the seasons) I durst undertake to have corne enough from the Salvages for 300 men, for a few trifles." Smith had already learned how to secure corn from the Indians, in Virginia. "And if they [the savages] should be untoward as it is most certaine they are, thirty or forty good men will be sufficient to bring them all in subjection, and make this provision; if they understand what they doe." In these words Smith disposed of what we have guessed was the deterrent to Champlain's settling in Massachusetts. It was easier for Smith to face this problem, since he had had far more abundant experience with it at Jamestown than had Champlain in Nova Scotia. Smith suggested again, however, that in dealing with the Indians it was essential to have someone with experience in such matters; success depended on having those who "understand what they doe."

He contended that the fishing season, being earlier in New England, could supply a European market earlier in the year than either the Newfoundlanders or the Icelanders. He was perfectly correct in saying that in Newfoundland one must stay aboard ship, whereas in New England, "fishing before your doors, [you] may every night sleep quietly ashore with good cheare and what fires you will, or when you please, with your wives and familie." In the matter of the fur trade, he believed that "of Bevers, Otters, Martins, Black Foxes, and Furres of price, may yearly be had 6 or 7000; and if the trade of the French were prevented, many more. 25000 this year were brought from those Northern parts into France; of which trade, we may have as good part as the French, if we take good courses." Of metals, he said: "I am no Alchymist, nor will promise more than I know; which is, who will undertake the rectifying of an Iron Forge—in my opinion cannot lose," since all the raw materials were ready at hand, a strange forecast of the bog iron furnaces which began to be set up before 1700.

Smith now went into specific detail about the cost of equipping ships for the fisheries, predicting the profits to be made according to prevalent prices. He even suggested that the voyage out to New England be made profitable by carrying supplies for colonists. "This would so increase our shipping and sailors, and so employ and encourage a great part of our idlers and others that want imployments . . . that could they but once taste the sweet fruites of their owne labours doubt lesse many thousands would be advised by good discipline, to take more pleasure in honest industrie, then in their humors of dissolute idelnesse." This is a return, of course, to his economic and social argument, and likewise an accurate prophecy of what actually happened in the subsequent decades. But more than either of these, it is to be remarked as an argument appealing to those who were not afraid of hard work, "honest industrie" and "good discipline." Smith is sometimes carelessly represented as somehow a man of weak moral fiber, in keeping with his characterization as a soldier of fortune. Yet in this and similar passages he sees fit to make his argument for colonization deliberately unattractive to lazy riff raff and to undisciplined adventurers. If one can read between the lines, his statements seem to suggest that he was thinking of the Virginia experience of unwillingness on the part of courtly gentlemen and riff raff alike to do the hard manual labor necessary to the success of a plantation.

We are beginning to become aware that John Smith was no ordinary man. From the internal evidence, in the fifteen pages of his little book which we have thus far considered, it has become apparent that he has not only failed to produce more than two or three minor errors of fact, but that he has built from his facts a structure of policy for the English nation worthy of Walter Raleigh. He has marshaled theories well justified by his observations into a doctrine which he is prepared to defend and proclaim. Not only does he produce a narrative and a map, but he has a program and specific plans for carrying it out. Such a program, conceived on the ground itself, and based on an apprenticeship in Virginia, was a tremendous advance over the tortuous imaginings of the politicians who had attempted to found Sagadahoc. I do not wish to detract from the credit due the furtherers of that earlier project, but I do wish to make clear the distinction between their equipment and approach and those of Captain John Smith. The fundamental weakness in their leadership forecast their failure. Their plans did not include any sufficient provision for a steady source of income to support the colony. Smith, however, has a definite plan built on the establishment of a trade which he has already tested. For the transportaton of the planters, "The ships that go there to fish may transport the first." He estimates that about a third of the crew who man a fishing vessel even at Newfoundland are superfluous except to "serve a stage, carry a barrow, and turne Poor John," that is, do the routine work of drying the fish on the flakes ashore. Nevertheless, "they must have meate, drinke, clothes, and passage as well as the rest." Smith proposes that these men be left as permanent colonists, and the supplies which they would normally consume during the return voyage be left with them, along with fishing equipment and small boats to carry on the fishing until the ships return the next year. The second year there would be a similar saving in passage expenses, which could be put into further equipment for colonists, to be paid for if necessary by products of the new country and by the work of the planters in drying fish.

This is no doubt an oversimplification of the problem of economic security for New England colonists, and I do not mean to suggest that this was the first time that a fishing economy had been suggested. But so far as is shown in the literature of the period available to us, Smith's plan was the first published outline for a sound project which from small beginnings, without the expenditure of great sums of capital, might grow into a thriving business while founding a colony. The losses which must have accrued to the Sagadahoc adventurers were enough to frighten any sound businessman, but in this ingenious project, a foothold might be established without great risk, on the basis of a trade that many knew was profitable. Such a foothold might begin to return dividends relatively soon. Instead of involving the heavy expense of a mass migration, it afforded the chance of a self-sustaining plantation from the first or second year. This was a shrewdly designed argument to tempt the smaller investor, who had watched his wealthier colleague go bankrupt in the Sagadahoc venture, but might still accomplish the same result through simpler means. Here again Smith made a contribution to the economic thought of the period, through his insistence that in this way fisheries were the true basis for a safe colonial investment. When we remember how important the fisheries have been in the subsequent history of New England, even though no colony was planted precisely by Smith's methods, we realize how well founded was his proposal. Certainly Smith's affirmation of the opportunity of profit in New England fishing was not lost upon the ears of the fishing fraternity, for they soon began to crowd into the Monhegan region, so that Edward Winslow in 1622 was able to provision Plymouth from the spare stores of the Monhegan and Damariscove fleet. Without having more adequate means of proof than the above speculations, I am convinced that these passages in Smith's book must have been of considerable influence in persuading merchants to reconsider their former rejection of New England as a field for profitable investment. Where for ten years only an occasional ship of Gorges and Popham had carried the English flag along these shores, now rather suddenly New England began to boom. One can find no other particular reason for this development than the work of John Smith, and the burden of proof rests on the man who denies Smith the credit for this achievement. His book and map were well conceived to attract the attention of navigators, fishermen, merchants, investors, and the oppressed unemployed alike, and they could not have gone unnoticed. It is my conviction that this book was the greatest single achievement in the founding of New England.

II. John Smith's Voyage

It has become quite apparent that Smith considered his voyage of secondary importance to his notions of colonization,

and used his title *Description of New England* as a vehicle for
the promulgation of his ideas. He has up to this point described
New England only incidentally. Having got his reader through
a consideration of his plans for New England, he is now ready,
however, to "returne a little more to the particulars of this
Countrey which I intermingle thus with my projects and reasons.

"The most Northern part I was at, was the Bay of Pennobscot, which is East and West, North and South, more than ten
leagues: But such were my occasions [that] I was constrained
to be satisfied of them I found in the Bay, that the River ranne
farre up into the Land, and was well inhabited with many people; but they were from their habitations, either among the Isles,
or hunting the Lakes and Woods, for Deer and Bevers. The Bay
is full of great Ilands, of one, two, six, eight, or ten miles in
length; which divided it into many faire and excellent good
harbours." Smith does not seem to have repeated Champlain's
ascent of the Penobscot.

"On the east of it are the Tarratines, their mortall enemies; where inhabit the French, as they report, that live with
those people as one nation or family. And Northwest of Penobscot is Mecaddacut, at the foot of a high mountaine (a kind
of fortress against the Tarratines) adjoining to the high mountaines of Penobscot, against whose feet doth beat the sea [Cam-
den Hills]: but over all the Land, Iles, or other impediments,
you may well see them, sixteene or eighteen leagues from their
situation. Segocket is the next: then Nusconcus, Pemmaquid,
and Sagadahock.

"Up this River [Kennebec], where was the Westerne plantation, are Aumuckcawgen, Kinnebeck, and divers others; where
there is planted some corne fields. Along this River 40 or 50
miles I saw nothing but great high cliffes of barren Rocks, overgrowne with woods; but where the Salvages dwelt, there the
ground is exceeding fat and fertill." Smith obviously followed
Champlain, Raleigh, Gilbert and Biencourt with a fourth ascent
of the Kennebec.

"Westward of this River is the countrey Aucocisco in the

bottome of a large deepe Bay, full of many great Iles, which divides it into many good harbours." This was probably the second voyage that entered Casco Bay, since Lescarbot says that Champlain visited it in 1606.

"Sowocotuck is the next, in the edge of a large sandy Bay [Saco Bay]; which has many Rocks and Iles; but few good harbours but for Barks, I yet know.

"But all this Coast to Pennobscot, and as farre as I could see Eastward of it, is nothing but such high craggy Cliffy Rocks and stony Iles that I wondered such great trees could growe upon so hard foundations. It is a Countrie rather to affright, then to delight one. And how to describe a more plaine spectacle of desolation, or more barren, I know not. Yet the Sea there is the strangest fishpond I ever saw; and those barren Iles so furnished with good woods, springs, fruits, fish and foule, that it makes me thinke though the Coast be rockie, and thus affrightable; The Vallies, Plaines and interior parts may well (notwithstanding) be very fertile. But there is no kingdome so fertile hath not some part barren; and New England is great enough to make many Kingdomes and Countries, were it all inhabited."

With these words Smith destroyed the unduly enthusiastic estimate of the central Maine coast which Rosier's narrative of the Waymouth voyage had first produced, and no doubt confirmed the impression which the survivors of the Sagadahoc colony had brought back with them. He substantiated the former accounts of the products to be obtained there, but clearly rejected it as a primary site for colonies. In this opinion he mirrored the conclusions of Champlain, who had called this region "very poor," and, as we know, also those of Pierre Biard. Thus Smith was no apologist for the country he was promoting so actively, but rather a discriminating observer.

"As you passe the Coast still Westward, Accominticus and Passataquack are two convenient harbors for small barks; and a good Countrie, within their craggie cliffes." This sounds like York Harbor.

"Angoam [elsewhere spelled Aggawom] is the next. This place might content a right curious judgement: but there are many sands at the entrance of the Harbour; and the worst is, it is inbayed too farre from the deep Sea. Heere are many rising hilles; and on their tops and descents many corne fields and delightful groves. On the East is an Ile of two or three leagues in length [Plum Island]; the one halfe, plaine morish grasse fit for pasture, with many faire high groves of mulberie trees gardens: and there also Okes, Pines and other woods to make this place an excellent habitation, beeing a good and safe harbor." Whether Smith's Aggawom refers to Ipswich or New-buryport seems to be in some doubt; perhaps both are here severally included. Early settlers confirmed his judgment that the region was indeed "an excellent habitation."

"Naimkeak though it be more rockie ground (for Angoam is sandie) is not much inferior, neither for the harbor, nor any-thing I could perceive, but the multitude of people." Cape Ann was apparently still as heavily populated as when Champlain left it in 1606.

"From thence doth stretch into the Sea, the faire headland Tragabigzanda, fronted with three Iles called the three Turks heads: to the north of this doth enter a great Bay, where wee found some habitations and corne fields. They report a great River, and at least thirtie habitations, doe possesse this Coun-trie. But because the French had got their trade, I had no leasure to discover it." Smith's was the second expedition to learn of the Merrimac from Cape Ann Indians after having passed it. Tragabigzanda was Smith's own name for Cape Ann, deriving from an alleged experience of his in the wars of Bohemia as a younger man. Prince Charles shortly altered Smith's name for the peninsula to Cape Anna, and with a minor change so it has remained.

"The Iles of Mattahunts are on the West side of this Bay, where are many Iles, and questionlesse good harbors: and then the Countrie of the Massachusets, which is the Paradise of all those parts. For heere are many Iles all planted with corne;

groves, mulberries, salvage gardens, and good harbours: the coast
is for the most part, high clayie, sandie cliffs. The Sea Coast
as you passe, shews you all along large corne fields and great
troupes of well proportioned people; but the French, having
remained heere neere six weeks left nothing for us [but] to
take occasion to examine the inhabitants relations, viz, if there
be neer three thousand people upon these Iles, and that the River
doth pearce many daies journies the intralles of that Countrey."
Smith's description of the region around Boston is of interest
from several angles. It agrees fully with Champlain's impression
of 1605 in respect to the abundant Indian population and the
amount of land planted by the Indians. The Pilgrims, on a trading voyage to Boston Harbor in 1621, reported that all the
islands in the harbor had been cultivated within a few years.
Smith probably did not penetrate very deeply into Boston Bay,
but he did realize that there was a river emerging from its
depths, which he called the Massachusetts River, but which
Prince Charles appropriated for his own. Smith saw Blue Hill
and named it Massachusets Mount, only to have it changed by
his princely patron to Chevyot Hills. Something closely resembling Quincy Bay appears on the 1616 map, with a peninsula
which might be either of those flanking the Wollaston shore.
The crowning achievement of his visit was unquestionably his
gift to us of the name of Massachuset, of which no record exists
before Smith's visit to Boston Bay. He was, of course, also the
originator of the name "New England." His note about the six
weeks' stay of the French traders suggests that Champlain's book
had not lain unread in France and records an otherwise unchronicled discoverer of Boston. His "high clayie cliffs" well
describe Point Allerton and Peddocks Island to this day. Smith
thus added to the existing knowledge of the region around Boston several details of significance, and may be said to have influenced the later settlement of the area through his calling
attention to the fact that it was "the Paradise of all those parts."
The French had published no such impression of it.

The narrative continues: "We found the people in those

parts verie kinde; but in their furie no lesse valiant. For upon a quarrel we had with one of them, hee onely with three others, crossed the harbor of Quonahassit to certaine rocks whereby wee must passe; and there let flie their arrowes for our shot, till we were out of danger." In his later *General Historie*, Smith added: "yet one of them was slaine, and another shot through his thigh." In return for this modest mention of Cohasset, its people have erected to Smith a memorial of the event. This seems to have been his first skirmish with unfriendly natives.

"Then come you to Accomack, an excellent good harbor, good land; and no want of any thing but industrious people. After much kindnesse, upon a small occasion, wee fought also with fortie or fiftie of those; though some were hurt, and some slaine; yet within an hour after, they became friendes." This was Plymouth Harbor, to which Prince Charles was to give the name "Plimouth" six years before the landing of the Pilgrims. Martin Pring, its discoverer, had called it "Whitson Bay"; Champlain, the "Bay of St. Louis." Later Indians called it "Patuxet." This same summer, Adriaen Block had named it on his map "Cranes Bay." Yet two more roving mariners were to enter it before the advent of the Pilgrims. John Smith appears to have had a serious altercation here, which is the second pitched battle recorded in the annals of Massachusetts, unless the one just previously at Cohasset be termed such also. The only additional information Smith gives us is a reference in the *General Historie* to what seems to be the same fight, in which he says: "we tooke six or seven of their Canowes which towards the evening they ransomed for Bever skinnes." We have spoken previously of the Europeans' thievishness in the matter of canoes: Smith here seems to consider rather their strategic value. This process of securing trade through ransom for crime seems to have been a new wrinkle in New England Indian policy, though Smith had used it in Virginia. This seems to have been the first instance in our narratives in which bloodshed was followed immediately by a negotiated settlement. Champlain had been content to overlook a murder at Eastham, but had later sought revenge by slaughter at Chatham. Smith here bought off his adversaries and returned their canoes to them. While this was scarcely an atonement for the Indians who were slain, it must have left in the Plymouth natives' minds a slightly greater respect for the possibilities of fair dealings with some Europeans. Smith neither turned and fled, as so many of his predecessors had done, nor did he seek retribution in unrestrained slaughter. Apparently he was able to stop the fight before the possibilities of a truce had been made hopeless. In this we see for the first time in New England the atttitude of a man who realized that it was necessary to make terms with the natives. One may speculate as to whether this instance had any effect on the later relations of the Pilgrims with Massasoit. Unfortunately its effect was to be largely nullified by the crime of Smith's associate Thomas Hunt only a few weeks after Smith's visit to Plymouth. Of this we shall read in our next chapter.

"Cape Cod," continued Smith's chronicle, "is the next [that] presents it selfe, which is onely a headland of high hils of sand overgrowne with shrubbie pines, hurts, and such trash; but an excellent harbor for all weathers. This Cape is made by the maine Sea on the one side, and a great Bay on the other in forme of a Sickle; on it doth inhabit the people of Pawmet and in the bottome of the Bay, the people of Chawum." Prince Charles tried to change Gosnold's "Cape Cod" to "Cape James," but the new name did not stick.

"Towards the South and Southwest of this cape, is found a long and dangerous shoale of sands and rocks. But so farre as I incircled it, I found thirtie fadom water aboard the shore, and a strong current; which makes mee think there is a Channell about this shoale: where is the best and greatest fish to be had, Winter and summer, in all that Countrie. But the Salvages say there is no channell; but that the shoales beginne from the maine at Pawmet, to the Ile of Nausit; and so extends beyond their knowledge into the Sea.

"The next to this, is Capawack [Martha's Vineyard], and those abounding Countries of copper, corne, people, mineralls:

which I went to discover this last year 1615; but because I mis-carried by the way, I will leave them, till God please I have better acquaintance with them."

Before leaving the description of the voyage, Smith sum-marizes by making certain general observations which would be of use to subsequent visitors. He describes the relations of the Indians among themselves: "The Massachusets, they report, sometimes have warres with the Bashabes of Penobscot; and are not alwaies friends with them of Chawum and their alliants: but now they are all friends, and have each other to trade with so farre as they have societie on each others frontiers. For they make no such voiages as from Pennobskot to Cape Cod, seldom to Massachewset." He notes that the more southerly peoples have so much corn that they "have what they will from them of the North. But the furs Northward are much better, and in much more plentie, then Southward." One is left with the im-pression that there was more trade among the Indians them-selves than we sometimes imagine. This idea is well borne out by the presence of materials and implements from other parts of New England on Massachusetts Indian village sites. It also perhaps explains the appearance of the Pemaquid sachem, Samo-set, in the Plymouth of 1621.

Smith clearly appreciated what the prominent landmarks along the coast were. "The highest Ile is Sorico [Isle au Haut], in the Bay of Pennobskot; but the three Iles and a rock of Matinnack are much furder in the Sea. Matinicus is also three plain Iles and a rock betwixt it and Monahigan." He here con-fused Metinic and Matinicus, a not unnatural error. "Monahi-gan is a rounde high Ile, and close by it Monanis; betwixt which is a small harbor where we ride. In Damerils Iles [Damariscove] is such another. Sagadahock is known by Satquin [Seguin] and foure or five Iles in the mouth. Smyth's Iles [Isles of Shoals] are a heape together, none neere them, against Accominticus. The Three Turks Heads are three Iles seen far to Sea-ward in regard of the headland [of Cape Ann.]" For mountain land-

marks he singles out the Camden Hills, White Mountains, Agamenticus and the Blue Hills.

Smith's inventory of the products of the country, its flora
and fauna is rather more complete and accurate than either
Brereton's or Rosier's, whose lists most nearly rival his among
his predecessors. Among the "Hearbes and fruits" he included
currants, raspberries, gooseberries, plums, walnuts, chestnuts,
small nuts, pumpkins, gourds, strawberries, beans, peas, and
maize. He mentions, as did Champlain, a "kinde or two of flax,
wherewith they make nets, lines, and ropes both small and great,
verie strong for their quantities." In listing the trees he saw he
comments about New England oaks that "there is great difference in regard of the soyle where it groweth." Who has not
marveled at the contrast between the oaks of the seaside and
those of the forest? Smith's list of sea birds is a flattering index
of his ornithological knowledge—he added six species to the
lists compiled by Brereton and Rosier. Like Champlain, he took
note of the "Moos, a beast bigger than a Stagge"; and so far as
I am aware he was the first to mention the "Musquassus," or
muskrat. Of fishing he adds to his previous remarks the following: "you shall scarce finde any Baye, shallow shore, or Cove
of sand, where you may not take many Clampes, or Lobsters,
or both at your pleasure; and in many places lode your boat
if you please: nor Iles where you find not fruits, birds, crabs,
and muskles, or all of them for taking, at a lowe water. And in
the harbors we frequented, a little Boy might take of Cunners
and Pinacks and such delicate fish, at the ships sterne, more then
sixe or tenne can eate in a daie; but with a casting net, thousands when wee pleased: and scarce any place, but Cod, Cuske,
Holybut, Mackerel, Scate, or such like, a man may take with
a hooke or line what he will. And in divers sandy Baies, a man
may draw with a net great store of Mullets, Bases, and divers
other sorts of such excellent fish, as many as his Net can drawe
on shore." This accent on the ridiculous abundance of small fish
in the harbors had never been as clearly presented by any
previous explorer. It must have softened the English picture of

the hardships of settlement, at least in so far as the food supply was concerned.

There is little fault to find with any of the descriptive material which Smith has given us. We have remarked already on his striking ability to observe and record details. Had he been the arch liar we have been accustomed to think him, it is almost inconceivable that he would not have betrayed himself by willful exaggeration or pretense in this book. Yet three centuries of our accumulated experience in New England have not produced occasion for quarrel in any significant degree with his succinct picture of this coast; in fact, we treasure as a portion of our New England heritage many of the Indian place names which he was the first to record. The *Description of New England* is still accurate. Smith's map is still a source of wonder to all who behold it. But the tragedy remains that the quarrel over his veracity, in Virginia, should so long have concealed not only the man's truthfulness as to New England, but also the far more important matter of his contributions to British colonial policy. John Smith was not only an accurate observer and geographer; he laid down the specifications for Britain's economic policy in New England and devoted the rest of his life to an insistent propaganda for his idea. In this sense he was a statesman. The opponents and critics of his Virginia policy succeeded during his lifetime in casting a cloud over this fact, but in the long run Smith's persistence won, through a journalistic career that should be set down alongside those of Milton and Daniel Defoe in the same century. We should now give some attention to this later career.

III. Smith's Campaign for New England Colonization

John Smith left the New England coast on July 18, 1614, after a stay of only eleven weeks. During that brief period he had amassed a tremendous amount of information, and had become inspired with a stubborn determination to make of New England a new paradise for English planters. This determination was to prove tough enough to survive the severest reverses of his personal ambitions, and to become the dominant motive of the remainder of his life. He was only thirty-five, and was possessed, doubtless, of an egotism that repeatedly thwarted his efforts in dealing with other men. It was this egotism which had already got him into quarrels and tactless recriminations as to the forcefulness of his character and ability. He was returning to an England that was thoroughly prejudiced against his notions of New England, and indeed against the hardships of colonization generally. Moreover, political jealousies constantly assailed any constructive program in England at this period. The religious feuds of the day were beginning to interfere seriously with the efficiency of all national projects that required cooperative effort. It was thus against a discouraging background of events at home that Smith entered on the promotion of a New England colony.

"Now, returning in the Bark, in the fift of August, I arrived at Plimouth; where imparting there my purposes to my honorable friend Sir Ferdinando Gorge, and some others: I was so incouraged, and assured to have the managing their authoritie in those parts, during my life, that I ingaged myselfe to undertake it for them." Would that more information were available about those conversations with Gorges! Unfortunately there is a gap of six years in the existing letters of Gorges in this period, and we have to speculate as to the true character of their dealings. It is obvious that this was an association of the two men who, more than any other individuals in England, were enthusiastic about the settlement of "Northern Virginia." Gorges had been the mainspring of the Plymouth Company for eight years, standing forthright for the idea of New England settlement through the preliminary explorations, the tragic failures of the Sagadahoc planters, and the ensuing anticlimax of aimless trading voyages. Gorges was a gentleman possessed of an ideal which he persistently fostered, though unable or unwilling to uproot himself from his responsibilities at home in order to further it. He was a military man attached to his post as governor of Plymouth and, whether because of family ties, economic necessities or military regulations we are not aware, he never seems to have attempted a voyage to the New World. Thus Smith was in most respects his opposite, being the bachelor adventurer all his life. Nevertheless, the two men must have enjoyed in common their military background and their mutual ambitions for the new country. Certainly the meeting of these two men seemed to augur well for New England.

"Arriving at London," continued Smith, "I found also many promise me such assistance, that I entertained [contracted with] Michael Cooper the Master, who returned with mee, and others of the company." Smith went to London to settle his affairs with the merchants who had sponsored his 1614 voyage, and while there succeeded in stimulating the interest of some members of the London Company. They seem to have offered him the command of four ships for a New England expedition for fishing and trade, but because of his previous contract with Gorges and the Plymouth Company, and the added circumstance that he was now bent on colonization rather than further fishing or exploration, he declined. This refusal made him some enemies in London. That the disagreement was serious was evidenced by the fact that Cooper, Smith's chosen skipper, saw fit to break his contract and sail with the London expedition. Smith's situation in relation to the London men had probably never been very strong after his somewhat dubious quarrels in Jamestown and the partial reconciliation which must have been necessary to persuade London merchants to support the 1614 voyage was now very likely destroyed. Circumstances therefore served to cast his lot even more definitely with the Plymouth Company and Gorges. At the time this was probably to Smith's liking, for it was after all the Plymouth Company who still held the New England charter. Later events made him wonder whether his choice had been the better one.

For the poverty of the Plymouth adventurers began to display itself immediately. The four ships which Gorges was to have had ready by Christmas of 1614 were not forthcoming.

But at length early in 1615 two small vessels, one of 200 and the other of 50 tons, were made ready by the combined efforts of Gorges, Dean Sutcliffe of Exeter, a few remaining London friends and some western merchants. The plan was to have Smith settle in New England, along with sixteen men, among whom were counted Thomas Dermer and Edward Rocroft, both of whom commanded subsequent New England voyages. This was to be a modest attempt, certainly; not another Sagadahoc of a hundred planters, but more comparable to the Gosnold manner of planting. This was indeed to be an acid test of Smith's theories. The little expedition set sail bravely, but hardly had it lost sight of land when a sudden squall carried away the masts of Smith's larger vessel and he brought her limping back into Plymouth for repairs. Ferdinando Gorges must have long ago determined that any expedition of his was necessarily wrecked or taken by pirates a few times before it ever got across the ocean. It took until June 24, 1615, to get matters straightened out, and this time Smith set sail in a single little 60-ton ship. The luck of the Plymouth Company again was with them, for this ship was captured by French pirates. The French privateer captain, believing that Smith was "him that burnt their Colony in New France"—this confusion of Smith with Argall indeed was plausible—made him a virtual prisoner aboard the French vessel and let the English crew and ship go free. During several months of a piratical voyage Smith made good use of his time by writing the account of his New England travels which was later published as the *Description of New England*, from which we have quoted so extensively. Eventually the privateer anchored in a port on the west coast of France, and Smith managed to escape. Returning to Plymouth, he found that his ship had returned without accomplishing anything, and some ill-mannered members of his crew had sought to excuse some of their own misfortunes by blaming Smith, who was thought dead. With characteristic forthrightness, Smith sprang to his own defense: "The cheeftaines of this mutinie that I could finde, I laied by the heels," he wrote, and he secured written affidavits from all he could to support his side of the story. Needless to say, Smith's reputation was injured in the process, for in such circumstances gossip is far more powerful than affidavits and those "laied by the heels" probably retaliated vociferously when they could. In short, this tragicomedy of errors seemed to have put the quietus on Smith's chances of settling New England on his own account. The series of his grotesque misadventures combined with the suspicious gossip of his crew to throw discredit on his whole project, and it seemed likely that he never again would be entrusted with the leadership of an expedition. Possibly he was regarded as a Jonah more often than as a ne'er-do-well, but the effect on Smith's leadership ambitions would be as sterile in either case. The Plymouth Company continued to send out fishing and trading ships, but there did not appear to be any hope of further attempts at a John Smith colony. Any ordinary person would have judged his career as a New England promoter finished.

Smith, however, was undaunted. Had he been purely and simply a man of action, he would probably have transferred his activities to some new field. Instead, we find him exploring new means of accomplishing the same end. He prepared for publication the manuscript of the New England book he had written while a prisoner on the French vessel. He had addressed the book at its first writing to the Privy Council of England, but thinking better of his plan, he seems to have secured the attention of the young Prince of Wales, Prince Charles, and in return for the dedication of the book to him, allowed the young prince the privilege of changing the Indian names of many of the places noted on the new map, to English names of Charles's own choosing. This interesting publicity stunt, which no doubt proved flattering to the sixteen-year-old Prince, gave us the modern names of Cape Ann, Plymouth, and the Charles River. About twenty additional names conferred by the royal heir have since disappeared, half of them reverting to their original Indian titles and the remainder having acquired subsequently a new nomenclature. The text of the book was printed prior to its presentation to the prince, and so retained its original names, but the new names were engraved on the map. Published probably at Smith's own expense, this book "did much," writes James Phinney Baxter, "towards disseminating the truth regarding a country which had been under a ban since the return of the unfortunate Popham colonists." In the meantime Smith bent all his energies toward enlisting the support of other adventurers. At length, early in 1617, in spite of all the history of fiascos that had gone before, and against what we have cited as seemingly insuperable obstacles of prejudice and enmity, he succeeded in marshaling some members of the Plymouth Company, and other merchants, in the support of a new venture.

Three ships and a colony of fifteen persons were assembled at Plymouth for a new trial at settlement. Here at last it seemed that the single-minded aims of this remarkable promoter were to be realized. All preparations were completed while the little fleet waited for a favorable wind for setting out. But that wait was a long one. For three months, along with several hundred other vessels, Smith's ships lay windbound in Plymouth Harbor, the merchants growing progressively more restive at the charges for maintenance being built up as the wind held contrary, and at the end of that time, with most of the stores used up and nothing to replenish them with, the whole project had to be abandoned. Baxter says that from this time all relations between Smith and Gorges ceased, and that in the various expeditions to New England which Sir Ferdinando Gorges fostered he henceforth entirely ignored the doughty captain. He concluded that Gorges did not regard Smith "with the admiration so fully bestowed upon him by contemporaries less experienced in the knowledge of men than the more practical Father of American Colonization," which title he bestows on Gorges. In truth it did seem that every project Smith attempted went sour even before it was begun. But Gorges had lived for twelve years with the bitter realization that every project of the Plymouth Company seemed to wilt in his hands. Seven futile New England colonies had been outfitted in Sir Ferdinando's Plymouth, and of the seven, he had seen fit to entrust the last three to the leadership of Captain John Smith. The original Plymouth Company never sent another. New England was settled despite the company, and John Smith's resignation from the leadership was not a discharge, but a recognition that the merchant sponsors had exhausted their patience and their resources. Had Gorges had such a poor opinion of Smith, it is hardly conceivable that he would have repeated his appointive error three times. Indeed, in his *Briefe Relation of the Discovery and Plantation of New England*, which he published in 1622, Gorges tells of Smith's capture by the French pirates, "to the ruine of that poore Gentleman Captaine Smith who was detained prisoner by them, and forced to suffer many extremities, before hee got free of his troubles." Thus seven years after the event, Sir Ferdinando's sympathies toward Smith were still active. No, let us amend Baxter's comment and leave to both Gorges and Smith the titles which their associates conferred on them—Gorges was the governor, and Smith the admiral, of New England. As for a "Father of American Colonization," neither of these men deserves so inclusive a title; it should be reserved for that great originator Walter Raleigh.

Forced into inactivity, John Smith's busy brain began a press campaign. In 1620 and 1622 he brought out a first and a revised edition of *New England's Trials*, which added to a rewritten *Description of New England* a survey of the succeeding voyages to those shores. These books constitute unquestionably the most important existing source books for a history of New England voyages during the 1614-1622 period, and establish for Smith a place as a competent historian along with his other contributions. They were intended as further arguments for colonization, a purpose from which Smith never wavered, and in this sense they are to be considered in the same category with Purchas's work as a continuation of the tradition of Richard Hakluyt's *Voyages of the English Nation*. In 1624 appeared Smith's voluminous *General Historie of Virginia*, which is a compendium of his previous works on Virginia and New England. All these works served their purpose in stimulating the colonial impulse. No doubt they assured Smith of immortality. Most books are written for that purpose. But apart from displaying some degree of egotism, the books sold New England to a discouraged Britain. To the oppressed debtor, the unemployed, the misfit in Stuart England, torn with religious inquisition and controversy, they brought a message of hope, of escape, which went over the heads of the nobility and the merchants and presented America as a land of freedom for the common man. It is inconceivable that this appeal was not a factor in setting the Puritan migration in motion. "I caused two or three thousand of them to be printed," wrote Smith, "one thousand with a great many Maps both of Virginia and New England, I presented to thirty of the chiefe Companies in London at their Halls." Almost immediately thereafter he wrote: "Upon these inducements some few well disposed Gentlemen, and Merchants of London and other places, provided two ships," which were the *Mayflower* and the *Speedwell*.

Indeed, it is wholly fitting that we should here restate what has usually been represented as the grotesque failure of Smith's career. Outwardly the current estimate is obviously true. Everything Smith attempted failed to come off. Candidly considered, his whole life was an extravaganza. His young manhood in the wars of Bohemia reads like a fairy tale, and its details as he alone describes them are impossible of historical confirmation. His experience at Jamestown was quarrelsome in the highest degree, and ended under a cloud. Of his single short New England voyage he made a heroic exploit seemingly out of proportion to its importance as a mere trading voyage. His grotesque failures of 1615 and 1617 likewise add up to a tragic anticlimax that led to a disappointed but egotistical old age. He died in obscurity in 1631. So runs the popular fable, and its circumstances are undeniable. He was never prominent in the court circles or accepted as an equal by the great men of his day. He was an inveterate climber and was constantly butting into feuds with his associates. All these things are self-evident. What, then, remains but to cast him out as a charlatan and a faker?

I believe that, granting all of the above, the achievement that John Smith produced in connection with his one New England voyage is enough to stamp him as one of the great founders of American colonial history. He probably also saved Jamestown Colony from extinction. But let the case rest on his New England record alone. Here was a man who made of his obscure trading voyage a springboard for a great geographical discovery, a clarification of British colonial policy, and a basis for a career of effective propaganda and accurate historianship that was unexcelled in his own generation. However much he may have prevaricated about Pocahontas, his chronicle of New England is as straightforward and trustworthy in the book of 1616 as it could possibly be, and of far more use to the British nation than the work of any maritime writer since Walter Raleigh. He recorded more valuable information and made more shrewd judgments about the New England shores during his eleven weeks than all the previous explorers put together. He laid a foundation of economic practicability for New England settlement which no previous explorer had even attempted. He set the standards of craftsmanship and training necessary for the success of any colonial undertaking. He showed that one could come to terms with the native inhabitants as no one previously had been able to do. Beneath the web of self-justification and self-congratulatory poetry with which his work is cluttered, there is a philosophy whose processes are clear and of the utmost service to his nation. Finally, his faith in the soundness of his position was sufficient to keep him fighting away in an apparently hopeless cause long after his associates had foresworn his leadership.

Curiously enough, I believe that in the long run he succeeded in what he set out to do. Although all his ambitious plans for personal participation failed egregiously, even as had those of Raleigh before him, I am convinced that, like Raleigh, his ideas were the chief influence on the subsequent generation

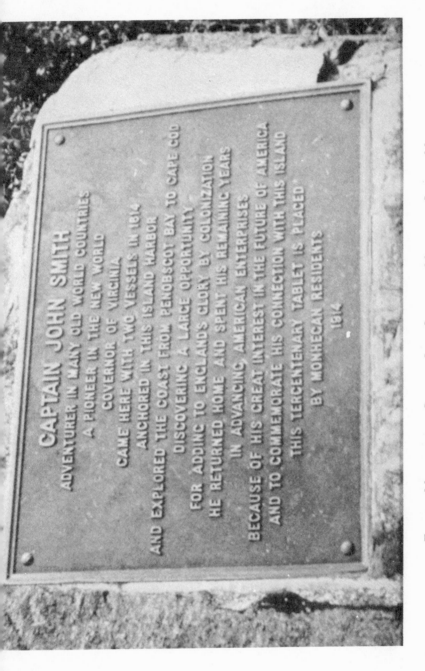

CAPTAIN JOHN SMITH
ADVENTURER IN MANY OLD WORLD COUNTRIES
A PIONEER IN THE NEW WORLD
GOVERNOR OF VIRGINIA
CAME HERE WITH TWO VESSELS IN 1614
ANCHORED IN THIS ISLAND HARBOR
AND EXPLORED THE COAST FROM PENOBSCOT BAY TO CAPE COD
DISCOVERING A LARGE OPPORTUNITY
FOR ADDING TO ENGLAND'S GLORY BY COLONIZATION
HE RETURNED HOME AND SPENT HIS REMAINING YEARS
IN ADVANCING AMERICAN ENTERPRISES
BECAUSE OF HIS GREAT INTEREST IN THE FUTURE OF AMERICA
AND TO COMMEMORATE HIS CONNECTION WITH THIS ISLAND
THIS TERCENTENARY TABLET IS PLACED"
BY MONHEGAN RESIDENTS
1914

FIG. 12—MEMORIAL TO CAPTAIN JOHN SMITH ON MONHEGAN ISLAND, MAINE.

which founded Boston in the year previous to his humble death. I feel morally certain that neither Pilgrims nor Puritans would have reached Massachusetts when they did had it not been for Smith and his *Description of New England.* His was indeed the signal individual achievement in the founding of Massachusetts. Out of the succession of disasters in his life he drew brilliant triumphs with his pen. If this is failure, what is success?

Chapter Thirteen

THE REMOVAL OF THE INDIAN MENACE

1. Declaration of War: Thomas Hunt and Nicholas Hobson

FROM THE time of the failure of the Sagadahoc Colony, the two great obstacles to English settlement of New England were the discouragement of the Plymouth Company adventurers, and the increasing apparent hostility of the Massachusetts Indians. We have seen how, almost unaided, the writings of Captain John Smith succeeded in revising the English estimate of New England as a field for commercial and colonial endeavors. This analysis involved not so much Smith's voyage in New England, as the use he made of it in influencing the state of mind of English adventurers, thus surmounting the first of the above obstacles. We should now turn our attention more directly to the developments in New England itself which bore on the second obstacle, the power of the Indians to resist colonization.

Let us review briefly the extent and character of the Indian threat to colonization up to the year 1614. I think it is fair to say that until the time of Champlain's voyage of 1606 there was strictly no New England Indian menace to settlement beyond what might be considered the normal hazard of explorers in the pursuit of trading relationships with any primitive race. This is equivalent to saying that there had been as yet no concerted attempt at colonization within the New England area. To be sure, Gosnold's voyage was bent on planting a settlement, but since it was the first voyage in a new area there was not time for the development of any momentum of antagonism among the Indians based on any previous experience. Furthermore, the impulse toward settlement in the Gosnold expedition was so weak that no real test of strength between the colonists and the natives ever arose up to the time of its abandonment. The Champlain voyage of 1606, at both Gloucester and Chatham, offered a contrast to anything that had gone before in that it involved a second visit to the same general area. The result, we remember, was a pitched battle, followed by a revenge slaughter and then abandonment of the enterprise. A Massachusetts Indian would with some justice esteem this a victory. Even the retreat from St. Croix to Port Royal would probably also appear a successful outcome to the Indians of Maine.

The Sagadahoc venture, viewed again with the Maine Indian's eye, was a serious invasion. Whether the Indian menace had anything to do with its abandonment depends on what credence one puts in Father Biard's report of his 1611 voyage as to the Indians having killed some of the Sagadahoc settlers. If his report be true, then these Indians probably believed that they had successfully rid themselves of the colony. Nonetheless, the Popham settlement was followed up by steadily increasing numbers of trading voyages in the same area, which, however profitable to individual natives, must have aroused steadily increasing fears of further encroachment in that area among the natives generally. The massacre by Hudson could only have increased this feeling further. In spite of this, the trade increased without reports of hostilities.

One important difference existed between the Massachusetts and the Maine Indians. The Maine coastal tribes were more migratory and less agricultural, and they were not numerous. As a consequence of this, they reacted less violently to the foreign threat than did the more populous farmers of Massachusetts, who, while they had no such notion of land ownership and titles as we are accustomed to, did possess and defend certain plantation areas from year to year in a communal attitude of ownership. They were, in short, a settled people among whom a threat to their geographical establishment seemed more ominous than to the natives of Maine. We recall the invitation of the Mount Desert Indians to the Jesuits to settle at Fernald's Point a few hundred yards across the water from their own village: no such invitation was ever issued in Massachusetts, so far as I am aware.

The quarrels of Champlain, Harlow and Smith with the Massachusetts natives become more understandable in the light of this reasoning. It required less provocation in Massachusetts to arouse Indian hostility than it did in Maine. Your property owner in a village has more at stake to quarrel about than your gypsy migrant who repeatedly takes what he can get in one area and then moves on. The Massachusetts Indian had his roots in Massachusetts soil, he had prospered and multiplied there, and he resented any competitor. This serves to explain, I think, Champlain's abandonment of Massachusetts, as well as the repeated setbacks suffered by English expeditions in this region. John Smith was an exception because he had dealt with agricultural Indians in Virginia and was not afraid of them. But every other English explorer who made any sustained contact with the Massachusetts Indians got into difficulties with them.

So far as Smith's participation in his 1614 voyage was concerned, there was little about it that might have prejudiced the natives against the English; indeed, we have already remarked that, at Plymouth, he was the first of the explorers to make peace after a battle, through negotiation. Where Gosnold, Pring, Champlain, and Harlow had run away after conflict, Smith had stayed to make peace. This might seem to offer a decided gain, at least at Plymouth, in the possibilities for reconciliation with the natives in the new country, had it not been for what very soon followed. Smith, we remember, had left his larger vessel at Monhegan, to pursue the fishing, under command of Captain Thomas Hunt. Within a week or two after Smith's departure from Plymouth, Hunt, himself sailing into Plymouth Harbor, in Smith's own words "betrayed twenty seaven of these poore innocent soules, which he sould in Spaine for slaves: to moove their hate against our Nation, as well as to cause my proceedings to be so much the more difficult." Smith elsewhere states that this occurrence was at Plymouth, and that "this wilde act kept him [Hunt] ever after from any more emploiment in those parts."

We get a somewhat fuller picture of this most unpleasant episode from Increase Mather, who drew much of his material from *Mourt's Relation* and other Pilgrim chronicles. "An unworthy Ship-master whose name was Hunt, being sent forth into these Coasts on the Account of the fishing Trade, after he had made his Dispatch and was ready to sail, (under pretense of trucking with them) 'enticed Indians into his vessel, they in confidence with his Honesty went aboard, to the number of Twenty from Patuxet, since called Plimouth, and seven from Nosset (now known by the name of Eastam) these did this Hunt seize upon, stowed them under Hatches, and carried them to the Straights of Gibraltar, and there did sell as many as he could of them for 20 £. to a Man until it was known whence they came; for then the Friars in those parts took away the rest of them, that so they might nurture them in the Popish religion."

In "Nosset" we recognize Champlain's Nauset Harbor or Mallebarre, where so far as we know the natives had dwelt in peace with European navigators since the last voyage of the Frenchmen eight years earlier. Thus Hunt seems to have set up two distinct focuses of antagonism on the Massachusetts coast. Even the usually mild-spoken chronicler, Samuel Purchas, termed Hunt's "Savage hunting of Savages a new and Devillish Project." In spite of the fact that Hunt's act was probably the means by which the Pilgrims' interpreter Squanto secured his European education, there is no occasion for excusing him. He unquestionably set up a chain of hostility that might for generations have put the lives of Englishmen in peril throughout the region had events proceeded normally among the Indians. In this sense there seems some justification for Smith's assertion that Hunt, for private gain, was bent on wrecking Smith's ambitions for a settlement. Possibly there was a feud between the two men. But whatever the reason, Hunt's act was a blot on the record of English navigators, and one not lightly to be dismissed. Waymouth's kidnapings had at least some semblance of justification; Hunt's were gratuitous barbarism. The episode was a setback to trade and colonization; and the fact that Hunt was never employed further in New England voyages suggests that the adventurers so considered it.

But what of the Indians' opinion of all this? The reaction seems to have been immediate. Later in this same summer of 1614, eventful already for the expeditions of Block, Smith and Hunt, still another vessel appeared in Massachusetts waters. Stimulated by the acquisition of Epenow, who we remember had been captured at Martha's Vineyard by Harlow in 1611, Sir Ferdinando Gorges had succeeded in organizing another of those voyages for trade and an attempted colony, this time in Gosnold's old territory around Martha's Vineyard. Captain Nicholas Hobson was in command of the expedition. Epenow seems to have held out canny assurances of a rich gold mine in that neighborhood, though he pretended that if his fellow-natives became aware of his having revealed that fact to the British "he was sure to have his Brains knocked out as soon as he came ashore." Gorges was apparently distrustful of the man, for he wrote: "I gave the Captain strict charge to endeavor by all Means to prevent his Escape: and for the more Surety, I gave order to have three Gentlemen of my own Kindred (two Brothers of Sturton's and Master Mathews) to be ever at hand with him, clothing him with long Garments fitly to be laid hold on if Occasion should require." However, when the expedition reached Martha's Vineyard, where earlier that same summer Adriaen Block had reported no hostilities, we get the following picture of the situation, in the language of Increase Mather: "Hunt's forementioned Scandal, had caused the Indians to contract such a mortal Hatred against all Men of the English Nation, that it was no small Difficulty to settle anywhere within their Territoryes. And whereas there were two Indians called

Epenow and Manawet, who having been carried out of these Parts of the World into England had learned to speak English, that were returned in Hobson's Vessel, as hopeing they might be serviceable to the Design on foot, it fell out otherwise; since being exasperated by what Hunt had done, they contrived with their Country-men how to be revenged upon the English. Manawet dyed within a short time after the Ship's Arrival. Epenow secretly plotted how to free himself out of the English Hands, which he effected, though with great Hazard to himself and other Salvages that were his fellow Conspirators, which came to pass after this Manner. Upon the Ship's Arrival, many of the Indians (some of them being Epenow's Kinsmen) came aboard and were kindly entertained by the Captain; at their Departure they promised to return the next day and bring some Trade with them. Epenow had not Liberty granted him to go on shore, only much Discourse and probably a contrivement for his Escape was between him and the other Indians in the Vessel which nobody but themselves could understand. The Indians returned at the Time appointed with twenty Canoos, but were shy of coming aboard. Epenow cunningly called to them as if he would have them come into the Vessel, to Trade, and suddenly did himself leap overboard: He was no sooner in the Water, but the Indians sent a Shower of Arrows into the Vessel, and came desperately near to the Ship, and (in despite of all the Musketiers aboard) went away with their Country-man Epenow. Divers of the Indians were then slain by the English, and the Master of the English Vessel and several of the Company wounded by the Indians.

"Hereupon the Captain and the whole Company were discouraged and returned to England, bringing nothing back with them, but the News of their bad Success, *and that there was a War broke out between the English and the Indians.*"

Gorges complained that the voyage was needlessly abandoned, since he had given instructions that another attempt should be made elsewhere if the first one failed. Mather remarks, however, that if the captain and others were badly wounded, there was probably good reason for the return to England. Yet another Plymouth Company venture thus came to grief, and yet more difficult became Captain John Smith's task of persuading merchants of Plymouth and Bristol to finance his 1615 voyage.

But what must one suppose was the purport of consultations on the American side of the ocean? After each harvest it was the custom of Massachusetts sachems to gather for a powwow—probably Champlain's meeting of the chiefs of Saco at Gloucester in 1606 was an example of such a conference. In the fall of the year 1614 we may imagine how many were the harangues centered about the experiences of the year. Epenow certainly was heard with greatest intentness as he described the streets of London, along which he had been paraded as a "wonder." Surely the sachems of Plymouth and Nauset and Quonahassit must have been aroused and vehement in their bitter denunciation of the English. Older heads that had witnessed the kindness of Champlain and Martin Pring must have been howled down by the relatives of men killed or kidnaped by Harlow, Hunt and Hobson. Thus far the dreaded Europeans had been successfully ejected and the power of arrows to resist muskets well proved. Yet the incursions of the visitors had steadily increased, and here had come five separate vessels, if the French reported by Smith be included, in a single summer into Massachusetts waters. And now for the first time here was one of their own who had reappeared as if from the dead from the homeland of these white traders.

"What counsel do you give us, Epenow? Is it war?" No fool was Epenow: of that he had given abundant evidence during his escape from Hobson's vessel, crying "Come aboard the Ship!" *in English* to his fellow natives while he told them to fire their arrows in the native language. Of what his recommendation was we can have no inkling, of course, but if we may speculate on the basis of the indications of his character at our command, he counseled wily and unremitting resistance to the invader wherever he appeared—perhaps a show of willingness to trade, but a jealous defense against any foothold for a settlement. "Secure weapons in trade for beaver, steal boats, acquire the means for a strong defense at any cost. Attack only in overwhelming numbers and always by surprise. Save your farm land for the Indian and under no circumstances allow this greedy race to build their houses and set up their towns among you."

We can have no proof that war was declared, but all the meager information supports that view. Unlike Virginia, Massachusetts natives had been given a dozen years in which to formulate their opinions of the newcomers, and every English explorer had brought back news of an increasingly hostile attitude. Hunt's treachery seemed to be all that was needed to destroy again the good preparations of Ferdinando Gorges and John Smith. These Indians had checkmated the French in 1606; Argall had again saved New England for the English in 1613. Were now the Indians in turn to stop the English thrust toward empire? Scarcely could these sachems in their harvest council know that within a scant eighteen months their unburied skeletons would be strewn in thousands over the untended gardens of their desolate towns.

II. Plague: The Voyage of Thomas Dermer, 1619

In 1615 there sailed Michael Cooper with four ships of the London Company. He it was who should have been John Smith's associate had Smith not already contracted with the ailing Plymouth Company. Smith's own voyage of the same year, we recall, was captured by French privateers, though his smaller vessel, perhaps skippered by Thomas Dermer, had a successful voyage and returned in August "well fraught," presumably with fish. All that we know of Cooper's voyage was that he fished at Monhegan from March until June, and that one vessel, headed with its cargo for Spain, was captured by Turks, another arrived safely in Jamestown, and the others in London.

The first records of the fishermen wintering at Monhegan appear also in 1615–1616. Richard Hawkins, president of the Plymouth Company, sailed for the Maine coast in October of

1615 and remained there until April of the next year when another vessel under command of Edward Brande found him still at Monhegan. Hawkins reported that a war was going on among the Maine tribes, and that "the principal natives were almost destroyed." Some suppose that Nahanada and Skidwares perished in this war. Hawkins went to Virginia and eventually sold his cargo of fish in Spain.

The 1615 voyage of greatest moment to our New England interest was that of Richard Vines, who also spent the winter on the Maine coast at the Saco village among the Indians. Vines seems to have been an employee of Ferdinando Gorges and had been several times to the Maine coast in previous voyages, perhaps as early as 1609. He may have spent earlier winters also on the coast, as had probably Humphrey Damerill for whom Damariscove (Damerill's Cove) is named. After the cumulative failures of Hobson and Smith in their colonization attempts under the Plymouth Company Gorges found himself unable to get other adventurers to finance his steadfast faith in repeated colonial efforts. Fishing voyages had been proved to pay well, as Smith had prophesied, but the projects for settlements were another matter. "Finding that I could no longer be seconded by others," wrote Gorges, "I became an owner of a ship myself fit for that imployment, and under colour of fishing and trade, I got a master and company for her, to which I sent Vines and others, my own servants, with their provisions for trade and discovery, appointing them to leave the ship and ship's company for to follow their businesse in the usuall place [Monhegan]."

When Vines arrived at the Saco village, the great plague among the Indians was at its height. No one knows what this disease was. It seems to have been one of the European contagious diseases to which at least adult Europeans were immune. Vines and his associates "lay in the cabbins" with the suffering savages, yet "not one of them ever felt their heads to ake while they stayed there." But the disease was so universally fatal among the Indians that "the country was in a manner left void of inhabitants" around the Saco region, which was its northern limit. Governor Bradford, writing in 1621, said that about Plymouth the Indians were "not many, being dead and abundantly wasted in the great Mortalitie which fell on all these parts about three years before the coming of the English [Pilgrims]; wherein thousands of them dyed, they not being able to bury one another. Their Sculls and bones were found in many Places lying still above the Ground, where their Houses and Dwellings had been. A very sad Spectacle to behold. But they brought Word that the Narighansets lived but on the other side of the great Bay, and were a strong People, and many in Number, living compacte together, and had not been at all touched with this wasting Plague." And so all the way from Saco to Narragansett Bay this awful pestilence swept away thousands upon thousands of the unfortunate savages. From the "Planters Plea" of 1630 comes the following: "And which is remarkable, such a Plague hath not been knowne or remembered in any age past; nor then raged 20 or 30 miles up into the land, nor seized upon any other but the Natives, the English in the heate of the Sicknesse commercing with them without hurt or danger." By a conservative estimate it is said that the Wampanoags and Massachusets, the two tribes who became the most immediate neighbors of Pilgrims and Puritans, were reduced from a population of nearly a hundred thousand to a total of about five thousand at the time of the English settlement. The disease swept a band of territory along the coast, and as the "Planters Plea" suggests, did not penetrate very far inland. The circumstances certainly indicate that some mariner aboard one of the coasting vessels, French or English, was a carrier of the disease and distributed it up and down the coast.

This theory is supported by an incident of which we have only the most fragmentary mention, and which further illustrates the warfare going on between Massachuset Indians and explorers of French as well as English origin. Thomas Morton, the jovial founder of Merrymount in the modern Quincy, wrote: "It fortuned, some few years before the English came to inhabit at new Plimouth in New England; that upon some distaste given in the Massachusetts Bay, by Frenchmen, then trading there with the Natives for beaver, they set upon the men, at such advantage, that they killed manie of them, burned their shipp, then riding at Anchor by an Island there, now called Peddock's Island in memory of Leonard Peddock that landed there (where many wilde Auckies haunted that time which hee thought had been tame), distributing them unto 5 sachems which were Lords of the severall territories adjoyninge. They did keep them, so longe as they lived, onely to sport themselves at them, and made these five Frenchmen fetch them wood and water, which is the generall worke that they require of a servant. One of these five men outlivinge the rest had learned so much of their language, as to rebuke them, for their bloudy deeds, saying that God would be angry with them for it; and that hee would in his displeasure destroy them; but the Salvages (it seemed boasting their strength) replyed and say'd, that they were so many that God could not kill them. But contrary wise in short time after, the hand of God fell heavily upon them, with such a mortall stroake, that they died on heapes, as they lay in their houses; and the living that were able to shift for themselves would runne away & let them dy and let there Carkases ly above the ground without buriall. For in a place where many inhabited, there hath been but one left alive, to tell what became of the rest, the livinge beinge (as it seems) not able to bury the dead, they were left for Crowes, Kites and vermin to pray upon. And the bones and skulls upon the severall places of their habitations made such a spectacle after my comming into those parts that as I travailed in that Forrest, nere the Massachusetts, it seemed to mee a new-found Golgotha." Thomas Dermer rescued two of these unfortunate French castaways in 1619.

It seems almost needless to point the moral of the plague. All up and down the coast, from Cape Cod to the Saco, there was laid open a band of territory ripe for English seizure. Without the plague, all the toil and losses of Gorges, Smith and the Pophams might have been in vain. The Indians were in revolt and prepared to stand their ground. Despite all the preliminary exploration, the demonstration of profitable fishing, and the widespread organization of voyages, I venture to say that the Indians of Massachusetts might have defended themselves against colonization for yet another century had it not been for the accident of measles, or scarlet fever, or whatever the disease was to which they had none of the Europeans' inherited immunity. Suddenly, within a year, their resistance in this band of territory dropped to zero. The only major obstacle to settlement just melted away.

In this situation a peculiar thing happened. In the presence of the most perfect opportunity that had been presented to the Plymouth venturers in twenty years no one was able to take advantage of it. Gorges had practically bankrupted himself, Smith was unable to get a vessel to sea, and the Plymouth Company was on the point of disintegration. During 1617 and 1618 a rather smaller group of fishermen than usual went to Monhegan. One would not have needed the equipment of Sagadahoc or its leadership to have succeeded during these years. A project of the caliber of Harlow's or of Hobson's would undoubtedly have made a go of it in Massachusetts Bay in 1618: yes, even Gosnold's fainthearted little company might have turned the trick. But no, there was no one available! I doubt if even Gorges realized what an opportunity lay before him. Smith, of course, tried, but was lying windbound in Plymouth Harbor all the summer of 1617. After that fiasco, his voyaging days were over.

Finally, after two years of idleness, a new ray of hope appeared for New England. At some time during the summer of 1618 Captain Thomas Dermer, who had been associated with John Smith in his abortive voyage of 1615, and perhaps had then made the New England voyage in Smith's smaller vessel, was living in Newfoundland. There he ran across an Indian named Squanto, who had been among those captured by Thomas Hunt at Plymouth in 1614. Squanto had in some manner been freed from the slavery into which Hunt had intended to sell him, and in some unknown way had got to London, where a certain John Slany, an officer of the Newfoundland Company, took him into his household. Eventually Squanto secured passage to Newfoundland and was now living there, apparently under the protection of Captain John Mason, the English governor of Newfoundland. Dermer immediately saw the possibilities of the situation, and secured from Captain Mason permission to take Squanto to New England as pilot for a voyage of exploration. Mason, who was a friend of Gorges, offered to do anything within his power to aid the expedition. Dermer thereupon wrote to Gorges suggesting that he send someone to meet him at Monhegan, but in the meantime on Mason's advice he set sail for England to talk the matter over with Gorges in person. Gorges received Dermer's letter before Dermer himself arrived in England, and promptly sent a Captain Edward Rocroft, also a member of Smith's 1615 company, to meet Dermer there. Rocroft accordingly reached Monhegan, and not finding Dermer he busied himself with seizing a French bark of Dieppe. Increase Mather writes: "Some of his own Ships Company conspired against him intending his Death, he having secret Intelligence of this Plot against his life, held his Peace until the Day was come wherein the intended Mischief was to be put in Execution, then unexpectedly apprehended the conspirators; he was loth himself to put any to Death, though they were worthy of it. But therefore he resolved to leave them in the wilderness, not knowing but they might discover something that might be advantageous. Accordingly he furnished them with Ammunition, and some Victuals for their present Subsistence, and turned them ashore to Socodahock [Sagadahoc] himself with the rest of his company, departing to Virginia. Those English Mutineers got over to the island of Monhegin, three leagues from the Main, where they kept themselves safe from the Fury of the exasperated Indians, until the next Spring." At Monhegan they spent the winter of 1618–1619 "with bad lodgings and worse fare." There Dermer found them when his ship arrived from England in May of 1619. Dermer now sailed southward, "searching every harbor and compassing

every cape-land to Virginia," where he found that Rocroft had
been shipwrecked and lost his life in a quarrel. Dermer's account
of this voyage, written for Samuel Purchas, is the last of the
New England narratives, preceding the voyage of the *Mayflower*.

"It was the nineteenth of May, before I was fitted for my
discovery when from Monahiggan I set saile in an open Pinnace
of five tun, for the Iland I told you of. I passed alongst the coast
where I found some ancient Plantations, not long since populous
now utterly void, in other places a remnant remaines but not
free of sickenesse. Their disease the Plague for wee might perceive the sores of some that had escaped, who describe the
spots of such as usually die. When I arrived at my Savages
[Squanto's] native Country [Plymouth] (finding all dead) I
travelled alongst a daies journey Westward, to a place called
Nummastaquyt [Middleboro], where finding Inhabitants I dispatched a messenger a dayes journey further west to Poconokit,
which bordereth on the sea; whence came to see me two Kings;
attended with a guard of fiftie armed men, who being well satisfied with that my Savage and I discoursed unto them (being
desirous of noveltie) gave me content in whasoever I demanded,
where I found that former relations were true." One supposes
that Massasoit was one of these "two kings," and inevitably one's
mind travels back to Verrazano's visit to this same region just
ninety-five years previously, and forward to Edward Winslow's
visit only two years later. "Here I redeemed a Frenchman, and
afterwards another at Mastachusit, who three years since escaped
shipwrecke at the North-east of Cape Cod." Dermer now goes
on to tell of his return to Monhegan, where he sent off his larger
ship to Virginia, again turning southward in the pinnace to
extend his explorations around Cape Cod. On the way, he left
Squanto, "who desired (in regard of our long Journey) to stay
with some of our savage friends at Sawatiquatooke [Saco]."
Thus Squanto was returned, I take it, to the coast of Maine,
whence he must have found his way back again to Plymouth,
possibly along with that Pemaquid native Samoset, who brought

him to the Pilgrims. Squanto seems to have crossed the ocean four times before getting back finally to his depopulated village. Who knows whether he, in the end, considered Hunt had done him a favor?

Dermer came near shipwreck somewhere near Cape Ann: "Wee had not sayled above forty leagues, but wee were taken with a Southerly storme, which drave us to this strait: eyther we must weather a rockie point of Land, or run into a broad Bay no lesse dangerous: *Incidit in Syllam* etc, the Rockes wee could not weather, though we loosed till we received much water but at last were forced to beare up for the Bay, and run on ground a furlong off the shoare, where we had beene beaten to pieces, had wee not instantly throwne overboard our provisions to have our lives; by which meanes we escaped and brought off our Pinnace the next high water without hurt, having our Planke broken, and a small leake or two which we easily mended. Being left in this misery, having lost much bread, all our Beefe and Sider, some Meale and Apparell, with other provisions and necessaries; having now little left besides hope to encourage us to persist: Yet after a little deliberation we resolved to proceed and departed with the next faire winde. We had not now that faire quarter amongst the Savages as before, which I take it was by reason of our Savages absence—for now almost everywhere where they were of any strength they sought to betray us. At Manamock [Monomoy] (the Southern part of Cape Cod, now called Sutcliffe Inlets) I was unawares taken prisoner, when they sought to kill my men, which I left to man the Pinnace; but missing their purpose, they demanded a ransome, which had, I was as farre from libertie as before: yet it pleased God at last, after a strange manner to deliver me, with three of them into my hands, and a little after the chiefe Sachem himselfe; who seeing me weigh anchor, would have leaped overboard, but intercepted, craved pardon, and sent for the Hatchets given for ransome, excusing himselfe by laying the fault on his neighbours; and to be friends sent for a Canoas lading of Corne, which received we set him free." No one apparently could get by Chatham without a fight. Cape Cod, being little affected by the Plague, was still possessed of hostile Indians.

"Departing hence, the next place we arrived at was Capaock [Martha's Vineyard], an island formerly discovered by the English, where I met with Epenow a Savage that had lived in England, and speakes indifferent good English, who foure yeares since being carried home, was reported to have beene slaine, with divers of his countrymen, by Saylors, which was false. With him I had much conference, who gave mee very good satisfaction in everything almost I could demand. Time not permitting me to search here, which I should have done for sundry things of speciall moment: the wind faire, I stood away, shaping my course as the coast led mee, till I came to the Westerly part where the coast began to fall away Southerly. In my way I discovered Land about thirty leagues, heretofore taken for Mayne [Long Island], where I feared I had beene imbayed, but by the help of an Indian I got to the Sea againe, through many crooked and streight passages . . . once the Savages had great advantage of us in a streight, not above a Bowe shot, and where a multitude of Indians let flye at us from the banke, but it pleased God to make us victours; neere unto this wee founde a most dangerous Catwract amongst small rockie Ilands, occasioned by two unequall tydes, the one ebbing and flowing two houres before the other: here wee lost an Anchor by the Strength of the current, (but found it deepe enough); from hence we were carried in a short space by the tydes swiftnesse into a great Bay (to us so appearing) but indeed is broken land, which gave us light of the Sea." In these words Dermer portrays for us the first English passage of Long Island Sound and Hell Gate, which Adriaen Block had traversed in the reverse direction five years earlier. Dermer's friendly contact with Epenow at Martha's Vineyard is of interest and seems to belie the inference that this sachem was at war with the English. Dermer's voyage is of particular importance in that it represents a link between Squanto and Epenow; the one representing the friendly alliance between the Pilgrims and Wampanoags, the other standing for enmity between the races. Dermer was to lose his life at Epenow's hands in 1620, but not until he had provided the Pilgrims with their most precious safeguard in the form of Squanto. Dermer should be remembered, but is not, as one of the founding fathers of Plymouth, for he made possible the peace of Massasoit.

Dermer returned to Virginia, where he produced a map of his discoveries which unhappily has not come down to us. In 1620 he explored the Delaware and Hudson rivers and worked his way northward to Monhegan. At Martha's Vineyard on the way back to Jamestown in an encounter with Epenow all his men but one were killed, and Dermer himself mortally wounded. He died of his wounds, in Virginia, the first martyr to the cause of New Plymouth. In Dermer Gorges lost one of his most resourceful leaders. His death was the final blow in a long series of disasters to the Plymouth Company. The accidental landing of the Pilgrims within the grant of the Plymouth adventurers was a happy but totally unforeseen circumstance to Gorges and his company. The Leyden emigrants were able to take advantage of all the preliminary work prepared for them by the Plymouth Company, together with the golden opportunity provided by the depopulation of Massachusetts by pestilence.

During this time the company was having trouble with its charter in Parliament and Dermer's was the last serious effort of the adventurers in New England before their reorganization. Nevertheless, their heartbreaking series of catastrophes, all unknown to them, had laid the groundwork for the permanent settlement of Massachusetts. In utter rout and hopelessness, they had already won the battle. And even while Dermer was fighting his last battle with the savages of Martha's Vineyard, the *Mayflower* was on her way across the Atlantic.

Chapter Fourteen

New Plymouth

THE DEATH of Thomas Dermer was at once a culmination of disaster for the colonial ambitions of the dying Plymouth Company and a final preparation, through Squanto's home-coming, for the Pilgrim triumph. It was the end of the era of New England's discovery, and the prelude to her colonial period. The design of this book has been merely to set down the sequence of events in New England's exploration in the order in which they occurred. This aim has been largely accomplished. We have learned what a long series of heart-rending catastrophes prepared the field for the final achievement. The shoals had been sounded, trials made of the fishing, and good maps made. Commodities had been tested and profitable commerce begun. The temper and populousness of the natives had been discovered throughout the coast. Descriptive brochures were now available for prospective tenants; disease had conveniently removed the country's defenders, and English-trained pilots and interpreters had been planted among the remnant. Increasing numbers of attempts to winter in the country had proved its habitability. Permanent bases had been established a thousand miles away in both Newfoundland and Virginia, and a semi-permanent fishing station set up at Monhegan. A practicable outline of an economy adequate to the support of colonies had been drawn up. Yet, says the popular legend, all the New England work heretofore accomplished was a failure. Only with the arrival of the Pilgrims at New Plymouth did success enter the picture. The verdict of posterity thus delivers all the credit for the championship to the substitute who in the last quarter intercepts a forward pass and races eighty yards to a touchdown. The team, the promoters, trainers and coaches, all are forgotten. It is important that we should here attempt an illumination of this paradox by some study of the founding of New Plymouth. For there is nothing in the story of the voyages from Gosnold to Dermer which could suggest to us that a single subsequent voyage could possibly be successful without dependence on the contributions of these earlier men.

Any description of New Plymouth as a plantation, as a new government or as a religious refuge is wholly outside the province of this book. These phases have been made so familiar by more competent writers that their repetition here would be redundant. It is sufficient for our purpose to note that at this point in New England's history one of those acts of God occurred. A group of religious exiles who had made no preliminary investigations in America, who knew practically nothing of the previous work of the Plymouth adventurers, and whose equipment, physical stamina and technical background for such a project were decidedly below standard, landed by accident in New England and despite a fifty per cent mortality rate in the first winter succeeded where others had failed. For an explanation of their success we need go no further than to reemphasize their extraordinary endowment with devoted Christian faith, courage and perseverance. But for an explanation of how their achievement has so thoroughly displaced all remembrance of the work of the Plymouth Company we need to study in some detail the circumstances under which they landed at New Plymouth.

The Pilgrims were themselves explorers for the first six weeks after their American landfall, and for this reason alone this book would do them an injustice were it to omit a record of their contribution to knowledge of the New England coast. Their journals collected by George Mourt and those written by William Bradford and Edward Winslow provide us with an interesting study of the Cape Cod area comparable in that region only to the earlier work of Samuel de Champlain. Insufficient attention has been paid to this portion of the Pilgrim chronicles; we are now possessed of a background for comparative study such as enables us to place it in its proper relation with the previous voyages. From it we can derive certain conclusions about the techniques, skill and judgment of the Pilgrims. From certain omissions we can assume that there were matters of which they were ignorant.

The *Mayflower* was the first ship to bring women and children to New England shores. She made a slow passage of more than nine weeks and at length on November 20, 1620, the cliffs of Truro were sighted. Captain Jones probably consulted the map of either John Smith or Adriaen Block in company with his pilot Robert Coppin, who had made a previous New England voyage, and rightly identified the shore as that of Cape Cod. This produced consternation among the Pilgrims, for as we have already noted, their patent had been obtained for a settlement in the territory of the southern Virginia Company. Some have supposed that the Dutch had conspired with Captain Jones to keep the colony away from that area.

"After some deliberation had amongst themselves and with the master of the ship," wrote Bradford, "they tacked about and resolved to stand for the Southward (the wind and weather being fair) to find some place about Hudson's river for their habitation. But after they had sailed that course about half the day, they fell amongst dangerous shoals and roaring breakers, and they were so far entangled therewith as they conceived themselves in great danger; and the wind shrinking upon them withal, they resolved to bear up again for the Cape, and thought themselves happy to get out of those dangers before night overtook them, as by God's providence they did. And the next day they got into the Cape-harbor where they rid in safety." Our memory goes back inevitably to the disagreeable experiences of Waymouth, Champlain, and Hudson on these shoals. Jones and Coppin may easily have shared the doubtful opinion of the geography in this quarter which the voyages of Harlow, Hobson and Smith had not sufficiently clarified. Even Dermer had been wrecked on that beach the year before.

During the time they were returning to the shelter of Provincetown Harbor, the Pilgrims composed and signed their famous compact in the attempt to legalize a government—in place of their now useless Virginia patent.

The writer of *Mourt's Relation* was enthusiastic about Provincetown, whose shores were then "compassed about to the very sea with oaks, pines, juniper, sassafras and other sweet wood. . . . There we relieved ourselves with wood and water, and refreshed our people, while our shallop was fitted to coast the bay to search for an habitation. There was the greatest store of fowl that ever we saw." The beaches of Cape Cod are still swarming with migratory waterfowl each November. But the great schools of blackfish which he then saw in Cape Cod Bay are gone: "And every day we saw whales playing hard by us, of which in that place, if we had instruments and means to take them, we might have made a very rich return; which to our great grief, we wanted. Our master and his mate, and others experienced in fishing, professed we might have made three or four thousand pounds worth of oil. They preferred it before Greenland whale-fishing, and purpose the next winter to fish for whale here." He goes on to say that at that season there were no codfish and that some of the Pilgrims got sick, like Thoreau, from eating sea clams.

"The Bay is so round and circling that before we could come to anchor we went round all the points of the compass. We could not come near the shore by three quarters of an English mile, because of shallow water, which was a great prejudice to us; for our people going on shore, were forced to wade a bowshot or two in going aland, which caused many to get colds and coughs; for it was many times freezing cold weather.

"The same day, as soon as we could, we set ashore 15 or 16 men, well armed, with some to fetch wood, for we had none left; as also to see what the land was, and what inhabitants they could meet with. They found it to be a small neck of land; on this side where we lay is the bay, and the further side the sea; the ground or earth, sand hills, much like the downs in Holland, but much better; the crust of the earth, a spits depth, excellent black earth; all wooded with oaks, pines, sassafras, juniper, birch, holly, vines, some ash, walnut; the wood for the most part open and without underwood, fit either to go or ride in. At night our people returned, but found not any person, nor habitation; and laded their boat with juniper, which smelled very sweet and strong and of which we burnt the most part of the time we lay there." It seems apparent that Provincetown's Wood End was better supplied with forest and with topsoil than is now the case.

"Monday, the [23rd] of November, we unshipped our shallop and drew her on land to mend and repair her, having been forced to cut her down in bestowing her betwixt the decks, and she was much opened with the people's lying in her; which kept us long there, for it was 16 or 17 days before the carpenter had finished her. Our people went on shore to refresh themselves and our women to wash, as they had great need. But whilst we lay thus still, hoping our shallop would be ready in five or six days at the furthest, but our carpenter made slow work of it, so that some of our people, impatient of delay, desired for our better furtherance to travel by land into the country (which was not without appearance of danger, not having the shallop with them, nor means to carry provision but on their backs) to see whether it might be fit for us to seat in or no; and the rather, because as we sailed into the harbor there seemed to be a river opening itself into the main land. The willingness of the persons was liked, but the thing itself, in regard of the danger, was rather permitted than approved; and so with cautious directions, and instructions sixteen men were sent out with every man his musket, sword and corslet, under the conduct of Captain Miles Standish, unto whom was adjoined for counsel and advice, William Bradford, Stephen Hopkins and Edward Tilley.

"Wednesday the 25th of November, they were set ashore, and when they had ordered themselves in the order of a single file and marched about the space of a mile, by the sea they espied five or six people with a dog coming towards them, who were savages, who, when they saw them, ran into the wood and whistled the dog after them. First they supposed them to be Master Jones, the master, and some of his men, for they were ashore and knew of their coming; but after they knew them to be Indians, they marched after them into the woods, lest other of the Indians should lie in ambush. But when the Indians saw our men following them, they ran away with might and main, and our men turned out of the wood after them, for it was the way they intended to go,—but they could not come near them. They followed them that night about ten miles by the trace of their footings and saw how they had come the same way they went, and at turning perceived how they ran up a hill to see whether they followed them. At length night came upon them, and they were constrained to take up their lodging. So they set forth three sentinels, and the rest, some kindled a fire, and others fetched wood, and there held our rendezvous that night."

The next day they proceeded on the trail of the natives, past the head of the creek now known as Pilgrim Lake, and then through bushes "which tore our very armour in pieces." In midforenoon they finally found some springs "of which we were heartily glad, and sat down and drank our first New England water with as much delight as we ever drunk drink in all our lives."

Returning to the bay shore, they built a fire to give notice to the ship of their whereabouts, and then proceeded southward to North Truro, "where we found a fine clear pond of fresh water, being about a musket-shot broad, and twice as long; there grew also many small vines, and fowl and deer haunted there; there grew much sassafras." Still farther southward they began to see some evidences of former Indian cornfields. At this point some of the party attempted to walk the beach, but soon found how tiring the loose sand is, and resumed their course on the higher land. Soon they "found a little path to certain heaps of sand, one whereof was covered with old mats, and had a wooden thing like a mortar whelmed on top of it, an earthen pot laid in a little hole at the end thereof. We, musing what it might be, digged and found a bow, and, as we thought, arrows, but they were rotten. We supposed there were many other things; but because we deemed them graves, we put in the bow again, and made it up as it was, and left the rest untouched."

Approaching the Pamet River mouth, the Pilgrims saw newly harvested cornfields and the site of a native house, with some planks and a European kettle near by. "There was also an heap of sand, made like the former, but it was newly done (that we might see how they had paddled it with their hands), which we digged up, and in it we found a little old basket full of very fair Indian corn; and digged further and found a fine great new basket full of very fair corn of this year with some 36 goodly ears of corn, some yellow and some red, and others mixed with blue, which was a very goodly sight. The basket was round, and narrow at the top. It held about three or four bushels, which was as much as two of us could lift up from the ground, and was very handsomely and cunningly made. But whilst we were busy about these things, we set out men sentinel in a round ring all but two or three which digged up the corn. We were in suspense what to do with it and the kettle, and at length after much consultation, we concluded to take the kettle and as much corn as we could carry away with us and when our shallop came, if we could find any of the people and come to parley with them, we would give them the kettle again and satisfy them for their corn. So we took all the ears, and put a good deal of the loose corn in the kettle for two men to bring away on a staff. The rest we buried again; for we were so laden with armor that we could carry no more." The program here decided upon was faithfully carried out, and the next year corn was returned to the Nausets in repayment for that which had been taken. The corn was of course of vital importance to the Pilgrims as it provided them with seed for their first harvest. The scrupulousness of these settlers was most striking, although their severity in punishment of Indian offenders was to become equally notable.

Not far from the cache of corn the Pilgrims found the Pamet River, in search of which they had originally set out, "dividing itself into two arms by an high bank standing right by the cut or mouth, which came from the sea. . . . Here also we saw two canoes, the one on the one side, the other on the other side." As they had designed to be out only two days, the party now turned back and camped that night in the rain near the pond at North Truro. On the way back to Provincetown the next day, "we came to a tree, where a young sprit was bowed down over a bow, and some acorns strewed underneath. Stephen Hopkins said, it had been to catch some deer. So as we were looking at it, William Bradford being in the rear, when he came looked also upon it, and as he went about it, it gave a sudden jerk up, and he was immediately caught by the leg. It was a very pretty device, made with a rope of their own making, and having a noose as artificially made as any roper in England can make, and as like ours as can be, which we brought away with us." Needless to say Bradford does not regale us with this delightful bit of indignity in his *Historie*. It is, so far as I know, the first mention of the Indian use of snares since Verrazano's report of them in 1524. "Thus," continues the narrative, "we came both weary and welcome home, and delivered in our corn into the store to be kept for seed."

During the next few days the Pilgrims occupied themselves "in seeking out wood, and helving of tools, and sawing of wood to build a new shallop," which we may suppose was the second boat to be built in New England, the first, of course, being Sagadahoc's *Virginia*, unless we are sufficiently generous with geography to include Champlain's St. Croix shallops and Adriaen Block's *Onrust*. "But the discommodiousness of the harbor did much hinder us; for we could neither go to nor come from the shore but at high water, which was much to our hindrance and hurt; for oftentimes they waded to the middle of the thigh, and oft to the knee, to go and come from land. Some did it necessarily, and some for their own pleasure; but it brought to the most, if not all, coughs and colds (the weather proving cold and stormy) which afterwards turned to the Scurvy, whereof many died." Here in Provincetown was the beginning of that scourge of respiratory disease that almost wiped out Plymouth.

At length twenty-four Pilgrims and ten of the sailors, with Captain Jones in command, set out in the shallop and longboat to pursue the explorations. Caught in a snowstorm, the party had to be landed short of its destination, which was the Pamet River, and the shore party proceeded by land six or seven miles before making camp, and was joined by the boats only after a bitter night in the snow. "It blowed and did snow all that day and night, and froze withal. Some of our people that are dead took the original of their death here." Embarking the next morning in the shallop, they entered the Pamet River mouth, and "landed our men between the two creeks, and marched some four or five miles by the greater of them, and the shallop followed us. At length night grew on and our men were tired with marching up and down the steep hills and deep valleys, which lay half a foot thick with snow. Master Jones, wearied with marching, was desirous we should take up our lodgings, though some of us would have marched further. So we made there our rendezvous for that night under a few pine trees; and as it fell out, we got three fat geese, and six ducks to our supper, which we eat with soldiers' stomachs for we had eaten little all that day. Our resolution was next morning to go to the head of this river, for we supposed it would prove fresh water. But in the morning our resolution held not, because of the hilliness of the soil and badness of the harbor. So we turned towards the other creek, that we might go over and look for the rest of the corn that we left behind when we were here before." So, returning to Cornhill, using an Indian canoe as a ferry—"She carried us over by seven or eight at once"—they found the remainder of the corn. The ground was "so hard frozen that we were fain with our curtlaxes and short swords to hew and carve the ground a foot deep, and then wrest it up with levers." Having obtained the seed, "in all about ten bushels," it was loaded aboard the shallop, and, along with a dozen sick Pilgrims, sent back to the *Mayflower*. Eighteen stayed obstinately encamped at Cornhill in the snow that night.

The next day, while waiting for the return of the shallop, the party came upon a curious burial mound, covered with boards and mats. It contained a bow, a carved painted board, bowls, dishes and two bundles. The larger of these bundles was wrapped in a "sailor's canvas cassock and a pair of cloth breeches" and contained the bones and skull of a man embalmed in a fine red powder reminiscent of the red-paint burials familiar to New England archaeologists. With this bundle were a "knife, a pack-needle and two or three old iron things." The smaller bundle contained the skeleton of a child together with "strings and bracelets of fine white beads" and "a little bow" and "other odd knacks." As an archaeological puzzle this would provide material for a long evening of speculation. For our historical purpose it provides only the evidence of another of the many unrecorded voyages which came to grief about Cape Cod, unless one chooses to suppose that these were relics of one of Champlain's mishaps a few miles to the south.

In the course of this same reconnaissance the party discovered some of the Indians' houses. These "were made with long young sapling trees bended and both ends stuck into the ground. They were made round like unto an arbor, and covered down to the ground with thick and well-wrought mats; and the door was not over a yard high, made of a mat to open. The chimney was a wide open hole in the top, for which they had a mat to cover it close when they pleased. One might stand and go upright in them. In the midst of them were four little trunches knocked into the ground, and small sticks laid over, on which they hung their pots and what they had to seethe. Round about the fire they lay on mats which are their beds. The houses were double matted, for as they were matted without so were they within with newer and fairer mats. In the houses we found wooden bowls, trays, dishes, earthen pots, hand-baskets made of crab-shells wrought together; also an English pail or bucket; it wanted a bail, but it had two iron ears; there was also baskets of sundry sorts, bigger and some lesser, finer and some coarser; some were curiously wrought with black and white in pretty works and sundry other of their household stuff. We found also two or three deer's heads one whereof had been newly killed, for it was still fresh. There was also a company of deer's feet stuck up in the houses, hart's horns and eagles claws and sundry such like things there was; also two or three baskets full of parched acorns, pieces of fish, and a piece of a broiled herring. We found also a little silk grass, and a little tobacco seed, with some other seeds which we knew not, without was sundry bundles of flags, and sedge, bulrushes and other stuff to make mats. There was thrust into an hollow tree two or three pieces of venison; but we thought it fitter for the dogs than for us. Some of the best things we took away with us, and left the houses standing still as they were." This is one of the most detailed descriptions of an Indian household in all the explorers' literature and deserves to stand alongside the chronicles of Champlain as a fine example of observation. It has the characteristics of the fine hand of Edward Winslow, and it is to him that we probably owe this portion of *Mourt's Relation*.

The narrative now continues with a discussion of the advisability of settlement about this Pamet River. The idea seems almost grotesque to one who knows the region, and this is best evidenced by its modern population of only a few hundred. But the Pilgrims were faced with a dilemma. It was almost mid-December; supplies were running low, and sickness was increasing. Their delays in England were forcing them to desperate remedies. For this reason Truro was seriously considered for their plantation site. No colonial expedition ever landed with worse prospects of success, what with their ignorance of the coast, their encumbrances with women and children and the sick, and winter at hand. Therefore they patiently catalogued the virtues of Truro; its "convenient harbor for boats, though not for ships," its "good corn-ground," its "good fishing," its likelihood of being "healthful, secure and defensible." And for its vices, the first was that "Angoum" (which was undoubtedly John Smith's Aggawom—Ipswich) was said to have a much better harbor, better soil and better fishing; secondly that there might be near by a better place; thirdly that the water supply was "but in ponds," and fourthly "the water must be fetched up a steep hill." Technically considered, this reasoning is pitiful, but given their desperate position it is comprehensible.

An inkling of their dubious situation as regards Captain Jones may be obtained from this remark in the course of the discussion: "It was also conceived, whilst we had competent victuals, that the ship would stay with us; but when that grew low, they would be gone and let us shift as we would."

Certainly their chances at Truro could have been no worse than Champlain's at St. Croix. Fortunately for them, however, they decided to explore farther. One of the chief proponents of such further investigations was Robert Coppin, the pilot, who "made relations of a great navigable river over against Cape Cod, being a right line, not much above eight leagues distant, in which he had been once, and because that one of the wild men with whom they had some trading stole a harping iron from them, they called it Thievish Harbor." Coppin perhaps had been in Boston Harbor. In any case his argument seemed to find favor, and he was among the company of eighteen who set out on yet a third voyage in the shallop.

Suffering a good deal from seasickness and cold, "for the water froze on our clothes, and made them many times like coats of iron," they at length made Wellfleet Harbor, where they landed, seeing many stranded blackfish on the beach and the Indians cutting strips of blubber from the carcass of one of them. It was a disappointment to find no river entering the

bay. After another cold night without shelter, the sentinels con-
tinuously watching for Indians, they explored the country.
They came on old cornfields and in one place a great Indian
burying ground, "encompassed with a large palisade, like a
church-yard with young spires four or five yards long, set as
close one by another as they could, two or three foot in the
ground. Within, it was full of graves, some bigger some less.
Some were also piled about. And others had like an Indian
house made over them, but not matted." In another place were
some Indian houses "lately dwelt in," yet "all this while we saw
no people."

"We went ranging up and down till the sun began to draw
low, and then we hastened out of the woods, that we might
come to our shallop. . . . They were exceeding glad to see us,
for they feared because they had not seen us in so long a time
. . . So being both weary and faint, for we had eaten nothing
all that day, we fell to make our rendezvous and get firewood,
which always cost us a great deal of labor." The site of this
encampment was later identified by the Pilgrims themselves as
at Nauset, or Eastham. It was now December 17th. "By that
time we had done and our shallop come to us, it was within
night; and we fed upon such victuals as we had, and betook
us to our rest, after we had set out our watch. About midnight
we heard a great and hideous cry; and our sentinel called 'Arm!
Arm!' So we bestirred ourselves and shot off a couple of muskets, and noise ceased. We concluded that it was a company of
wolves or foxes; for one told us he heard such a noise in Newfoundland.

"About five oclock in the morning we began to be stirring
and two or three, which doubted whether their pieces would go
off or no, made trial of them and shot them off, but thought
nothing at all. After prayer we prepared ourselves for breakfast
and for a journey; and it being now the twilight in the morning,
it was thought meet to carry the things down to the shallop.
Some said it was not best to carry the armor down. Others said,
they would be readier. Two or three said, they would not carry

theirs till they went themselves, but mistrusting nothing at all, as it fell out, the water not being high enough, they laid the things down upon the shore and came up to breakfast. Anon, all upon a sudden, we heard a great and strange cry, which we knew to be the same voices, though they varied their notes. One of our company being aboard came running in and cried, 'They are men! Indians! Indians!' and withal their arrows came flying amongst us. Our men ran out with all speed to recover their arms; as by the good providence of God they did. In the meantime Captain Miles Standish, having a snaphance ready, made a shot; and after him another. After they two had shot, other two of us were ready; but he wished us not to shoot till we could take aim, for we knew not what need we should have; and there were four only of us which had their arms there ready, and stood before the open side of our barricado, which was first assaulted. They thought it best to defend it, lest the enemy should take it and our stuff, and so have more vantage against us. Our care was no less for the shallop, but we hoped all the rest would defend it. We called unto them to know how it was with them, they answered 'Well! Well!' every one, and 'Be of good courage!' We heard three of their matches. One took a log out of the fire on his shoulder and went and carried it unto them; which was thought did not a little discourage our enemies. . . .

"There was a lusty man, and no whit less valiant, who was thought to be their captain, stood behind a tree within half a musket shot of us and there let his arrows fly at us. He was seen to shoot three arrows, which were all avoided; for he at whom the first arrow was aimed saw it, and stooped down, and it flew over him. The rest were avoided also. He stood three shots of a musket. At length one took, as he said, full aim at him after which he gave an extraordinary cry, and away they went all. We followed them about a quarter of a mile; but we left six to keep our shallop, for we were careful of our business. Then we shouted all together two several times, and shot off a couple of muskets, and so returned. This we did that they might see we were not afraid of them, nor discouraged.

"Thus it pleased God to vanquish our enemies and give us deliverance. By their noise we could not guess that they were less than thirty or forty, though some thought that they were many more. . . . We took up 18 of their arrows, which we sent to England by Master Jones; some whereof were headed with brass, others with hart's horn, and others with eagle's claws. Many more no doubt were shot, for these we found were almost covered with leaves; yet by the especial providence of God, none of them either hit or hurt us, though many came close by us and on every side of us, and some coats which hung up in our barricado were shot through and through."

It would be naïve to claim that these Indians had had no provocation. However partial we may feel toward the Pilgrims we must recognize that for more than three weeks they had been rifling the Indians' food supplies, their houses and their graves. It is therefore not surprising that this first meeting should have taken the form of an ambush. A settlement at Pamet would have faced inevitable war added to so many other woes that survival would have been a miracle. Despite the many burials, Cape Cod was not depopulated by the plague, and would doubtless have offered as bitter opposition to the Pilgrim planters as it already had to French and English geographers. The Pilgrims, of course, acquitted themselves well in this episode, though after a tactical blunder. But they seem to have accepted the hint that further explorations in this neighborhood would prove unprofitable, for their narratives contain no further speculations upon settling at Wellfleet or Nauset or any other portion of Cape Cod. "So after we had given God thanks for our deliverance, we took our shallop and went on our journey. . . . From hence we intended to have sailed to the aforesaid Thievish Harbor, if we found no convenient harbor by the way." The Indians of Cape Cod had again successfully asserted their powers of self-defense. They thus conferred a favor on the Pilgrims.

It is worth pausing at this point to consider how futile had been the use the Pilgrims had made of their first month in America. No previous expedition had ever required two weeks to assemble a shallop, or accomplished so little with the shallop in the first two weeks after it was made ready. All the work thus far done was in an area no more than twenty miles long, and lacking in most of the requirements for a good plantation site. Despite the fact that they had in Robert Coppin a man who knew Massachusetts Bay, they had failed to circumnavigate it, though Champlain had done so in five days. It was high time they were about their business of further exploring the shores.

"Having the wind good, we sailed all that day along the coast about 15 leagues; but saw neither river nor creek to put into. After we had sailed an hour or two, it began to snow and rain and to be bad weather." It was no doubt the storm which obscured to them the opening of Barnstable Harbor. "About the midst of the afternoon the wind increased, and the seas began to be very rough; and the hinges of the rudder broke, so that we could steer no longer with it, but two men with much ado were fain to serve with a couple of oars. The seas were grown so great that we were much troubled and in great danger; and night grew on. Master Coppin bade us be of good cheer, he saw the harbor; as we drew near, the gale being stiff, and we bearing great sail to get in, split our mast in 3 places and were like to have cast away our shallop. Yet, by God's mercy recovering ourselves we had the flood with us and struck into the harbor.

"Now he that thought that had been the place, was deceived, it being a place where not any of us had been before; and coming into the harbor, he that was our pilot did bear up northward, which if we had continued, we had been cast away. Yet still the Lord kept us, and we bare up for an island before us; and recovering of that island, being compassed about with many rocks, and dark night growing upon us, it pleased the divine providence that we fell upon a place of sandy ground, where our shallop did ride safely and secure all that night." Bradford adds that Coppin and his master's mate "would have run her ashore in a cove of breakers before the wind. But a lusty seaman which steered, bade those which rowed, if they were men, about with her, or else they were all cast away; the which they did with speed. So he bid them be of good cheer and row lustily, for there was a fair sound before them and he doubted not but they should find one place or other where they might ride in safety. And though it was very dark and rained sore, yet in the end they got under the lee of a small island and remained there all that night in safety." This of course was Clark's island. Fortunately, it was uninhabited. They spent the next day, which was Sunday, in drying their clothes and resting from their sufferings of the voyage. "On Monday they sounded the harbor and found it fit for shipping; and marched into the land and found divers cornfields, and little running brooks, a place (as they supposed) fit for situation; at least it was the best they could find, and the season, and their present necessity, made them glad to accept of it. So they returned to their ship again with this news to the rest of their people which did much comfort their hearts."

It was thus that the Pilgrims rediscovered Plymouth. Not one among them, not even their pilot, knew of its existence except for their possible examination of Smith's map, and they came upon it in the last extremity of freezing cold, near shipwreck, Indian hostility, hunger and disease. Despite the facts that during the previous eighteen years at least six expeditions had entered this harbor, and that it had been mapped for fifteen years and named Plymouth for six years, not one among the Pilgrims had ever heard of it. Members of the ship's crew seem to have been at Newfoundland and Greenland but, so far as we know, Robert Coppin was their only link with the previous New England voyages, and he of doubtful value. Is it any wonder that Captain John Smith wrote in 1622 that it was *"for want of experience"* that they ranged to and fro for six weeks before "they found a place they liked to dwell on"? In the same period of time Smith himself had explored and mapped five hundred miles of coast. The Pilgrims had made a courageous acquaintance with perhaps fifty miles, much of it on foot. Had they

made even the circuit of Massachusetts Bay, they would probably have settled in Boston Harbor, as they admitted during
their voyage there in 1621. That they did not was no reflection
on their courage, but it was a commentary on their lack of
experience.

Nevertheless, they were rapidly accumulating experience,
and nowhere is there a more concentrated picture of the haz-
ards of New England exploration than in the chronicle we have
just reviewed. They were quick to learn, and without question
their newly acquired knowledge of the Indians, particularly of
some of their means of subsistence, together with the seed corn
and beans obtained on these foraging expeditions, was to save
the colony more than once. They were now forewarned as to
the sort of defense they must maintain. They had had a taste
of the weather and of what exposure to it meant to their health.
Finally they had come on unquestionably a much better site for
a new plantation than any part of Cape Cod would have been.

It has by now become apparent that the Pilgrims were of
no mind to belittle the work of previous explorers. So far from
their minds was any such intention that they made obvious in
these narratives their utter ignorance of all the previous New
England work. Yet it is precisely because of their ignorance that
some of us have fallen into the error of considering their voyage
the beginning of New England's history, for it is from these
accounts of Mourt, Bradford and Winslow that the early history of New England has in the past been largely drawn. Their
omission to mention the efforts of the Plymouth Company has
in turn encouraged our ignorance. Most of their mistakes in the
six weeks on Cape Cod stemmed from their ignorance, and
indeed it determined their choice of Plymouth for their settlement.

Thus we should derive from these narratives the clear
appreciation that this voyage was in no sense a sequel to the
work of Dermer or Hobson, or even of John Smith or Ferdinando Gorges. In its inception during their years in Holland it
was perhaps stimulated more by the voyages of Henry Hudson,

Adriaen Block and the Dutchmen who followed them in New Netherland than by the English voyages to New England. The Pilgrims had in fact made a futile application to the Dutch for a New York settlement. But they had never made even a preliminary inquiry of the Plymouth Company. The Pilgrims came to New England by accident. We should therefore consider this enterprise, judged by its origin, as belonging among the Jamestown or New Amsterdam series of voyages rather than among the New England ones. It is significant to remember how early trading relations were established between Plymouth and New Amsterdam, and how long the Pilgrims remained ignorant of the English fishing fleet around Monhegan. Surely there should be no mystery about the Pilgrims' ignorance of New England; whatever studies of the coast they had made must have been centered around the Delaware or the Hudson River, where even Bradford states they had intended to settle. It was not the Pilgrims who stole the glory of New England's discovery from their predecessors, but we, who have reconstructed the "stern and rockbound coast," the untouched wilderness, from the insufficient evidence of the Pilgrim journals.

Despite their ignorance of the previous New England work, they inherited many advantages that were the result of that work. We know how the scythe of pestilence had cleared away their potential enemies. We know how Squanto was educated ready to their need. We know that, difficult as it may have seemed to William Bradford, financial support was available in England for New England ventures. We know that the French had been effectively dispersed from New England colonial activities and that Pilgrims no longer need fear conflict from that quarter. As time went on the hardily developed English confidence in New England fishing, fur trading and other commerce would support their colony as a port of call for such activities and give them a market, communications, and a source of needed supplies which their own adventurers could not furnish. There would be friendly ships from unexpected quarters, and means of assistance when they were in famine. None of these things would have been as easily available to them on the Hudson River. These were the gifts from the English failures of twenty years past.

For the rest, the Pilgrims had to improvise their assets. That they did so in no small measure is the reason we honor them. Among their chief advantages were their distaste for a return to Europe, their true emigration in whole families, their invincible religious faith, and an uncompromising justice in their government and Indian relations. This was a group lacking almost all the advantages possessed by the Sagadahoc planters, but endowed to an extreme degree with the virtues the hapless Popham colonists had most lacked. Champlain's colonies were twice at the point of abandonment after experiences of New England winters; few of the Pilgrims ever returned to Europe except on the colony's business. Neither famine nor disease nor poverty could shake their resolution. With waning numbers they boldly punished Indian conspiracy at Wessagussett, and flung down the gantlet to the powerful Narragansetts when the latter sent them a sheaf of arrows. They maintained their self-respect among tricksters like Weston and Lyford. They established a just peace with their Indian neighbors, which was as much supported by kindly interest in their welfare as by the punishment of crime. They kept their portals open to the exiles of all creeds, so long as the community was not injured by so doing. In all these matters they demonstrated a self-discipline under their own laws which no American colony before or since has ever equaled. That they succeeded in their project was due mainly to the purity of their motives and the steadfastness of their courage. With them New England civilization began, and much of American civilization as well. We who have inherited their traditions cannot render them too high homage.

Yet history necessarily dramatizes the moral issue of this event at the expense of accuracy. The idealistic nature of the Pilgrim victory is a blinding light through which we perceive but darkly the previous quarter century of American struggle that made it possible. It belied the evidence which had painfully been built up over a generation, that equipment and men, chosen for their training and apprenticeship, were the secret of success. So completely had the moral quality of Pilgrim faith, justice and democracy dominated the stage of history that most Americans have forgotten actually the name of Ferdinando Gorges. The adventurers who financed the Pilgrim voyage have been distorted into villains of the piece, largely because their exhaustion in the attempt to support American colonization presented a few obstacles to William Bradford. It is a strange anticlimax that a group of men who had in no way participated in the bitter failures of laying New England's foundations should at last have fallen heir to nearly all the glory for the achievement.

Let us keep clear in our minds the fact that the Pilgrims in their turn were the inheritors of a struggling merchant tradition that was set in motion by Sir Walter Raleigh, Richard Hakluyt, Sir Ferdinando Gorges and Captain John Smith. Let us recognize their indebtedness to Portuguese and French and Dutch and English seamen who prepared the way through long years of disappointment and bitter struggle. Let us also do homage to unknown hundreds who perished at sea, like the men on Argall's pinnace, and at the hands of New England natives, like Thomas Dermer, in the single attempt to open the seaways of New England commerce. The Pilgrim contribution was more fundamental to our subsequent political and social development but it could not have succeeded without the earlier contributions of the Plymouth Company. The indomitable courage of the Pilgrims was more spectacular than the dogged persistence of such men as Gorges and John Smith, but it would be difficult to adjudge one as being superior to the other. If today some zealous American minority group were to establish a successful permanent refuge in Antarctica, our attitude toward them in contrast to Admiral Byrd's expeditions might approximate what England must have thought of the Pilgrims in the seventeenth century. Such a historical parallel is useful as a demonstration of the actual relationship of New Plymouth to the Plymouth Company, and thus also as a basis for a rational apportionment of credit to the several agencies involved in the founding of New England. For even as Admiral Byrd has established in Little America whatever grounds there may be for its future use, and perhaps permanent occupation, so had the English explorers from Gosnold to Dermer done in New England. Their work had made apparent that New England must inevitably someday be colonized, regardless of the failures thus far suffered. If it had not been the Pilgrims, some other group would certainly have accomplished that end. To give the Pilgrims all the credit is, it seems to me, entirely equivalent to claiming for our hypothetical group of modern exiles all the glory for the work of opening up Antarctica to American civilization.

BIBLIOGRAPHY

A. Primary Original Sources

1. *Leif Eriksson, Discoverer of America A.D. 1003*, Edward F. Grey. New York: Oxford University Press, 1930.
2. *The Principal Navigations, Voyages, Traffiques and Discoveries of the English Nation*, collected by Richard Hakluyt, edited by Edmund Goldschmidt. Edinburgh 1889 edition.
   This includes most of the pertinent material in the Hakluyt's *Divers Voyages touching the discovery of America*, 1582, as well as that in his *Principal Navigations* of 1589.
3. *Hakluytus Posthumus, or Purchas His Pilgrimes, contayning a history of the world in sea voyages and lande travells by Englishmen and others*. Glasgow: MacLehose, 1905–1907. Originally published 1625.
4. *American Historical Prints*. Early views of American Cities, etc., from the Phelps Stokes and other collections by I. N. Phelps Stokes and Daniel C. Haskell. New York: New York Public Library, 1933.
   Catalogue of best collection of early maps of North American coasts.
5. *History of the Discovery of Maine*, J. G. Kohl. In *Documentary History of the State of Maine*, ed. by William Willis, Portland, Me.: Bailey and Noyes for the Maine Historical Society, 1869.
   Contains much otherwise inaccessible material, maps, etc.
6. *Sailors' Narratives of Voyages along the New England Coast 1524–1624*, edited by George Parker Winship. Boston: Houghton Mifflin Co., 1905.
7. *Forerunners and Competitors of the Pilgrims and Puritans*, etc., edited by Charles H. Levermore. Brooklyn: New England Society of Brooklyn, 1912.
8. *Old South Leaflets:* Boston, Old South Association n.d. (1920).

Vol. V contains Archer's account of Gosnold's Settlement at Cuttyhunk.

9. *Voyages of Samuel de Champlain,* translated from the French by Charles Pomeroy Otis, with Historical Illustrations and a Memoir (204 pp.) by the Rev. Edward F. Slafter A.M. (2 vols.). Boston: Prince Society, 1880.

10. *The Works of Samuel de Champlain,* reprinted, translated and annotated by six Canadian scholars under the general editorship of H. P. Biggar. Toronto: Champlain Society, 1922–1936. Maps edited by W. F. Ganong.

11. *The Voyages and Explorations of Samuel de Champlain 1604–1616,* narrated by himself; transl. by Annie Nettleton Bourne. Together with "The Voyage of 1603" reprinted from *Purchas his Pilgrimes,* edited with introduction and notes by Edward Gaylord Bourne. New York: A. S. Barnes & Co., 1906.

12. *History of New France,* Marc Lescarbot; transl. by W. L. Grant. Toronto: Champlain Society, 1914.

13. *Rosier's Relation of Waymouth's Voyage to the Coast of Maine, 1605,* Henry S. Burrage. Portland, Me.: Gorges Society, 1887.

14. *The Second Book of the First Decade of the Historie of Travaille into Virginia Brittania,* William Strachey. Collections of Massachusetts Historical Society, 4th Series, Vol. 1, pp. 231–246, 1849.

15. *Genesis of the United States,* Alexander Brown. Boston: Houghton Mifflin Co., 1890.

16. *Narratives of New Netherland 1609–1664,* edited by J. Franklin Jameson. Original Narratives of Early American History Series. New York: Scribner's, 1909.

Includes all the sources for the voyages of Adriaen Block and Henry Hudson.

17. *Relation de la Nouvelle France,* P. Biard. Lyon: P. Muguet, 1616(?)

18. *Extracts from the Letters of the Jesuit Missionary in Maine, Father P. Biard,* from Carayon's Letters. In ed. 1612–1626, translated by Fred M. Warren.

In collections and Proceedings of the Maine Historical Society, 2nd Series, Vol. II, pp. 411 *et seq.* Published by the Society, Portland, 1891.

19. *A Description of New England*, Captain John Smith. London, 1616.

20. *New Englands Trials*, Captain John Smith. London, 1620.

21. *The Generalle Historie of Virginia, New England, and the Summer Isles*, Captain John Smith. London, 1624.

22. *Captain John Smith's Works 1608–1631*, edited by Edward Arber. Birmingham: English Scholars Library, 1884.
      Includes the foregoing three items with comparative notes.

23. *Early History of New England*. Increase Mather, with an introduction and notes by Samuel G. Drake. Boston: printed for the editor and sold by him at 13 Bromfield St., 1864; originally published, 1677.

24. *The New English Canaan*. Thomas Morton; edited by Charles Francis Adams. Boston: Prince Society, 1883; originally published, 1632.

25. *Chronicles of the Pilgrim Fathers*. New York: E. P. Dutton Co., 1910 (Everymans Library). Contains *New England's Memorial*, by Nathaniel Morton, 1669; *Cushmans Discourse*, 1662; *New Englands Trials*, John Smith, 1662; *Winslow's Relation*.

26. *Chronicles of the Pilgrim Fathers of the Colony of Plymouth from 1602 to 1625*, Alexander Young. Boston: Charles C. Little and James Brown, 1841.

B. Secondary Sources from Historians

27. *The Northmen in Maine, and The Discovery of Massachusetts Bay*, Rev. B. F. De Costa. Albany: Joel Munsell, 1870.

28. *Dighton Rock*, E. B. Delabarre. New York, 1928.

29. *The Precursors of Jacques Cartier 1497–1534*, A Collection of Documents relating to the early history of the Dominion of Canada, edited by H. P. Biggar. Published under the authority of the Minister of Agriculture, under the direction of the Archivist Ottawa, Government Printing Bureau, 1911.

30. *The Discovery of America, with some account of Ancient America and the Spanish Conquest*, John Fiske. Boston: Houghton Mifflin Co., 1889.

31. *Narrative and Critical History of America*, edited by Justin

Winsor. Esp. chapters by George Dexter and De Costa: "Cartier and his Successors."

32. *Pioneers of France in the New World*, Francis Parkman. Boston: Little, Brown & Co., 1906 (1885 ed.).

33. *The Beginnings of English Overseas Enterprise*, Sir C. P. Lucas. Oxford: Clarendon Press, 1917.

34. *Early History of Naushon Island*, Amelia Forbes Emerson. Privately printed, 1935 (Boston).

35. *A History of Pemaquid, with sketches of Monhegan, Popham and Castine*, Arlita Dodge Parker. Boston: MacDonald and Evans, 1925.

36. *The Beginnings of Colonial Maine 1602–1658*, Henry S. Burrage, State Historian. Printed for the State. Portland, Me.: Marks Printing House, 1914.

37. *The Sagadahoc Colony*, Rev. Henry O. Thayer. Portland, Me.: Gorges Society, 1892.

38. *Gorges and the Grant of the Province of Maine 1622*, A Tercentenary Memorial, Henry S. Burrage, State Historian. Printed for the State, 1923.

39. *Tercentenary of the Landing of the Popham Colony at the Mouth of the Kennebec, Aug. 29, 1907*. Portland: Maine Historical Society, 1907.

40. *Sir Ferdinando Gorges and His Province of Maine*, including The Brief Relation, The Brief Narration, His Defense, The Charter Granted to Him, his Will, and his Letters, edited by James Phinney Baxter. Boston: Prince Society, 1890.

41. *Mount Desert: A History*, George E. Street; edited by Samuel A. Eliot. Boston: Houghton Mifflin Co., 1905.

42. *The Connecticut River and the Valley of the Connecticut*, Edwin M. Bacon. New York: Putnam's, 1906.

43. *Handbook of the American Indians*, edited by Frederick W. Hodge, Washington, D. C.: Smithsonian Institution, Bureau of American Ethnology, 1912.
    Catalogue of Indian Place Names.

44. *Territorial Subdivisions and Boundaries of the Wampanoag, Massachusett, and Nauset Indians*, Frank G. Speck. New York: Museum of the American Indian, Heye Foundation, 1928.

45. *The Pilgrim Republic. An historical Review of the Colony of Plymouth*, John A. Goodwin. Boston: Tichnor and Co., 1888.

C. Miscellaneous Collateral Material

46. *Miguel Cortereal: The First European to enter Narragansett Bay*, Edmund B. Delabarre. Rhode Island Historical Collection, Vol. XXIX, October, 1936.

47. *Voyages of Elizabethan Seamen*, edited by Edward J. Payne. Oxford University Press (Macmillan), 1893.

48. *Elizabethan Sea-Dogs, A Chronicle of Drake and his Companions*, William Wood. Vol. 3, Chronicles of America Series. New Haven: Yale University Press, 1920.

50. *The Discovery and Colonization of North America*, John Fiske, 1905. Boston: Ginn & Co., 1905.

51. *Antiquities of the New England Indians*, Charles C. Willoughby. Cambridge: Peabody Museum, 1935.

52. *Some Indian Events of New England*, A Collection of Interesting Incidents in the Lives of the Early Settlers, etc., compiled by Allen Forbes. Boston, 1934.

53. *Captain Martin Pringe, The Last of the Elizabethan Seamen*, James Hurly Pring. Plymouth (Eng.): W. H. Luke, 1888.

54. *A Vindication of the Claims of Sir Ferdinando Gorges as the Father of English Colonization in America*, John A. Poor. New York: D. Appleton and Co., 1862.

55. *Captain John Smith*, E. Keble Chatterton. New York: Harpers, 1927.

56. *The Dutch and Quaker Colonies in America*, John Fiske. Boston: Houghton Mifflin Co., 1899.

57. *Pioneers of the Old South*, Mary Johnston. New Haven: Yale University Press, 1920.

58. *Nooks and Corners of the New England Coast*, Samuel Adams Drake. New York: Harpers, 1875.

59. *Cape Cod, the Right Arm of Massachusetts*, Charles F. Swift. Yarmouth, 1897.

60. *The Beginnings of New England, or the Puritan Theocracy in its Relations to Civil and Religious Liberty*, John Fiske. Boston and New York: Houghton Mifflin Co., 1900.

61. *Good Old Dorchester, A Narrative History of the Town 1630–1893*, William Dana Orcutt. Cambridge: The University Press, 1908.

316   BIBLIOGRAPHY

62. *A Cruising Guide to the New England Coast*, edited by Robert F. Duncan. New York: David Kemp & Co., 1938.
63. *Ranging the Maine Coast*, Alfred F. Loomis. New York: W. W. Norton & Co., 1939.
64. *The Voyages of the Cabots and the English Discovery of North America*, James A. Williamson. London: The Argonaut Press, 1929.

INDEX

A

Acadia (see Nova Scotia)
Accomack, 245, 258
Accominticus, 245, 255, 260
Agamenticus, 245, 261
Aggawom, 185, 245, 256
Agriculture, experiments, 60–1, 73, 88, 177, 194, 208, 214, 249–50 (see also under Indians)
Albany, 30, 174
Aldworth, Mount, 70
Aldworth, Robert, 70
Algonkian, 11
Allefonsce, Jehan, 29, 59, 69, 80, 177
Allen's Island, 88
Allerton Point, 257
Almouchiquois, 101, 192
Amadas, Captain, 43
Amenquin, 161
Amsterdam Trading Company, 231
Anassou, 122
Anchor Bay, 224
Androscoggin River, 99
Anglican, 189
Angoam, 256
Annapolis (see Port Royal)
Annisquam, 131
Anticosti, 28
Antons, Sieur des, 123
Archangel, 85
Archer, Gabriel, 56–65, 102, 146, 168
Archipelagus, 221
Argall, Sir Samuel, 165, 179–83, 191, 208–20, 265
Armada, Spanish, 42, 44, 45
Armouchiquois, 192–200
Arundel, Thomas, 84, 85
Assacomet, 186
Asticou, 207
Aubert, Thomas, 9
Aucocisco, 245, 254
Aumoughcawgen, 245, 254
Azores, 6, 7, 43, 55, 85, 215

B

Baccalaos, 9, 32
Back River, 99
Bailleul, 213

Bangor, 81
Barlowe, Captain, 43
Barnstable, 132, 304
Bashabes, Bassaba, Betsabes (see Bessabez)
Baxter, James Phinney, 164, 267
Beauport, Le (see Gloucester)
Bedabedec, 82
Belle-Isle, Straits of, 28
Bellinger, Stephen, 43
Bessabez, 80, 81, 94, 155–7, 161, 162, 201, 202, 260
Biard, Pierre, 163, 190–217
Biddeford Pool, 102
Biencourt, 171, 190–204, 206, 209, 214–6
Biggar, H. P., 23, 26
Birds, 33, 60, 74, 103, 120, 261, 292
Block, Adriaen, 219–33, 243
Block Island, 11, 223
Blue Hill (Massachusetts), 257, 261
Boats, American-built, 60, 98, 124, 162, 163, 178
Bobadilla, Isabella de, 31
Boone Island, 57
Boston, 25, 105–9, 189, 230, 257, 306
Bradford, William, 76, 183, 281, 291*ff*, 294, 296
Brande, Edward, 280
Brant Rock, 110
Brereton, John, 55–65, 261
Bridges, Thomas, 71
Bristol, England, 6, 45, 68–70, 147, 150
Broken Hook, 230
Browne, Richard, 41
Brown's Bank, 9, 96
Burrage, Henry S., 88
Buzzards Bay, 60, 225

C

Cabahis, 81, 83
Cabot, John, 5–9, 38, 45, 52, 68, 175
Cabot, Sebastian, 6, 59, 68, 168
Cachaquant, 224
Cam, Thomas, 87
Camden Hills, 34, 80–1, 87, 153, 254, 261
Canada, 14, 30, 33, 104, 143–5, 154
Cap Blanc (Cape Cod), 116, 122
Cap Corneille, 123

318 INDEX

Capawe, Capawack, Capaock, Cape Ack (see Martha's Vineyard)
Cape Ann, 16, 69, 103, 108, 115, 129, 230, 256
Cape Bevechier, 228
Cape Breton, 9, 27, 43, 69
Cape Cod, 20, 25, 26, 58–60, 116–21, 132–73, 179, 182, 184–6, 225, 227, 228, 230, 231, 259, 260, 285, 291–309
Cape Elizabeth, 156
Cape Hatteras, 7
Cape James, 259
Cape Neddick, 56, 69
Cape Porpoise, 103
Cape of Shoals (see Nantucket)
Cape St. James (see Cape Cod)
Cape St. Louis, 109
Carolina coast, 14, 31, 42, 44
Cartier, Jacques, 28, 29, 42, 78, 144, 175, 177
Casco Bay, 25, 68, 101, 129, 156, 245, 255
Castine, 81
Catholic, Roman, 85, 109, 188–90, 197, 202–4, 213
Cecil, Sir Robert, 163
Challons, Henry, 75, 150
Champdoré, 122, 123
Champlain, Lake, 83
Champlain, Samuel de, 37, 70, 78–83, 98–145, 156, 157, 166, 174, 175, 189–90, 205, 206, 216, 227, 228, 231, 243, 272–5, 278
Charles V of Spain, 14
Charles, Prince, 233, 256–8, 266
Charles River, 108, 257, 266
Charters, 51–3
Chastes, Amyar de, 78
Chatham, 59, 119, 132–4, 141–3, 145, 230, 287
Chawum, 245, 259, 260
Chesapeake Bay, 176
Chevyot Hills, 257
Chiboctous (see Matawamkeag)
Chouacoet, 101–3, 122, 129, 231, 246
Christiaensen, Hendrick, 219, 225, 231
Church of England (see Anglican)
Clark's Island, 116
Claudia, 223
Codfish, 6, 7, 27, 58, 68, 110, 169, 171, 237, 238
Cohasset, 110, 236, 245, 246, 258
Coligny, Admiral, 32
Colonial personnel requirements, 52, 165, 166, 177, 178, 243, 244, 250, 251, 308
Colonial sites, requirements for, 98, 102,

Colonial sites, requirements for, continued 116, 121, 130, 131, 134, 194, 207, 236, 247, 248, 255, 256, 299, 300, 303
Colonies, attempts to found, 9, 27, 43–5, 60–7, 150, 154–66, 206, 265, 267, 276, 280
Columbus, 5, 6, 175, 244
Commercial background for colonization, 13, 14, 43, 67, 96, 144, 147, 162, 163, 166, 170, 188, 236, 237, 243, 249, 250, 252, 253, 289
Commodities, 61, 66, 68, 73, 74, 88, 101, 102, 163, 221, 236, 237, 246, 248
Compact, 292
Companies, English trading, 45, 51–4
Concord, 55
Coneconam, 185
Connecticut, 174, 225, 232
Connecticut River, 25, 175, 221, 222
Cooper, Michael, 264, 279
Copper, 15, 20–2, 40, 59, 63, 64, 71
Coppin, Robert, 291, 300, 304, 305
Cornhill, 298
Cortes, Hernando, 14, 175, 244
Cortereal, Gaspar, 6–9, 26, 59
Cortereal, Miguel, 7, 8, 21, 59
Cos Haven, 230
Cousin, Captain, 6
Cramolet, 122
Cranes Bay, 228, 258
Crosses, setting up of, 88, 95, 140, 153, 160, 189, 200, 208, 214
Cuttyhunk, 60, 62, 65, 67

D

Dale, Sir Thomas, 178, 208, 213
Damariscove, 165, 183, 260, 280
Damerill, Humphrey, 280
Dameril's Isles, 260
Dartmouth, 85, 86, 96, 174
Davies, James, 152, 156, 167
Davies, Richard, 156
Davies, Robert, 153, 162, 167
Davis, John, 42, 177
Davis Strait, 26, 84, 169
Dauphine, 14
De Costa, 30, 43
Dehanada (see Nahanada)
Delabarre, Edward, 8
Delaware Bay, 170, 173, 231
Delaware, Lord, 178, 179, 182
Dermer, Thomas, 70, 165, 186, 265, 279, 282, 283–90
De Soto, Hernando, 31, 175, 238, 244
Dieppe, 6, 9, 30, 78, 190, 211, 284
Dighton Rock, 8, 21
Discoverer, 68

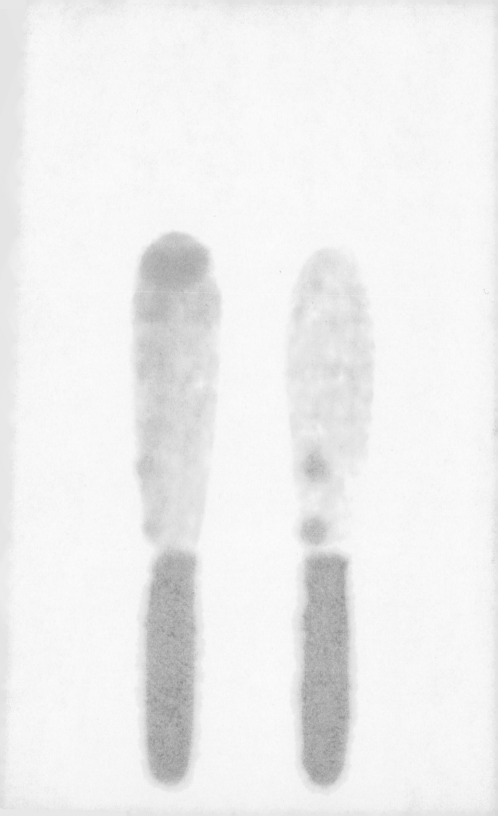

84502

F
7
H85

HOWE, HENRY
    PROLOGUE TO NEW ENGLAND.

DATE DUE	

Fernald Library
Colby-Sawyer College
New London, New Hampshire

GAYLORD   PRINTED IN U.S.A.